The Waterways of Britain
a social panorama

Boatpeople were a special people – Rose Skinner and her late husband Joe

The Waterways of Britain

a social panorama

D. D. GLADWIN

text illustrations by J. K. Ebblewhite

B. T. Batsford Ltd
London

By the same author:
ENGLISH CANALS
THE CANALS OF BRITAIN
THE CANALS OF THE WELSH VALLEYS
VICTORIAN AND EDWARDIAN CANALS
FROM OLD PHOTOGRAPHS

© D. D. Gladwin 1976
First published 1976

ISBN 0 7134 3159 8

Filmset by Servis Filmsetting Ltd, Manchester
Printed in Great Britain by Biddles Ltd, Guildford, Surrey
for the Publishers B T Batsford Ltd
4 Fitzhardinge Street, London W1H 0AH

Contents

The Plates

The Plates

My thanks are due to the following copyright holders for
permission to use photographs:
British Waterways Board, L. A. Edwards, W. K. V. Gale,
P. Garrett, Geographical Magazine, D. James, Sir John Knill,
National Museum of Wales, A. & J. Picken, Price, Pearson
Refractories, The late G. H. Pursell, D. G. Russell, P. L.
Smith, Waterways Museum, M. Webb, P. White.
My gratitude to other helpful souls who lent photographs is
no less sincere despite their omission.

8

Acknowledgments

Over the years any researcher runs into the private individual, learned institute or corporate body that, squirrel like, hangs on to its hoard, refusing to help in any way in the clarification of some minor problem. To these I owe many thanks; by forcing both myself and my colleagues to look elsewhere, their attitude has led to the uncovering of much unusual material, which is to some degree reflected in the contents of this book.

For every person who is unco-operative a hundred are helpful: only a few of whom are mentioned below, but omission does not render my thanks the less sincere.

Hugh Barker (proof reading), George Bate, B.E.M., J. K. Ebblewhite (illustrations), W. K. V. Gale, Phil Garrett, Janet Harris, the late Jack James, F. W. Jones of Solihull (photography), J. V. Shepard, Stan Turner, Phil White, the late Mrs. B. Bunker (Inland Waterways Protection Society), Miss S. Doeg (*Waterways News.* British Waterways Board), Roger Calvert, M.A. (National Council for Inland Transport), Martyn Denney (Waterways Research Centre), L. A. 'Teddy' Edwards (East Anglian Waterways Association), Brigadier and Mrs. Fielding (Salvation Army), P. L. German (Pickfords Removals Ltd.), P. L. Smith (Canal & Barge Development Association), the Assistant Secretary, Institution of Mining Engineers, Miss B. Barley, F.L.A. and staff, Worcester & Hereford County Library Service, Miss D. McCulla, F.L.A. and staff, Local Studies Department, Birmingham Public Libraries, the Archivist and staff, British Transport Commission, Historical Records, Public Record Office, London, the Librarian, House of Lords Library. Librarians, Archivists and staffs of the following Libraries and Record Offices: Abingdon, Bath, Bristol, Dorchester, Dudley, Gloucester, Littlehampton, Newport (Gwent), Portsmouth, Southampton, Swindon and Taunton.

The facts were provided; if I have misinterpreted them, then the errors are all mine. Finally, my greatest debt is to my wife who in between running a household and a permanently bankrupt Research Centre, finds the time to brew my coffee, howbeit it is often made on a steaming typewriter.

9

Prologue

The history of Britain's waterways is many faceted. There is the basic and often dry-as-dust economic story, drawn almost entirely from Minute Books and financial statements. An alternative approach is to take the engineering data of each separate waterway. A third scheme is to specialize in the life-and-death course of one specific navigation. Unfortunately, by their nature, each of these options must include a vast and sometimes disproportionate amount of data on Acts of Parliament, opening and (too often) closing dates, stocks and shares, and the financial intricacies of railway take-over bids.

This book is an attempt to tell the story from the other side of the coin: that of the people concerned. It took people to put up the money, to obtain the authorizing act, to plan and build the waterway. Similarly, boatmen, who were neither the animals that George Smith would have us believe, nor yet the angels other writers have portrayed. They were people – a special people perhaps, but still men and women. Maintenance men appear only here and there, for their story is really integral with that of engineering – their mode of life requires a particular approach which can only be understood in the context of the engineering works entailed.

The financial figures quoted in the text for food and materials in the times depicted are representative. Even today there is a distinct variation in prices throughout Great Britain; the cost of living and the wages paid are higher in London than in Lancaster, or in, say, Longbridge than in Lechlade. Conversely though, the cost of living in the Orkneys – or for that matter even in the lowlands of Scotland – is very high, and wages are relatively poor. These differences were far more marked in the eighteenth and nineteenth centuries and, therefore, where a craftsman's or labourer's wage is given, I have tried to relate them to a specific area. Most food and material prices, unless otherwise stated, are national averages.

Politically, I have tried not to show bias. Navigations have always been the playthings of politicians. They are loved in time of war – the Royal Military Canal was planned in part so that troops could be moved along it easily in the event of Napoleon crossing the Channel, while in the First World War many boatmen and their boats appeared in France, moving ammunition and supplies, and at home the transport of coal by water became vital. At Dunkirk, more recently, narrow boats and barges played their part, and quite a few of their crews were present at the D-Day landings, while others once again played their part at home. In peacetime waterways were reviled and neglected. Recently, due to direct political influence, the bulk were eliminated as a possible transport medium. True they now serve for amenity purposes, but how long will this last?

Not a decade ago many caravans were bought, now the 'in thing' is to buy a boat. Too often the buyer is disappointed. Aside from rising prices of both the craft, its fittings, fuel, moorings and licence, the greatest cruising pleasure – that of finding peace – is at the mercy of the tiny one per cent of canal users who are hooligans. Mainly because of their ruthless approach, canal boatmen were rarely bothered with this problem; perhaps the logical answer is for both pleasure and commercial interests to work together towards a Greater Britain where all the heavy traffic goes by water, whether canal, river or coastwise.

Falling off of traffics

1 *Changing Times*

To comprehend the effect upon Great Britain of building
turnpikes and canals, we can reduce the social scene to the
microcosm of one village. Near this village, Upper Whitford,
there is a bell-pit or winning hole where one man, part time,
digs out sufficient coal, no more, no less, to cater for the
immediate neighbourhood. In his spare time he works for
Farmer Giles. Ten miles away is another village, Middle
Whitford, but because of a lack of transportation, the Middle
Whitfordians have to rely on wood for their fires. On the other
hand they do have a mill. The coalman, anxious to expand his
trade, proposes a turnpike from Upper Whitford to Middle
Whitford, a motion seconded by Farmer Giles who wishes to
send his wheat more easily to the mill. On completion of the
project, two effects promptly occur. Having now to cater for
the demands of two villages, the coalman works full time, and
Farmer Giles has to take on another labourer. This labourer
and the toll-keepers of the turnpike, together with the people of
Middle Whitford, all require coal, which necessitates the coalman taking on a labourer. But the cost of the tolls, the maintenance cost of the turnpike, and of the coalman's carter

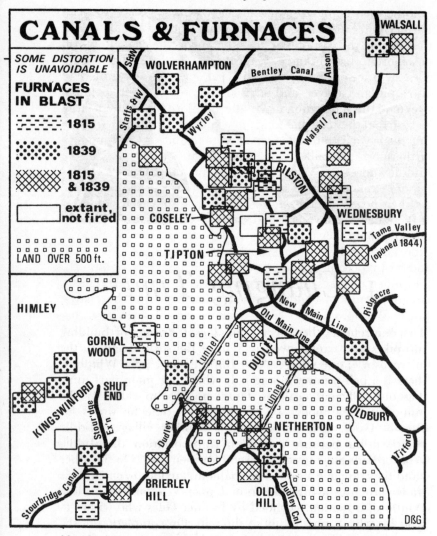

CANALS & FURNACES

SOME DISTORTION
IS UNAVOIDABLE

**FURNACES
IN BLAST**

1815

1839

1815
& 1839

extant,
not fired

LAND OVER 500 ft.

WALSALL

WOLVERHAMPTON

Bentley Canal

Anson

Staffs & W'ton

Wyrley

Walsall Canal

BILSTON

WEDNESBURY

Tame Valley
(opened 1844)

COSELEY

TIPTON

HIMLEY

New Main Line

Old Main Line

Ridgacre

DUDLEY

Tunnel

Tunnel

GORNAL
WOOD

OLDBURY

KINGSWINFORD

SHUT
END

Stour'dge Ex'n

Dudley

NETHERTON

Titford

Stourbridge Canal

BRIERLEY
HILL

OLD
HILL

Dudley Cnl

DßG

Map showing canals and furnaces, based on a drawing by Davies and Hyde in
'Dudley and the Black Country' (1760–1860) slightly simplified for clarity
(Courtesy of the Dudley Libraries)

(another new employee) all contrive to put up the cost of coal. Farmer Giles increases the price of his wheat to compensate, thus raising the cost of living, which means the coalman must pay more to his workmen, and in tolls to the turnpike, so up goes the price of coal . . . Nearby, at Lower Whitford, there is also a pit, and a river, and plans are mooted by their coalman to extend this navigation to Middle Whitford by means of flash locks so that they can undercut our coalman of Upper Whitford. But this river is often flooded in winter and dry in summer, furthermore the miller who grinds all the wheat for Upper, Middle and Lower Whitford is unhappy about the project for reasons explained later. So he, the coalman and Farmer Giles get their heads together and decide that if they can build one of these new deadwater canal navigations ignoring the river, not only could they then reduce their own costs, they could also export coal and wheat to a nearby city. They build their canal and the pit becomes a colliery, swallowing up Upper Whitford; the miller changes to steam and opens a linen mill (cheap labour, plenty of children about); Farmer Giles purchases Lower Whitford and its river, demolishing the one and using the other to water his cattle, which feed the inhabitants of Middle Whitford, who now work at the mill, or the colliery, or for him. This, more or less, is the theory of what happened in Britain.

From theory to the practice is only a short step. Thoughts of profit were rarely far from the minds of canal shareholders, but save only such expressions as 'no canal of the same extent is likely to prove of greater advantage to the public or its adventurers' (Basingstoke);[1] 'It is happy for the world, that public interest is grafted upon private and that both flourish together' (Birmingham Canal Navigations);[2] and '. . . this undertaking is worthy of a great commercial nation, and does great credit to the exertions of the individuals who have promoted and completed a work of such magnitude . . .' (Thames & Severn Canal);[3] by 'disinterested' third parties, the motive was seldom expressed. Instead, the proprietors and their friends pontificated upon the virtues of the work and the advantages that would accrue to the local populace.

Their principal objectives varied according to the locality and the neighbouring cities; the Bude, for example, was built to 'facilitate the introduction of Welsh Coal, and the carrying of Shelly Sand from the coast, to be used in the interior as manure',[4] while the Carlisle was an endeavour to improve communications between the city and the sea following the silting of the Solway Firth and the inefficiency of the River Eden Navigation.[5] Goods carried, to the benefit of townsfolk, included lime and coal. Lime (before the 'benefits' of artificial manures) was a vital ingredient in agriculture; where not available sea-sand, night-soil and almost anything decomposable was used. The Glamorganshire and its tramroads[6] was built to 'facilitate the export of the vast quantity of coal, ironstone, and other ores and minerals which are worked in great abundance on its line, and in particular at Merthyr Tidvile and its immediate vicinity.'[4] The ill-fated Glasgow, Paisley and Ardrossan Canal[7] was designed to run between the harbour of Ardrossan, via Paisley to Glasgow. In the outcome, due to financial difficulties, only that part from Glasgow to Johnstone was built by canal, while the rest was built by tramroad, but a commentator of 1831 envisaged that despite the difficulties of double-handling,

'By means of this canal and railway, great facilities will be given for exporting coal, from the extensive mines in the line, for the supply of the north and eastern coasts of Ireland, and to receive, in return, supplies of corn for the consumption of the populous places of Glasgow, Paisley, &c. Moreover, it will have the effect of shortening considerably the distance, and rendering more safe the transit of exported manufactured goods from the above-mentioned towns, by avoiding the circuitous route by the River and Firth of Clyde.'[4]

More obvious traffics – and hence 'advantages' to all, were mentioned in a notice of 1770.

'We hear that the Country is surveying from the Coventry Canal by Colehill, Castle Bromwich, Aston, Perry, Hamstead and West Bromwich, to the Coal Pits near Wednesbury and Bilston, and to the Lime Pits near Walsall, and we are informed that a Canal in that Tract would very much reduce the Price of Coal and Lime in the Eastern Parts of Warwickshire and the adjoining Counties; and that a Cut therefrom

1 Motor barge and butty on the Leeds and Liverpool Canal at
Bootle about 1950. *(Courtesy of the late G H Pursell)*

2　Privately owned motor boat with liner funnel on the Grand Union Canal about 1948. Note the boat is clothed-up. *(Courtesy of Sir John Knill)*

3　Cutting firewood on the Worcester and Birmingham Canal at Bittell Cutting during the great freeze of winter 1962/3, when the ice reached a depth of 20 inches. *(Courtesy of David James)*

to Birmingham would occasion the Price of Corn to be cheaper than by Land Carriage.'[8]

Another canal that ran out of luck (and money) was the Hereford & Gloucester, but nevertheless in 1794:

'The advantages which must result from this inland navigation to Ledbury and the adjoining country are incalculable. In the article of coal the inhabitants of this district will reap an important benefit by the immediate reduction in price of at least 10s. per ton.'[6]

A newspaper of 1794[10] had no doubt as to which trade item was the most important.

'We have the satisfaction of informing the public that the Leicester Navigation Water Levels and Railways are now fully and completely open for the carriage of COALS (as well as Merchandize and Goods of all sorts). This long wished for event was celebrated here on Monday last by the ringing of bells, &c. . . . In addition to the above, we are happy to have it in our power also to say, in so forward a state is the UNION CANAL, that on the same day a boat load of coals proceeded along that line to Blaby, an extent of six miles. The advantages arising from this early communication with the Leicester Canal to the country around and the subscribers, is of the greatest importance, and reflects the highest credit on the Conductors, for the speedy completion of the works to that distance.'

Sometimes commentators – cynics would say they were shareholders anxious to boost the value of their shares – were clearly starry-eyed.

'It may not be improper here to introduce some account of what promises to be of the greatest utility to this country, viz. a navigable canal from the town of Basingstoke to the river Wey in Surrey . . . Considering this undertaking only in this limited view; no canal of the same extent is likely to prove of greater advantage to the public or its adventurers; yet if we extend our ideas to what future associations may accomplish, the utility would be unbounded, viz. to continue it quite across the island to the Bristol channel on the one side; and into the British Channel, by Southampton or Christchurch, with an arm to Salisbury on the other; but perhaps this is more a matter of speculation than can be made practicable; else how useful in time of war would such communication be . . .'[11]

The 'blurb' was probably unsuccessful: 'This canal has, though improving, been as yet unproductive to the shareholders.'[12] Occasionally, honesty or disillusionment crept in,

'. . . the Huddersfield Canal has answered better for the town and for the country through which it passes, than for the proprietors. It has been a loosing speculation; and ages will probably pass away, before it pays common interest, for the money invested in the undertaking.'[13]

However, having convinced the public that they were on a good thing, the proprietors fought tooth and nail to stop any rivals emerging, irrespective of how the rest of the populace might be affected – although in the later canal age, rate wars probably kept many from starving, or freezing.

'In the neighbourhood of Loughborough are some pleasant seats . . . but the spirit and life of this place is its Navigation, which was compleated in 1778. The people of Loughborough, be it recorded to their credit, are remarkably studious for the interest and prosperity of the town. The navigation they procured with ease; and it has enriched its inhabitants, aided the population of the place, and continues a source of multiplying blessings to almost every individual therein. With a foresight that does their judgement credit, they have struggled hard to prevent its extention to Leicester, where its inhabitants, with an equal degree of industry, but with a less enterprising spirit, are, now their eyes are open to its utility, labouring and have been so far some years, to obtain an advantageous navigation, which they might have had with ease when the people of Loughborough obtained theirs. If the people of Leicester now succeed in the application to Parliament, it must be at a costly sacrifice of wealth; a humiliation bordering upon civility; a disgraceful inconvenience in a circuitous passage; and a tonnage, which will forever remain a burdonsome tax upon the many, to the great advantage of a few individuals who possess an earlier laudible enterprising spirit.'[14]

While prior to the canal age, workmen's living conditions may have been relatively poor, it is nevertheless difficult to apportion the blame for the often appalling existence many were to lead while the industrial revolution was at its height. Did canals come as a result of demand for easy trade channels, or did the trade induce the growth of the canal network? Even before the day of Bridgewater and Brindley, Egremont and Telford, 'enclosures' were taking effect; men were being forced to move from their patch of land for the ultimate profit of the landowner; turnpikes, by way of tolls where previously there were none, made the carriage of fertilizers for the small farmer that much more expensive. But a man and his family could still keep body and soul together, both as a family and part of the community. Aside from the pig looking over the sty rail at the end of the garden, meat might be rare, coals well-nigh unknown, but wood was plentiful, fish only something seen (however smelt!) when the hawker made his monthly visit. But a roof, and a steady income, clothing, beer, milk, the odd candle, these kept the cottager happy. Occurrences like the enclosures, the people had met before – the Black Death, the Reformation, and Civil War – all had been either shaken off or assimilated in a new way of life. But what kind of dog had the villager become by 1819 when he could be evicted without committing a crime?

'John Balaam, farmer's man. I came from Stowmarket, and belong to the parish of All Newton, Suffolk. Having a large family of children, I had occasion to apply for parish relief . . . John Moor [Poor-law Guardian] said, if I would come into the manufacturing district, I might get a good living, save money, and have the pleasure of eating plum-pudding and roast beef. Tracts were circulated in our neighbourhood stating that labourers were very much wanted in the manufacturing districts, and several families had gone into different parts. If they were badly clad, the masters bought them new clothing, and they liked them so well, that they advanced their wages; they added, that working in the mill was such easy employment that the children had grown quite healthy and fat. . . . In consequence of what I had heard stated, and had read in pamphlets . . . I made up my mind to come with my family into Lancashire, to better my condition, as I thought . . . [An agreement guaranteeing wages was signed] We sold the bulk of our furniture and leaving Stowmarket on the 5th day of May last, came by waggon to London, and then by Pickford's boat to Huddersfield. Slept in a warehouse on straw, and the next morning walked to Halifax; from thence went to Richworth, by a cart. When we arrived at our destination, we were put into a house that had not been occupied for some time, and had nothing but bare walls. We purchased 3s. worth of straw for our beds. For three months Mr. Stead stood by his agreement; and then he got it from me, and said I was not worth 12s. per week; so I agreed to work for 9s. Since then, at a moment's warning, he said he could not find me any employment. He has only found me one ten days' work this last fifteen weeks, and only paid me 1s. per day for it. Then he turned my daughters, Mary Ann and Hannah, to piece work, and they have never averaged 4s. per week each since. So the last fortnight, which ended on the 21st January, instead of receiving according to agreement £2.10s. we only received £1.1s.4d., for ten human beings to subsist on for one whole fortnight.' This family was in a wretched condition. 'On Saturday the 21st instant, the father, mother, and the oldest daughter, did not taste victuals till night. The three that went to the mill had ½d. worth of bread to their dinner, each half a cake to subsist on till night; the other four youngest had only a 1d. cake divided amongst them. The mother states that they have not had half an ounce of butter since Christmas. This family has often been without victuals these last two months, and their clothing is fast wearing out, and no probability of getting new. All the family are so reduced that they have not a change of linen. Their bed consists of the 3s. worth of straw they purchased, with not a single sheet to cover them. One of the children has been without shoes these several weeks. . . . But, rather than see her family starve, she will go round the neighbourhood and try the charitably disposed. They actually declare they never was in such a wretched condition in all their lives. When they were at Stowmarket, they were well to do, considering, having occasional relief under the Old Poor-law; but might have been better, had not the Irish labourers come into the neighbourhood during harvest time. . . . But, notwithstanding their wretched condition, they state that they should not like to go back to their own country, for fear of having to go into the workhouse. The parish having been at the expense of bringing them here, they would be looked upon with disrespect.'[15]

William Burleigh says, 'I came from Stradbrook, Suffolk, about the 21st of March, 1836; am a husbandman, I now drive Mr. Well's cart, at 8s. per week. I had 10s. per week at Stradbrook, and house and garden rent free. The house had four rooms: garden about nine rods. I grew as many vegetables as served my family. . . . About twelve months ago, I was sent for to the Board at Stradbrook, and there found Dr. Kay; and he looked at me well once from head to foot, and said, 'Well, Burleigh, you are just now the right age to go into Lancashire', and that he understood that I was a man of good character. I said, 'I could not like to be sent away, I had done nothing that I ought to be transported for'. . . . A short time afterwards one of the Guardians met with me, and said, 'Burleigh, I hope you have made up your mind to go to Lancashire'. I answered him, 'No, sir, I should not like to go yet'; but he over-persuaded me, until I gave consent. . . . I did not like the terms of the contract; but they [the Board of Guardians] promised that, if I would come, they had no doubt that Mr. Wells would advance my wages to 12s. per week, and every lad 1s. per head more. . . . I sold my furniture, except my beds: I brought them with me. The parish officers sent me and family by waggon to London, and put us in a boat at Pickford's Wharf, and we came thus to Huddersfield. Mr. Wells sent a horse and cart to meet us, and we got here that night. I have had my regular wages of 8s. per week ever since. [He was told] that the best beef was 4d. per pound, and flour 1s. 6d. per stone, and coals brought to the door for almost nothing; and clothes also. . . . We had five pints of milk for 1d. in Suffolk. I never made any agreement with any one, but came under the direction of the Guardians of the Poor . . . [and] that in case I should become troublesome to the parish, I should be liable to be shoved into a workhouse, and my wife into another, and the children into another. The operatives did not like us at first, they mobbed us. The earnings of the whole family of nine persons is 31s. a week.'[15]

Were these people men or cyphers? Without canals the mill would not have needed them; without canals even, they could not have been moved so easily.

The greatest advocate of a return to rural simplicity was William Cobbett. His *Cottage Economy*, written in 1822, dealt wholly with the means by which a labourer and his wife could enjoy a happy and well fed life. As he said, 'To live well, to enjoy all things that make life pleasant, is the right of every man who constantly uses his strength judiciously and lawfully.' But already it was too late, oh how much too late for:

'Patience Kershaw, age 17, Halifax: Go to pit at 5 o'clock in morning, come home in evening. Get Breakfast, porridge and milk first. Take dinner with me, a cake and eat it as I go. Do not stop or rest any time, until I get home, have potatoes and meat, not every day meat . . . Bald place on head made by thrusting the corves [coal-trams] – hurry the corves a mile or more underground and back, they weigh 3 cwt. Move eleven a day. Wear a belt and chain. Getters I work for are naked except their caps. Sometimes beat me if I am not quick enough. Boys take liberties sometimes, pull me about, I am only girl in the pit. 20 boys and 15 men, all naked.' Note by Sub-Commissioner Scriven: This girl is an ignorant, filthy, ragged, and deplorable looking object, and such a one as the uncivilized natives of the prairies would be shocked to look upon.'[16]

The Duke of Bridgewater, as we shall show in Chapter 4, although a visionary, was nevertheless the heir to an estate, including coalfields at Worsley. While he may have treated his men well, to what degraded state had they sunk?

'Peter Gaskell, a collier in the Worsley pits, Lancashire, when asked "How often do the drawers wash their bodies?" replied "None of the drawers does wash their bodies. I never wash my body: I let my shirt rub the dirt off, my shirt will show that; I wash my neck and ears and face, of course". To the further question "Do you think it is usual for the young women to do the same as you do?" he replied, "I don't think it is usual for the lasses to wash their bodies, my sisters never wash themselves, and seeing is believing: they wash their faces and necks and ears".'[16]

The towns of the Black Country were pleasant enough places in the 1750s but with the coming of canals, the resulting expansion of both ironworks and coalfields led to their over-rapid growth, and the ensuing degredation of both labourer and master.

'The labourer, having nothing in common with the employer, is continually striking to get more out of him – and hence the "strikes" by which the trade is continually suffering. On the other hand the employer is led to treat the workman as a mere machine; as a machine without wants or feelings; as a machine in which he is only so far interested as he can work it. A remarkable proof of this position is to be found in the fact that although accidents in the pit-work are in the fearful proportion of no less than seventy-two per cent. per annum to the number of labourers, yet there is not in the Town of Dudley, or in the country round about it, a hospital, or even a dispensary! All cases requiring peculiar care must be sent to Birmingham, twelve miles off!'[17]

An appeal to sanity, considered far too radical at the time, was made by Samuel Cook in 1848.

'Nail Masters, Iron Masters, Coal Masters, Cotton Lords, Woollen Lords, and all other manufacturing Lords and Masters – Get fair profits, and be content – give reasonable wages, and let live, as well as live. Be not avaricious, and go not beyond your tether. Try not to undersell each other, and keep the markets steady. Then the Australian, the East Indian, the Brazilian, and American, and other buyers will know how to order.'[17]

Consider the description by Howitt of a farm labourer in 1838.

'They are mighty useful animals in their day and generation, and as they get bigger, they successively learn to drive plough, and then to hold it; to drive the team, and finally to do all the labours of a man. This is the growing up of a farm servant. All this time he is learning his business, but he is learning nothing else – he is growing up into a tall, long, smock-frocked, straw-hatted, ankle-booted fellow, with a gait as graceful as one of his own plough-bullocks. He has grown up and gone to service; and there he is, as simple, as ignorant, and as laborious a creature as one of the wagon-horses that he drives. The mechanic sees his weekly news-paper over his pipe and pot; but the clodhopper, the chopstick, the hawbuck, the hind, the Johnny-raw, or by whatever name, in whatever district he may be called, is everywhere the same – he sees no newspaper, and if he did, he could not read it; and if he hears his master reading it, ten to one but he drops asleep over it. In fact, he has no interest in it . . . He is as much an animal as air and exercise, strong living and sound sleeping can make him, and he is nothing more.'[18]

and contrast it with the 'mechanic' of 1851 :

'. . . savages, without the grace of savages, coarsely clad in filthy garments, with no change on week-days and Sundays, they converse in a language belarded with fearful and dis-gusting oaths, which can scarcely be recognized as the same as that of civilized England.'[19]

On the whole the position seems to have been tacitly accepted by nearly all those concerned.

'It is also conceded that factory labour is not so healthy, on the whole, as that of agriculture, nor the operatives of the former to be compared with the latter in well developed robust bodies, healthiness, and longevity . . . Such is the condition of men, such the inevitable lot of all but a favoured few, that they must eat the bread of hard, often deleterious labour, all the days of their lives.'[20]

At Liverpool, that city which received its initial growth impetus from the St. Helens Canal, instructions were issued for the use of the Corporation Baths:

'Many of the clothes are full of vermin, which boiling does not destroy; the clothes of the clean should therefore be boiled together, and those of the dirty together, in a second boiler when it is not wanted for infectious clothes. The woman [in charge] must be very cautious . . . or she will give great offence.'[21]

The apparently insatiable demand for 'more'; more brass, more iron, more coal, more money, led to the employment of children, not picking stones in a field, or turnips, or gleaning in the fields, but in the brickfields:

'The evil of the system of employing young girls at this work consists in its binding them from their infancy, as a general rule, to the most degraded lot in after life. They become rough, foul-mouthed boys before nature has taught them that they are women. Clad in a few dirty rags, their bare legs exposed far above the knees, their hair and faces covered with mud, they learn to treat with contempt all feelings of modesty and decency. During the dinner-hour they may be seen lying about the yards asleep, or watching the boys bathing in some adjoining canal. When their work is over they dress themselves in better clothes and accompany the men to the beershops.'[22]

in the pits, where Mary David, near seven years old, keeper of an air-door in a pit in South Wales, was described by Sub-Commissioner Franks as:

'A very pretty little girl, who was fast asleep under a piece of rock near the air-door below ground. Her lamp had gone out for want of oil; and upon waking her, she said the rats or some one had run away with her bread and cheese, so she went to sleep. The oversman, who was with me, thought she was not so old, though he felt sure she had been below near 18 months.'[16]

or on the canals:

'Thomas William, aged 10. I drive the horse that draws the boat along the canal. I drive with my brother; he is 16 or 17. We work from 6 in the morning, and sometimes before, until 6 in the evening and often later; but we don't work at night.

I have good health, but am out in all weathers along the canal. I lose no time from my work. I have met with no accidents. My work is not very hard. I go to Sunday School every Sunday.'[16]

How true was another Cobbett statement in his address to the journeymen and labourers.

'The real strength and all the resources of a country ever have sprung, and ever must spring, from the labour of its people, elegant dresses, superb furniture, stately buildings, fine roads and canals, fleet horses and carriages, numerous stout ships, warehouses teeming with goods; all these, and many other objects that fall under our view, are so many marks of national wealth and resources. But all these spring from labour. Without the journeyman and the labourer, none of these could exist.'

Short boat to Wigan Power Station

2 *More (or less) Navigable Rivers*

Canals have at various times and for various reasons been under construction, in the process of modification and/or closed, in Great Britain for nearly 2,000 years, but it is difficult to know what effect, for example, the Caer Dyke, built by the Roman occupying forces c. A.D. 120, had upon the neighbourhood of Peterborough. No doubt it drained some land (although the Romans probably promptly grabbed this), no doubt some goods were moved by water (but would the peasants have cared?), and most of all, troops would have been boated about in Mark I packet boats. The Foss Dyke, still extant albeit improved, and the Caer Dyke are the two best known Roman canals, but there were others:

'Quitting the Abbey meadow, and passing the North Lock [of the Soar] we still continue our walk . . . Approaching the Bow Bridge, we pass a plot of ground insulated by the Soar, called the Black Friars . . . That arm of the river which flows under the west bridge, is by some supposed from its passing under the site of the old Roman town, to be a canal formed by that people for the convenience of their dwellings. It is now called the New Soar . . .'[1]

After this period not much is known of artificial cuts being built, save for such oddities as a by-passing of a Thames loop at Abingdon by Aethelwold 'to serve and purge the offis of the abbey', the old river line then falling into disuse and being known as the 'Swiftch Ditch'. No doubt the bargees tut-tutted at the resultant effluent. Geoffrey de Lacy, Bishop of Winchester around 1189, made the Itchen navigable from Southampton to Winchester but at the head 'constructed a dyke'. This almost certainly wasn't a pound lock but the sort of thing Edward III had in mind in 1350 when he approved an Act of Parliament which stated:

> 'Whereas the common passages of boats and ships in the great rivers of England be often times annoyed by the inhancing of gorces, mills, weirs, stanks, stakes and kiddles, etc., which be raised in the time of King Edward the king's grandfather and after . . . shall be cut and utterly pulled down without being renewed. And that no man take for passage of water, going or coming, beyond what is rightful, under fixed penalty.'

A later Act (1371) set the penalty or fine at 100 marks.

Here we have the first of the problems which were to beset the 'adventurer' until comparatively recent times. Despite icehouses in lieu of refrigerators, fish was the one item of food that could be got fresh all the year round. Meat, badly cured and of poor quality, was all very well for the villein or serf – if he could get any, but not good enough for the up and coming nobleman or Abbot whose estate happened to be bisected by a fresh-water river, up which proceeded eels, salmon, tench, perch and (especial delicacy) carp. Initially, he might have sent men to catch these fish with hand nets but perhaps they were slack, or hungry, and he decided to build a permanent net, which would trap the fish, from which they could be removed by his bailiff as and when required, or be placed in fish pools – this latter was a common adjunct to Abbeys. But what of a bargee who wanted to pass along the river with a cargo? He could not, until the owner built a passable section in his weir or net. And then, suddenly, the bargee had another toll to pay.

Precisely who invented pound locks is a matter of some debate, but flash locks were extant 'since time immemorial', records go back to the twelfth century.

Basically the principle of these was simple (see drawing 31). Unfortunately they were extremely dangerous and in October, 1585, one John Bishop complained that:

The names	Mylls weares and locks men do them call
of the	that doe annoy that worthy streame
wrongs	Against the laws they doe stande all
	but still they drownde those symple men

A Locke of	One ffarmer hath a Lock in store
great	That hath made many a Childe to weepe
Murther	Their mothers begg from dore to dore
(Marlow)	Their ffathers drownde in the deepe

Swine and	Then being drowned they bury them there
dogges do	where doggs and swyne then do them finde
eat mens	Their fleshe they eat and all to teare
fleshe	which is contrarie to mankinde

Four murthers	At ffarmers lock foure men be loste
of late don	of late I putt you out of doubt
att ffarmers	Three were drowned the streams then toste
Lock	the fourth he had his braines knocked out[2]

The necessity of river navigation was, and is, all too apparent to any right thinking person and the preamble to an Act of 1624[3] relating to the River Thames only clarifies this. The first objective was a reduction in the price of fuel and other essential commodities, the second export of produce, and the third the saving of the roads which 'were during the winter so broken up as to be extremely dangerous to travellers, and could not be kept in a passable state without enormouse expense'.

During the period 1600–1750 no less than fifty-five Acts[4] were passed for the improvement of rivers in England alone. In some cases, nothing happened, as the riparian landowners were often able to halt the works, or mill-owners, who relied upon the river for their water, claimed such exhorbitant compensation, either by demanding outright purchase at an enhanced fee, or by claiming vast tolls every time a boat drew water from the mill feeder (as the bargee must in summer) that the 'adventurer' was discouraged and went away. The problem of mill owners versus bargees, both of whom wanted the same water, highlights the wastefulness of flash locks and unfortunately for the bargee, while he was necessary, the miller who ground flour to make bread to feed the workers who loaded the barges was absolutely essential in a village community. In winter, when all should have been at peace, a miller downstream of a lock would bitterly remonstrate when a flood of water released by the bargee choked his wheel – most it will be remembered were undershot and hopelessly inefficient compared with the overshot pattern which developed later. Small wonder then that in 1666 'the owner of Tottenham Mill on the Lea refused water with the result that barges lay aground for fourteen days',[4] while Yarranton[5] tells us that on the Thames it was a matter of no great surprise that barges often lay aground for four or even six weeks, the bargemasters having to feed their crew whilst there.

The first navigation in Britain to utilize pound locks, that is those where water is empounded between two sets of gates, was probably the Exeter, built by John Trew in 1564. A mere $1\frac{3}{4}$ miles long, it could not, as De la Garde explains[6] have had much impact, as the double handling of goods within such a short distance would be prohibitively expensive.

To make matters worse this form of lock was expensive to build compared with a flash – in 1632 'turnpike' or pound locks at Iffley, Sandford and Swift Ditch on the Thames cost $9\frac{1}{2}$p to pass whereas for a flash the going rate was a mere $2\frac{1}{2}$p, a 280 per cent rise which was passed on to the shipper and, no doubt inflated, to the rest of the community.

A curious half-way house navigation, which initially embodied all the problems of a river but was later to become a good example of a deadwater navigation, was the Stroudwater. The first Act was passed in 1730 (3 Geo. II, c. 13) to form a navigation along the River Frome on account of 'the great trade and populousness of the country', from Stroud to the River Severn but 'from an apprehension afterwards of injuring the clothing mills upon the river, it was never carried into execution'. However in 1759[7] a new idea was propounded, still

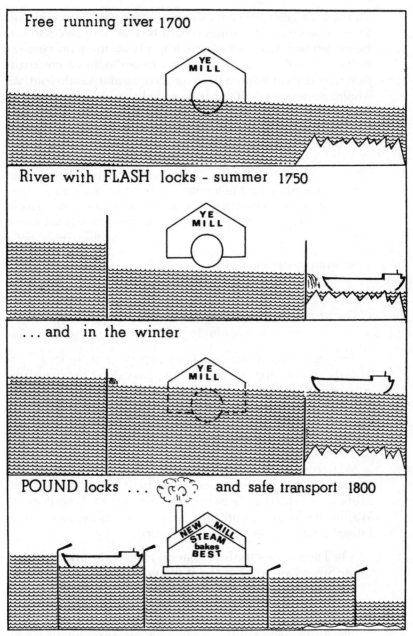

The progress of the navigation

utilizing the river, whereby double acting (two armed) cranes were to be used 'all loading should be lain in square chests to be placed in boats, two of which to ply on the river between every two mills . . . at each mill a crane should be erected to shift the chests of loading from one boat to another through the whole navigation'.[8] This, surprisingly, was attempted. Its failure was 'on the cards' for a comparative timing shows how costs to shipper, consignee, consignor and the ordinary person would rise to ridiculous levels!

		Hr	Min	Sec
(a)	40-ton barge for 8 miles =	8	22	50
	time to pass and repass 20 locks =	1	20	00
		9	42	50
(b)	ditto 10-ton crane boat	8	22	50
	time to pass and repass 20 mills			
	using crane	20	00	00
		28	22	50

Towing labour alone rose from 22p to 142p. Indeed T. S. Willan[4] tells us that 'no boat was to pass along the river from August 14th to October 15th without the consent of the major part of the mill owners, and there were nineteen mills', for all the fact that the towns of Malmesbury and Bristol had both declared their support for the scheme 'to reduce the cost of coals'.

Matters were then left in abeyance until 1776 when an Act[9] amending the previous one permitted the making of an artificial navigation between the Severn at Framilode to Wallbridge near Stroud and, slowly but more surely than hitherto, parts of the work were opened.

'On Tuesday last the first stone was laid of the first lock upon the Stroud Water river, by William Dallaway, Esq; and the name given the lock was the Framilode Lock. Besides a great concourse of other spectators, there was present the major part of the chief proprietors in the navigation; and many also of the neighbouring gentlemen honoured the meeting,

4 Two 'Sheffield' size barges at Doncaster Power Station on the Sheffield and South Yorkshire Navigation. *(Courtesy of P L Smith)*

5 Waddington's barge *Enterprise* at Rotherham on the Sheffield and South Yorkshire Navigation. *(Courtesy of P L Smith)*

6 After taking coal to Worcester, empty boats tow a BWB maintenance boat below Astwood Locks on the Worcester and Birmingham Canal

7 A loaded motor and empty butties on the Shropshire Union Canal during the 1950s. *(Courtesy of M Webb)*

and attended the usual ceremonies. Some coins of the year were put under the stone. After which the gentlemen all dined together, at Mr. Hall's, at Framiload's Passage. After dinner suitable healths were drank, particularly the Mayor and Aldermen of Gloucester for the time being, as standing Commissioners appointed by the act of parliament which was obtained for making the river navigable. The whole was conducted with great decency, accompanied with cheerful shouts, and other acclamations of real joy, expressive of the satisfaction that was felt by those present, upon seeing so necessary a work, so long wished for, thus begun; and in so promising a way of being speedily completed (unless retarded by the malignant spirit of opposition). A work of the utmost utility to the clothing trade of this county; and which will be a great relief to the poor in the article of firing*; and likewise an ease to the neighbouring estates in the saving of the roads. And it may with justice be added, a work, which begins an important era of the British annals; and which will keep in view, 'till really accomplished that great national object.

> Of which the bards have sung, in visionary dreams,
> The union of Sabrina's floods with silver Thames.'

Before the true canal age, Henry Berry was to build the St. Helens Canal. This waterway came into existence for the same reason as many others – turnpikes were being built, thereby increasing the cost of coal from pithead to customer, by the levying of tolls where previously there were none; in this case between the St. Helens collieries and Liverpool, at that time an up and coming seaport. Furthermore salt from the Cheshire fields was necessary as an export trade. But with the relatively crude evaporative methods in use, 10,000 tons of coal a year were necessary at the saltfields, and for the first five miles of its journey this was taken by packhorse. Without coal, salt could not be produced; without salt Liverpool could not expand its

---

* When this navigation is completed to Wallbridge, the same coals, which now at the lowest rate are sold for 13d. per hundred, will, on the same spot, be then sold for 8d. per hundred, to the poor.

It is proposed, when this navigation of the Stroud-Water is completed, to join it by a new canal to the Thames at Cricklade. This, upon a survey by an able Engineer, has not only been found to be practicable, but easy to be effected.[10]

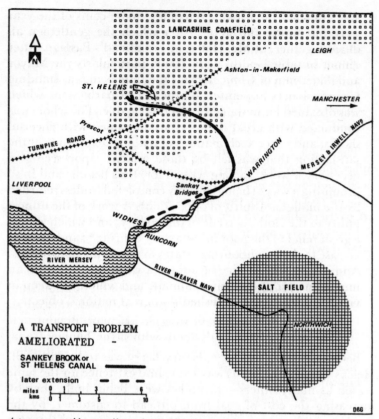

A transport problem ameliorated (slightly simplified for clarity)

trade; without trade nobody could buy either salt or coal.

So it was to everyone's benefit to consider building a navigation, initially by canalizing the Sankey Brook from the Mersey–Weaver route to the coalfields.

In 1754, in *Whitworth's Manchester Magazine* – so relatively insignificant was Liverpool, it did not then even have its own paper – a meeting of those interested in subscribing was called at Liverpool Exchange. The date is important for it was just six years before the much hailed Bridgewater Canal was to be commenced. The assenting Act[11] was passed the following year to make a river navigation. But we find

34

'after an attentive survey, he [Berry] found the measure [making the Brook navigable] impracticable and, knowing that the object they had in view could be answered by a canal, he communicated his sentiments to one of the proprietors (John Ashton) who, approving the plan, the work was commenced on 5 September 1755, it being apprehended that so novel an undertaking would be met with their opposition'.[12]

The whole work (as authorized) was completed by 1759, ten miles and nine locks, more than halving the cost of coal to the needy housewives of Liverpool, at 37½p a 'long' (30 cwt) ton. Pithead cost was 21p, the balance being accounted for by tolls 4p, carriers charges to the wharf 10p, and the local carter 2½p.

Interestingly, as the canal got into full swing, so the costs came down.

'Many and (it is to be feared) just complaints having been made, by House-keepers and others, of imposition, and unjust dealing, by delivery of short measure and other unfair practices, of the common dealers in that most useful article COAL, whereby the coal coming down the Sankey Canal may have fallen into disrepute: To obviate all such complaints, and to secure to all Persons a certainty of having the full quantity, and to secure to all such COAL, which they may hereafter pay for, the Proprietors of Sankey Navigation have come to a resolution of Delivering Coal by sworn Agents, in whom the Public may confide. And for public encouragement, with respect to price, the said Proprietors have studied the means of reducing it, and find that by a saving on the first cost, by paying ready money to the Coal Owners, by reducing the freight and cutting off the unfair profits and advantage hitherto taken by the Dealers or Retailers, Coal (sic) may be and are ready to be delivered, for the use of the Town, at the door of Housekeepers, and for Shipping, at the respective rates and prices undermentioned, and every buyer may rest assured that every Ton of Coal so delivered shall contain Twenty Hundred weight, reckoning 120 pounds to the Hundred, certified by a ticket from the keeper of the weighing machine with each cart, for Ready money only.

	Delivered to Housekeepers	Delivered to Shipping
Peter Leigh Esq.'s Coal	7s. 2d. per ton	6s. 6d. per ton
John Mackay Esq.'s Coal	7s. 0d. per ton	6s. 4d. per ton
Thos. Case Esq.'s Coal	6s.10d. per ton	6s. 2d. per ton
Sir Thomas Gerard's Coal	6s. 6d. per ton	5s.10d. per ton

Any person taking a Flat load, may have any of the above said Coal, paying the cost at the pits, river dues, freight and cartage; And to accommodate poor Housekeepers, or such as cannot purchase a Ton at a time, smaller quantities will be delivered at the yard, at fourpence halfpenny per hundred of 120 pounds. Sworn Agents will attend constantly at the Coal Office, adjoining the weighing machine on Nova Scotia, upon Mann's Island, to whom the public may apply. By order of the proprietors.'[13]

James Brindley and John Rennie

3 *The Men who Planned*

The preamble for an Act of Parliament, passed in 1720, for 'making navigable' the Mersey & Irwell Navigation stated[1] 'That it would be very beneficial for trade, advantageous to the poor, and convenient for the carriage of coal . . . and would tend very much to the employing an increased number of watermen and seamen, and be a means of preserving the highways.'

Contained within such Acts were various clauses for the protection of the public but unusually

> 'since the River Mersey has been before navigable from Liverpool to Bank Quay all Goods, Wares and Merchandize passing between those two Places, are not to be liable to the Rates.' Between Bank Quay and Hunt's Bank, Manchester, the true artificial cut, a rate of 3s. 4d. (17p) per ton was applicable. '. . . all the necessary works were done, and a navigable communication made between Liverpool and Manchester, to the incalculable benefit of those towns . . .'[2]

The Mersey & Irwell Navigation which was improved, in so far as a river navigation can be, by a further Act[3] in 1794, was successful but 'the want of water . . . which was severely felt in

37

dry seasons, has been [a] source of expense to the undertakers . . .'² Furthermore, by 1842:

'The river is really unsightly. Gas drainings, the refuse of
factories, unite with countless other abominations to con-
taminate the stream, and render it equally fatal to animal
and vegetable life. The barges which pass up and down add
to the sombre effect of its dark colour; they are clumsy,
heavily constructed vessels, and are generally propelled by
poles or shafts. The eye accustomed to the dashing steamers
and trim-built wherries of the Thames, can receive little
pleasure from contemplating the navigation of the Irwell.'⁴

The primary object of the Duke of Bridgewater was

'. . . to open his valuable collieries at Worsley, and to supply
the town of Manchester with coal, at a much cheaper rate
than could be done by the imperfect navigation of the
Mersey and Irwell.'⁵

Commencing with an acknowledgment to the Duke of Bridgewater:

'As you have early in life begun and already finished a work
which few Princes would have ventured to engage in, as an
Englishman you have my hearty thanks for the great good
done in the Kingdom and particularly to those parts of it
which from my infancy I have most esteemed. Distant
counties already see the mercantile profits that will arise
from your navigation and are striving who shall be the first
to imitate your works which by men of great understanding
were deemed impracticable, and others skilled in the
mathematical sciences have much admired the execution of
them . . .'⁵

and going on to state that a statue to the Duke's glory should
be erected, this intriguing exposition on the Bridgewater Canal,
written in 1769, shows extremely clearly the all-round advantages of the new stillwater navigations:

'When we consider that the wants and necessaries of life of
mankind, are particularly supplied by trade and commerce
it will appear of the utmost importance to render their

communication with each other for those solitary purposes as easy and commodious as possible, thus navigation joins as it were the whole world in a social intercourse of benefits. It conveys the super-abundance of the productions of one country or climate to another, destitute of those productions or manufactures . . .'[5]

Then there was the increase in trade leading to new buildings and hence increased labour utilization, and at the time nearly all work whether in factories, ironworks, or collieries, was labour intensive.

'The Navigation of the Are [sic] and Calder in Yorkshire will elucidate the great utility of inland navigations in the increase of established manufactures and in setting up of new ones, as it is well known that the navigations to Manchester and the salt works in Cheshire have contributed to the present flourishing state of the port of Liverpool.'[5]

Landowners of the period were to welcome the new navigations for the advantages they created by forming new outlets for the produce from their land, and during the digging of the waterways, special bonuses were paid to men who found minerals; one suspects that this contingency was not only covered but hoped for, particularly coal.[6]

As the landowners also had money invested in toll roads, they were not sorry that canals 'prevent the burdening of them with vast quantities of heavy goods which do them most injury so that from this relief they may become the finest roads in Europe'.[5]

Taking on an Act of Parliament had its hazards, at very high costs to the proprietors. As the Duke's Act was a model for those to come, it is as well to understand that although he could

'. . . enter lands, dig, and remove obstructions and then to make towing paths on the side of his canal, gutters, and watercourses, walks, etc. etc. weighing beams, bridges, arches, etc., for setting up posts, rails, etc. . . .'[5]

he must first placate the owners of the land through which it was desired to cut the canal. Because of the existing navigation '. . . no water to be taken out of the river Irwell into his cut or canal'.⁵ While he could survey the route and force the land-owners to disgorge '. . . the lands so to be let out shall not exceed 16 yards in breadth . . .'.⁵ Where he might build wharves was geographically defined and an arbitration machinery set up. Simply expressed, if any seven or more landowners and the Duke failed to agree terms '. . . juries may be empanelled to assess the purchase monies . . .'. The selling price of coal from his mines was settled at '. . . 4d. per hundred at Manchester, the navigation to be "free" [open to anyone] upon payment of the appropriate tolls, while tonnage rates were not to exceed 2/6d. per ton . . . on any part of, or on all of his Navigation.' However, 'All kinds of Manure, and Stones for repairing the Roads, are exempt from the Payment of Toll'. These tolls, while kept to in the Duke's time, were wrongly interpreted later,* and may have encouraged the building of the Liverpool and Man-chester Railway. Oddly, the Marquis of Stafford – successor to the Duke of Bridgewater – of whom it was said in 1831, the waterway had '. . . increased his annual income to the enor-mous amount of £260,000'² was to take up 1,000 of the 4,233⅓ shares in the Liverpool & Manchester Railway in 1825; a piece of business acumen second only to the Duke's in building the waterway.

During this work, although we have spoken of it as 'the Duke's canal', the planning, building and general running was carried on by a tripartite group, Bridgewater, John Gilbert his agent and James Brindley his engineer.

James Brindley is often described as 'Britain's First (and/or) Greatest Engineer', he was no such thing, but the part he played in the construction of our present canal network must never be underrated, while his life is an excellent example of how a 'do-it-yourself' man could, with a little luck, rise from total obscurity to fame. Born in 1716, he received some educa-tion and was not apprenticed until the relatively late age of 17. However, he rapidly found himself involved in much mill work, and it is probable that this gave him at least some of his con-fidence in the handling of 'hydraulic fluids'. From 1750 to 1756 he was involved in a scheme to eliminate flooding in the Wet Earth Colliery at Clifton near Manchester.⁷ For this work he

* For details see Gladwin, D D, *The Canals of Britain*, B T Batsford.

received 2/– (10p) per day, but during his subsequent work (scarcely better paid) at a windmill in Burslem (1758–9), for J. & T. Wedgwood, he contracted a misalliance with a Mary Bennett, their son being baptized 31 August 1760 – the great great grandfather of Arnold Bennett. In his remaining spare time he was employed by Earl Gower – one of the Duke of Bridgewater's guardians – to survey a canal line between the rivers Trent and Mersey; and it is in no wise fanciful to presume that the Earl suggested his name as engineer when the Duke of Bridgewater was considering his canal project, to run from Worsley to Manchester.

Those who are accustomed to the suave aloof canal engineers of today may find in Brindley an amusing contrast: 'In appearance and manners as well as acquirements a mere peasant. Unlettered and rude of speech, it was easier for him to devise means for executing a design, than to communicate his ideas concerning it to others.'[8] His method of working was unusual:

'When any extraordinary difficulty occurred to him, in the execution of his works, having little assistance from books, (for it is not true that he never learned to read or write) or from the labours of other men, his resources lay within himself. In order, therefore, to be quiet and uninterrupted, while he was in search of the necessary expedients, he generally retired to his bed, and he had been known to lie, one, two or three days, till he had attained the object in view. He would then get up, and execute his design without any drawing or model. Indeed, it was never his custom to make either, unless he was obliged to it, to satisfy his employers. His memory was so remarkable, that he has often declared, that he could remember and execute all the parts of the most complex machines, provided he had time, the several departments, and their relations to each other.'[9]

He had an equally unorthodox approach to his personal problems; when he had toothache it is said[10] that he would alternately pour jugs of hot and cold water over the tooth, on the basis, 'If it spites me, why then I'll spite it'. We all worry teeth with our tongues, but that was downright masochistic! The Duke of Bridgewater was, during the building of the canal, reduced to living on £400 per annum, while Brindley received roughly £120 plus free board. After the opening of this water-way in 1761, Brindley tried to stretch himself in too many directions, although accruing a reasonable income in the process – for his work on the Staffs & Worcs Canal alone he received £500 p.a. and '. . . [he] does not attend one month in twelve'.[11] On the main line of the Trent & Mersey canal he received 7/– (35p) per day at which time a labourer received 1/– (5p) in winter and 1/2d. (6p) in summer; on the Coventry £240 p.a.; on the Birmingham £200 p.a. On top of this were his surveying fees, etc., although in fairness from this must be deducted both his own costs and the pay of at least one assistant.

On 8 December 1765, at the age of 49, he married 19-year-old Anne Henshall, whose brother Hugh was to appear later as both the General Manager of the Trent & Mersey Canal and as a carrier; the interlocking of the 'old boys' club' was never better exemplified. In September 1772, Brindley was called upon by Josiah Wedgwood and the management of the Trent & Mersey to survey the line of a branch canal to Froghall. Pig-headed as ever, after getting soaked he went to an inn and dried off by parboiling himself in front of the fire. Soon after he retired to a damp bed. On 26 September 1772, Wedgwood wrote to his partner Bentley that:

'Poor Mr. Brindley has nearly finish'd his course in this world – He says he must leave us, & indeed I do not expect to find him alive in the morning. His disorder I think I told you before is a Diabetes, & this malady he has had upon him for seven years past most probably, which occasion'd his constant fever and thirst, though I believe no one of his Doctors found it out till Dr. Darwin discover'd it in the present illness, which I fear will deprive us of a valuable friend, and the world of one of the greatest Genius's who seldom live to see justice done to their singular abilities, but must trust to future ages for that from their fellow mortals. Poor Mrs. Brindley is inconsolable, & will scarcely be prevail'd upon to take either rest or food sufficient to support nature, but she has promis'd me to exert herself in bearing this afflicting stroke in her power, for the sake of her Aged Parents and her helpless Children.'

Brindley died on the 27 September at 12 noon, having earlier been given a drink by Wedgwood, after supping at it he exclaimed: 'It's enough, I shall need no more' – a direct expression from a direct man.

Thomas Telford was another country man, hailing from Glendinning in the Lowlands of Scotland where he was born on 9 August 1757. Unfortunately his father died within a few months and, living in a tied cottage, like many a later canal family in similar circumstances, the Telfords were ejected. After attending parish school Telford was apprenticed, eventually, to a stonemason, and on becoming a journeyman he left Eskdale, and in 1782 went to London, where he worked on both Somerset House, and the Portsmouth Docks. In a letter (1 February 1786), he describes how he normally got up at 7 a.m., getting progressively earlier until 5 a.m. became his normal summer rising hour. He then did his paperwork until 9 a.m., when he had breakfast, and arrived at the Yard at ten o'clock. After conferring with various people, and as Clerk of the Works-cum-Surveyor, visiting sites, he took lunch from 2.0–3.30 p.m., then continued his rounds again until 5, when tea was taken. From 6 till 9.30 he studied, 'then comes Supper and Bed Time'. He was proud to boast: 'I am powdered every day, and have a clean shirt 3 times a week', as proof that he did not neglect himself.

In 1787 he was appointed County Surveyor for Shropshire and as such was responsible for the design of Shrewsbury gaol where he met John Howard the great reformer, one result of which was the hitherto almost unknown usage of prisoners on outside labour: in this case the excavation of the Roman city of Uriconium. Among his other works were the church of St. Mary Magdalene at Bridgnorth, another at Madeley and the first of the bridges – that at Montford – that were to earn him the nickname of 'Pontifex Maximus'. At this time, 1790, he was also writing poetry, a contrast with Brindley who, when he attended the play Richard III with Garrick playing the lead, was overcome with excitement and retired to bed for several days. Sensibly, the honest Brindley never went to see play-acting again. As Brindley found London, so did Telford Birmingham which, he says, was '. . . famous for Buttons, Buckles and Locks and Ignorance and Barbarism. Its prosperity [like Britain today perhaps] increases upon the corruption of Taste and Morals.'

In September 1793, he was appointed 'General Agent, Surveyor, Engineer, Architect & Overlooker of the Canal & Clerk to the Committee & Sub-Committees when appointed' to the Ellesmere Canal Company which, inter alia, was planned to tap the coalfields of Wrexham. His was not the only application for the position, but he had not only the support of the ironmasters Abraham Darby and William Reynolds, but also of John Wilkinson, called by Telford 'King of the Iron Masters'. His salary was to be £500 p.a., out of which, as with Brindley's appointments, he had to find his own clerk and assistant. William Jessop, already a famous engineer, who had previously been involved in the surveys of the route was to prove a staunch friend to Telford until his (Jessop's) death in 1814 – a rare example of a partnership untarnished by jealousy.

In early 1795 Telford was appointed engineer to another canal, the Shrewsbury, which was to run from the 'Town of Shrewsbury to the Coalleries in the neighbourhood of the Wrekin at a place called Ketley'. In the same year work commenced on the famous Pontcysyllte Aqueduct, the foundation stone being laid on 25 July 1795, but it was ten years before it was opened on 26 November 1805: 'This day the stupendous aqueduct of Pontcysylte, upon the Ellesmere canal, was opened with great solemnity . . .

'Before 2 o'clock, the aqueduct having been filled, the procession began. The earl of Bridgewater's barge led the way, in which was his lordship and the countess, sir Watkin Williams Wynne, bart., sir Foster Cunliffe, bart., col. Kynaston-Powell and lady, and several other ladies and gentlemen. In the prow of the barge, the serjeant-major of the Shropshire volunteers, in full uniform, carried a flag, on which was painted a representation of the aqueduct, the Dee, and the valley . . . Next followed other members of the committee, and Mr. Telford, the projector of the aqueduct and general agent to the company in col. Kynaston-Powell's barge, carrying two union-jacks. In the third was the numerous band of the Shropshire volunteers in full uniform, playing "God save the King" and other loyal airs.

. . . As soon as the first barge entered the cast-iron water-way, which is 126 feet above the level of the river Dee, the artillery company of the Shropshire volunteers fired 16 rounds, from two brass field-pieces, which were taken at Seringapatam, and presented to that regiment by the earl of Powis. In the intervals of the discharge from the guns, the procession received the repeated acclamations of the numerous work-men, and a prodigious concourse of spectators. . . . The company from the barges landed, and the earl of Bridge-water, as chairman of the committee, conducted the ladies and their friends to a house belonging to the company, where they partook of a cold collation . . . The company went back to their barges, and the procession returned in the same order as it came. The two boats laden with coals followed the procession; the first having a handsome flag, thus inscribed: "This is the first trading-boat which passed the aqueduct of Pontcysylte, loaded from Plaas-Kynaston collieries, on the 26th day of November 1805." The discharge from the guns, as the procession returned, the plaudits of the spectators (calculated at full 8000) the martial music, the echo rever-berating from the mountains, magnified the enchanting scene; and the countenance of every one present bespoke the satisfaction with which they contemplated this very useful and stupendous work . . .'[12]

In a literal sense this was the high point of Telford's career.

'Pontifex Maximus' was for a while mainly involved in bridge and road building in Scotland and elsewhere, accompanied by his coterie of mainly Scottish assistants. Unmarried and grow-ing harder as he grew older, the unpleasant side of his character was shown in his treatment, while in the Highlands, of his ex-assistant on the Ellesmere Canal, John Duncombe. Somewhat inefficient, Duncombe was clearly unhappy in Scotland and ageing; for in October 1809 Telford wrote: 'He seems to be getting into dotage . . . I have for 10 weeks past stopt his salary . . .', and when he died in Inverness Gaol the following year all Telford could say was: 'I am quite vexed about the old fool – his dying will not be a matter of regret, but in Jail at Inverness is shocking.'[13]

In 1801/2 Telford first surveyed the line of the Caledonian

Canal, the work commencing in 1804, although it was not opened until 1822, partly because Telford took on an immense amount of other work.

To combat the slump which followed the peace of Waterloo the Government set up the Exchequer Loan Commission in 1817, which could make low interest loans to projects which would give employment. As engineering adviser, Telford was to be involved in many canal schemes he might otherwise not have worried about; each had to be inspected, and when it is considered they varied from the Bude in Cornwall to the Great Level of the Fens, it will be seen he had plenty of work. Not the least of his problems was the Gloucester & Berkeley, which was to have been a ship canal $17\frac{3}{4}$ miles long. Robert Mylne, another Scot and stonemason (Blackfriars Bridge, London, is his best known work) was appointed Surveyor and Engineer in 1793 and quoted £121,329.10.4d (£121,329.52p) as the cost. Initially he was paid £350 p.a., while an advertisement was placed for a:

RESIDENT ENGINEER
of ability and character,
qualified to superintend the
compleating and cutting the
said Canal, and the several
works and buildings
thereon . . .[14]

One Denis Edson was employed at £210 p.a. Two years later Edson was dismissed, his workmanship (and that of James Dadford, his successor) being criticized by Rennie: 'I have in my estimate gone on the supposition that all the new works are to be executed in a much more perfect and substantial manner than those already done on this Canal.'[15] While Mylne himself had his earnings cut to £4.20 per day (plus expenses) only payable for the days when he attended the works: this in 1797. Shortly afterwards he retired from the scene. At 64 he may have felt unable to face the travelling to and from his home in London. In 1799 the canal company had expended £112,000 and completed $5\frac{1}{2}$ miles. In 1807: 'The Canal . . . remains unfinished, and generally speaking, canals are unpopular in Gloucestershire . . . Canal and road-making should be the national work of the soldiery and provincial criminals, and petty offenders: and the shares should be the property of those whose lands are cut through.'[16] Aside from the last paragraph this 'national work' became so when the Exchequer Loan Commissioners, at Telford's recommendation, lent them in all £160,000 between 1817 and 1826. In 1818 the foundation stone of Sharpness docks was laid:

> 'To extend the advantages of commerce into the Interior of the Kingdom and to facilitate the intercourse with Foreign Countries, the Gloucester & Berkeley Canal Company projected this work. The approbation of the most illustrious and dignified Personages of the realm sanctioned the undertaking; and the countenance of His Royal Highness William Frederick, Duke of Gloucester, assisted by the noble House of Berkeley, was particularly evinced in graciously condescending to lay the first stone of this Harbour, the fifteenth day of July, 1818. Long may it remain unmoved, a Monument of national enterprise, a benefit to the proprietors, and a secure Harbour for the commerce of the World,'[15]

and John Woodhouse appointed engineer at £525 per annum (inflation there even!). Subsequently, following a trifle of, if not misappropriation, at least misdirection of funds – to his son – Woodhouse was dismissed, Telford writing in May 1820: 'I am of opinion that it is absolutely necessary to employ as Resident Engineer a person wholly unconnected with Contractors for Material or Labour in any shape,'[15] and J. Fletcher was appointed, staying on until the opening on 26 April 1827. Five years previous to this Telford embarked on a survey of the Birmingham Canal and found '. . . adjacent to this great and flourishing town, a canal little better than a crooked ditch with scarcely the appearance of a haling-path, the horses frequently sliding and staggering in the water, the haling-lines sweeping the gravel into the canal and the entanglement at the meeting of the boats incessant; while at the locks at each end of the short summit crowds of boatmen were always quarrelling, or offering premiums for a preference of passage, and the mine owners, injured by the delay, were loud in their just complaints.'[17]

After straightening works had been carried out under his direction (1827), being described as 'second to no other Canal

Works whatever in the Kingdom', a couple of years later he asked a passing boatman what he thought of the new cut, 'Sir,' he replied, 'I wish it went all the way to Manchester,' which must, indeed, have pleased Telford. A move towards this had already taken place in 1826, when the Birmingham & Liverpool Junction, the last of his canals, obtained its Act.[18] And what a contrast this was and is to the meanderings of Brindley's pastoral canals. No longer was attention paid to wandering from this village to that, taking produce, coal or fertilizer to and fro, instead Telford's directive was to move goods quickly from port to factory, from factory to docks, raw materials in, finished out, no longer any need to worry about villages, they were already depopulated to make way for the landowners 'shoots', pretty gardens and great estates. The villager, bereft of his plot of land, his cow and his pig, was now factory-fodder; no longer had he the illusion of independance: now he was one of the faceless working class.

'It is manifest enough that the population of this valley was, at one time, many times over what it is now . . . it is an exchange of labour in Wiltshire for labour in Lancashire . . . those who labour, no matter in what way, have a large part of the fruit of their labour taken away, and receive nothing in exchange . . . By some means or other there must be an end to it, and my firm belief is that that end will be dreadful. In the meanwhile I see, and I see it with pleasure, that the common people know that they are ill-used; and that they cordially, most cordially, hate those who ill-treat them.'[19]

Telford had come the full circle, he began his canals in Shropshire and ended working there again. In September 1830 the first train ran on the Liverpool & Manchester Railway, on 2 September 1834, Telford died. Deaf for the last three years, he had outlived most of his friends, had seen the railways coming, but had left behind the waterways we travel today; his last, and in many ways his greatest, the Birmingham & Liverpool Junction not being opened until 2 March 1835.[20]

Canal tokens

4 *The Men who Dug*

'On Monday last a disturbance, of a serious nature, occurred at Sampford Peverell. The annual fair, for the sale of cattle, &c. was held there on that day. On the Saturday preceding, a number of the workmen employed in excavating the bed of the Grand Western Canal, assembled at Wellington for the purpose of obtaining change for the payment of their wages, which there has been lately considerable difficulty in procuring. Many of them indulged in inordinate drinking, and committed various excesses at Tiverton, and other places to which they had gone for the purpose above stated. On Monday the fair at Sampford seemed to afford a welcome opportunity for the gratification of their tumultuary disposition. Much rioting took place in the course of the day, and towards evening a body of these men, consisting of not less than 300, had assembled in the village. – Mr. Chave [a local worthy] . . . was met on the road, and recognized by some of the party. Opprobrious language was applied to him . . . [and] . . . The rioters followed him to the house, the windows of which they broke; and apprehensive of further violence, Mr. Chave considered it necessary to his defence to discharge a loaded pistol at the assailants. This unfortunately took effect, and one man fell dead on the spot. A pistol was also fired by a person within the house, which so severely wounded another man, that his life is despaired of. A carter, employed by Mr. Chave, was most dreadfully beaten by the mob. Additional numbers were accumulating when our accounts were sent off, and we understand their determination was to pull down the house.'[1]

The oddest note to the modern ear is that the men, 'navvies', met 'for the purpose of obtaining change for the payment of their wages'. The normal rate of pay for a navvy was one calculated on a 'butty' or gang rate, not dissimilar to that in use contemporaneously in the Staffordshire coalfields. 'The masters employ butties to get the coal; these butties employ the men and pay them as they please: they make them work half a day for a quarter's wages.'[2] Up to the end of the first quarter of the nineteenth century there was an inadequate supply of small coinage – or indeed of money – partially because insufficient was minted to meet the demand (for example between 1815 and 1820 no copper coins were struck), and equally because the small banks of that day could not keep too much money on the premises, being forced to send elsewhere when a demand came.

This shortage could lead to all manner of troubles. On 22 October 1804, John Telford (no relation) wrote to Thomas Telford that (on the Caledonian Canal):

'Last Saturday . . . was pay day and a very disagreeable one it was; notwithstanding the men were all informed when you were here that those upon days wages [they] would only receive 1/6d per day, they refused to take it. Nor do I suppose it will be settled without going before a Justice. Mr. Wilson and myself were in eminent danger of our lives; yet notwithstanding we would not give way to one of them, tho they threatened much and were on the point of using violence several times. This prevents me getting the Pay Bill filled up to send by this post but shall transmit it the first post after matters are adjusted with every particular of this disagreeable business.'

The Scots employed on the work, were described by Telford – himself a Scot – as 'a people just emerging from Barbarism', who, when aggravated or questioned would claim they spoke no English; another problem for our contractor!

One result of this kind of behaviour was the issue of copper tokens – only exchangeable at the Tommy Shop or Public House – often by the canal company or one of the proprietors. Alternatively, large coins were quartered or halved. John Pinkerton, contractor for the building of the Basingstoke Canal, rather unusually, for halfpennies and pennies were more usual, issued copper (not silver) shillings, which were only exchangable at local public houses from whom Pinkerton received a commission.

The contractor, to whom we shall return later, would employ a 'butty', or ganger, who would enlist a band of men to carry out a certain amount of work. This system applied when discharging a collier into barges on the river.

'The whole system which is by law, provided for the discharge of the Colliers into the Barges is altogether defective. The allowance made by law to the Whippers, amounting to 3s. for each score of 20 chaldrons, being higher than the present market rates of wages of labour, much abuse has arisen in the distribution of the excess. It appears by the evidence . . . that the Undertakers, who usually provide the gangs of Whippers for unloading the vessels, connect themselves with publicans and shopkeepers, and compel the men whom they choose to employ to purchase liquor and goods of those persons upon very disadvantageous terms.'[3]

During 1770 the coal-heavers were bitterly complaining that the undertakers were charging them ½d. per score rent for shovels,*required that they spent 6d. (2½p) a day at their pubs and, to compound their misery, charged them 4d. per quart

* As late as 1948 workmen on the nationalized waterways were required to provide their own shovel.

for beer worth only 1d.!

A similar method of gang working was applied at Sapperton tunnel on the Thames & Severn canal.

'We now approached the great tunnel, which forms part of the communication between the Severn and the Thames . . . one end penetrates the hill at the village of Sapperton, the other comes out in Heywood; we turned on our left to visit the former and saw the shafts busy in several places, at a distance of about 230 yards from each other; by this means they wind up the materials from the cavity and expedite the work. The earth is principally a hard blue marle, and in some places quite a rock which they blow up with gunpowder, the depth of these pits are upon an average eighty yards from the surface. The first contractor receives £7 per yard from the company, and the labourers rent it at the rate of about £5 per yard, finding candles, gunpowder, &c., the workers are in eight gangs, having two or three reliefs and continue eight hours at a time, day and night.'[4]

The work of a navvy was far from easy, for virtually all the work of digging out a canal, embanking, draining tunnels, and locks, was carried out by hand. The chain of command in canal excavating was simple. The proprietors hired an engineer, he probably, but not necessarily, delegated the work to a resident engineer, who then appointed contractors, usually in co-operation with the Company Secretary, to carry out a certain part of the work. Normally, but not always, a number of contractors would tender for the length or cubic quantity; the better engineers, Telford for example, insisted a contractor should take on one hard length and one easy. The engineer was not bound to take the cheapest tender, as the results would be upon his head, nor indeed need he accept a particular contractor for one specific job if he doubted his ability to carry it out, but he could be overruled – if young and unestablished – by a parsimonious Company Secretary.

The contractor might then employ his men direct, or alternatively use a 'butty'. A fairly typical advertisement, which shows the number of men required, even on a small job, appeared in the *Bath Chronicle*, 5 July 1804.

The Men who Dug

To CANAL DIGGERS, &c.

WANTED, Six or Eight Hundred Men, to be immediately
employed in Cutting the NEW DOCKS and CANAL for
Improving the HARBOUR of BRISTOL, where every
encouragement will be given to men, and the prices
as under for some or greater part of the works, viz.
3½d. and in some places 4d. per yard, for the first
stage of 20 yards, and 1d. per yard for every 20
yards in length after the first 20 yards; and 3d.
per yard for filling Carts. To receive Four Shillings
per day subsistence, and a final settlement every
month. The ground consists of clay and silt, and the
materials are all ready for that number of men. Men
coming from great distance shall receive something
for their travelling expences.

Labour was a problem: in the Midlands there were colliers,
ironworkers and their kind to draw on, but on the more remote
navigations where the men were unaccustomed to the particular
disciplines of a navvy's life, not even the promise of high wages
could draw or retain men of a reasonable physique.

> 'The contractor, agreeable to the request of the company of
> proprietors, gives the preference to all the natives who are
> desirous of this work, but such is the power of use over
> nature, that while these industrious poor are by all their
> efforts incapable of earning a sustenance, those who are
> brought from similar works, chearfully obtain a comfortable
> support.'[4]

Similarly, horses to operate the 'gins' might not be available,
or only at an improbably high price, and oxen substituted.
Navvies themselves, in times of great demand, could be uncommonly uppity and if they heard of better wages elsewhere
would pack up and go, leaving only their women and children
to mark their passing. The mobility of such men was to bedevil
many waterways, although not to any extent those of, say,
Telford or Outram, both of whom received the men's loyalty in
exchange for relatively civilized conditions. Interestingly, the
navvies, most of whom were illiterate, relied upon and paid a
'navvy newspaper' to keep them abreast of developments. Not

a newspaper as we know it, but a navvy who had met with an accident, 'Wingy', 'Hoppity Rabbit', 'Dai Half', have all been recorded as performing the task of making their way from one camp to another bringing tidings, good or bad and, unfortunately, in the 1800s, cholera.

In the year 1832:

'The Asiatic cholera, which had been raging throughout the length and breadth of the land, acquired at this time a firm and fatal hold in this district. In June it appeared in Tipton, and on August 4th at Bilston, where, in little over three weeks, 565 of the inhabitants were swept away. On one of the early days of this latter month it appeared in Walsall, conveyed, in the opinion of the medical men of the town, direct from Bilston by the water of the canal.'[5]

The poor old canal was, of course, the scapegoat:

'The first victim that perished by it in Walsall was a man who lodged in a house on the bank of the canal terminus; he was well and dead in twenty-four hours. Another man working in a boat shared the same fate. The whole neighbourhood that stood within the breeze of wind from this part of the canal became immediately infected with the disease . . . So terrifying was the number of deaths daily that no one cared to put them into their coffins, neither could bearers be obtained to carry the dead to be buried, so that a man was employed by the authorities to go round the neighbourhood from house to house twice a day to carry off each corpse as soon as possible.'[5]

Apart from the constant risk of death or being maimed for life, the navvy stood in special risk of getting certain nasty ailments and given even 'That Mr. Robert Rean of East Looe be Surgeon and Apothecary to attend the Laborers working on this Canal and that six pence per month be deducted from the wages of each person employed, as a Remuneration to him for his Services'[6] their chances of a cure were almost non-existant.

'In 1801, when a fever was raging in all the higher parts of the town [Nottingham] and in its vicinity, there was but one tanner's yard in that street; yet, but very few dangerous symptoms appeared in it during the time the fever was raging. But while people could be found, sufficiently credulous to believe, that the scrofula could be cured by the touch of a king, no wonder they should also believe, that the plague was wholly arrested in its progress by the effluvium arising from the tanner's ouze.'[7]

With such faith, if they suffered from Yellow Jaundice, common enough, 'for which the Doctors, &c. . . . could give no Relief'; 'Rhumatic Pain . . . could not go without Crutches'; 'Ague and Fever' so badly that 'everyone that saw him hourly expected his Death' or 'the Sore Throat and Fever, which hath raged so violently'; all these ailments could be cured, in the words of a contemporary advertisement, by 'Bateman's Pectoral Drops' and they were 'soon restored to Health and Strength'.[8]

The opinion of the public relating to navvies was, justly or unjustly, one of disgust, repugnance, nausea, loathing or at very least resentment at his existence. As an example of this view we have a report in the *Carlisle Patriot*, dated 27 February 1846:

'During these trials the utmost interest prevailed in court – and among the spectators were to be seen a great number of navigators. They seemed much surprised at the severity of the sentence on Hobday – fifteen years transportation for maiming another navvy – but that worthy turned around and laughed at them. The prisoner Hobday is a remarkable man, and may be considered a type of the class to which he belongs. His stature is rather below the common height, but his broad frame gives evidence of immense strength. His countenance is forbidding in the extreme. Every feature indicates habitual crime:

> For evil passions, cherished long,
> Have ploughed them with expressions strong.

while his rough matted hair completed the aspect of the finished ruffian. We understand he has said that for nine years he has never slept in a bed, or worn a hat; that his custom was to put on his boots when new, and never remove them until they fell to pieces, and his clothes were treated very much in the same way, except that his shirt was changed once a week.'

With the 'better' classes not seeking to hide their feelings, it is not really over surprising that many navvy songs are bitter, the last verse of *Played Out* reads:

> 'They pulled it out of the ditch in the dark,
>   as a brute is pulled from its lair,
> The corpse of a navvy, stiff and stark,
>   with the clay on its face and hair.'[9]

Even when the canal was dug and drinks for all were on the table: the tables for 'them' (navigators) and 'us' (promoters) were kept well apart. On the opening of the Wey & Arun Junction canal, 28 September 1816, the Earl of Egremont

'... with a numerous company of friends and shareholders, attended by the Mayor and Aldermen of Guildford, assembled at Alford, where, after having provided a plentiful roasted ox and 200 gallons of ale [for the use of navvies] they embarked on the canal in four barges, enlivened by two bands of music ... About four o'clock, the interesting spectacle reached Guildford Bridge, when the Mayor and Aldermen landed, and having assumed the regalia of the corporation, and being joined by the other branches of it, accompanied by one of the town Members, neighbouring gentry, and magistrates, and attended by a band of music and colours, they welcomed the arrival of Lord Egremont and his friends. The whole then went in procession to the White Hart inn, where one hundred and thirty persons partook of a sumptuous dinner ...'[10]

Alford and Guildford are eleven miles apart, a sufficient distance to ensure the navvies' effluvia did not reach them.

In the end, any summing up of a navvy's existence depends upon your viewpoint. A writer of 1839, who wished to see the end of the navvy system tells us that:

'In the making of canals it is the general custom to employ gangs of hands who travel from one work to another and do nothing else. These banditti, known in some parts of England by the name of 'Navvies' or 'Navigators', and in others by that of 'Bankers', are generally the terror of the surrounding country; they are as completely a class by themselves as the Gipsies. Possessed of all the daring recklessness of the Smuggler, without any of his redeeming qualities, their ferocious behaviour can only be equalled by the brutality of their language. It may be truly said, their hand is against every man, and before they have been long located, every man's hand is against them; and woe befal any woman, with the slightest share of modesty, whose ears they can assail. From being long known to each other, they in general act in concert and put at defiance any local constabulary force; consequently crimes of the most atrocious character are common, and robbery, without an attempt at concealment, has been an everyday occurrence, wherever they have been congregated in large numbers. . . .'[11]

While a newswriter of 1811, indubitably a forerunner of modern 'comic' leader writers, and probably bored anyway, referring to the disturbance at Sampford Peverell (p. 49) expresses his feelings thus:

'It is impossible not to feel the deepest abhorrence for the proceedings of a savage ungovernable banditti, whose ferocious behaviour we hope will be visited by the heaviest punishments of the Law . . . It is a most extraordinary circumstance that the whole village and neighbourhood should have been kept in a state of the greatest terror and commotion for more than twenty-four hours, and no effects of the Police or Military made to quell the tumult. In the name of Justice, where are the Magistrates!'[12]

The navvy could only poke fun at himself:

> 'And the demon took in hand
> Moleskin, leather, and clay,
> Oaths embryonic and
> A longing for Saturday,
> Kneestraps and blood and flesh,
> A chest exceedingly stout,
> A soul – (which is a question
> Open to many a doubt),
> And fashioned with pick and shovel,

And shapened in mire and mud,
With life of the road and the hovel,
And death of the line or hod,
With fury and frenzy and fear,
That his strength might ensure for a span,
From birth, through beer to bier,
The link twixt the ape and the man.'[9]

However, when all is said and done it is an incontrovertible fact that we must all die and, as the navvy would sing:

'Perhaps some mortal in speaking will give us a kindly thought –
"There is a muckpile they shifted, here is a place where they wrought,"
But maybe our straining and striving and singing will go for nought.'[9]

Contractors had problems during the period of canal building aside from purely physical ones.

The estimate for the cutting of the Manchester, Bolton & Bury was jointly agreed by Hugh Henshall, consulting engineer, and Matthew Fletcher, mining engineer-cum-coalowner-cum-technical adviser, at an average of £4 per yard. The minute book of 1790 then shows this as altered to £5 per yard. Locks were quoted at £500 per 12 foot rise, and the whole of the canal, including tunnels and reservoirs, at £40,000 for the 15¾ miles and 17 locks. Unfortunately, while planned as a narrow canal '. . . an agreement entered into in 1794, with the Leeds and Liverpool Canal Company, for making a junction at Redmoss, the proprietors of the Manchester, Bolton and Bury Canal were induced to make their canal capable of navigating vessels 14 feet wide, the same as those on the Leeds and Liverpool Canal.'[13] This meant the contractors, in some parts 'John Seddon of Little Hulton, labourer', had to rebuild most of their work to take boats of the larger size, and acrimonious disputes arose between the contractors and the proprietors as to how much work was 'extras'.

In the middle, was the resident engineer; Charles Roberts, a Londoner, who found his £300 per annum rather suddenly gone, in 1793: 'Resolved that this Committee have no further occasion for the service of Mr. Roberts . . . that he be acquainted with their Sentiments and desired to provide for himself.'

Accidents during the building of this canal were uncommonly numerous, the navvies being 'buried in slips', 'crushed', 'run over' (presumably on the barrow runs) and 'bereft of hearing' (due to blasting). In 1796 the committee agreed that Robert Holmes should be '... repaid £4. 2s. 6d. Money by him expended in assisting poor Persons who have been lame and rendered Sick in the Service of the Company and unfit to work and in burying others being Strangers in the Country'.

By 1794 money was running out and the committee estimated they needed another £12,132. 8s. 5¾d. to finish the waterway, cheerfully giving the excuse:

> 'Since the time of the original estimate the wages of workmen and labourers have increased coincidentally and still continue at a higher rate than they were when the estimate was taken, which brings us back to our poor old contractor. Inflation in 1974/5 is supposed to have run at rates that varied (according to source) between 9% and 23% but that wasn't anywhere near what happened during the 1790s. In 1794: "A few years back, men worked, in some places, all the year round, for 6d. a day, finding their own victuals . . . About the same time, strong women worked in the fields during hay harvest, &c. for three-pence a day, finding their own breakfast and dinner, if they had any . . . The price of labour is however stirring, even here a labourer, having 1s. per day in summer . . .".'[14]

and Berkshire magistrates urged farmers to 'increase the pay of their Labourers in proportion to the present price of Provisions'.[15] These wage increases were essential to cover the rising price of staple foods; butter 2.7p and cheese 1.6p per lb. in 1790, had risen to 4.6p and 2.6p respectively, furthermore, as the latter figures related to bulk buying, specifically to provisions purchased for the Royal Hospital Greenwich, smaller quantities would have been proportionately dearer. A pair of shoes costing 20p in 1790 could not be purchased for less than 28.5p while, similarly, coals (per caldron) rose from £1.72p to £2.75. Bread, indispensible, costing on average 2.75p per 4 lb. loaf between 1790 and 1794, rose during the next decade to 4.8p; while the price of candles rose during the same period from 38.7p to 51.6p per dozen pound. The bricklayer in 1800 earned 3.3p more per day and a carpenter 1.6p than they had in 1790, and they needed to! The contractor could not have foreseen this trend when he wrote out his estimates.

One contractor is supposed to have said 'God preserve me from bad engineers', and one can only have sympathy for both engineer and contractors who were involved in the building of the Southampton & Salisbury Canal. This waterway seems to have started under a cloud:

> 'Southampton's wise sons found their river so large,
> Tho' Twould carry a Ship, 'twould not carry a barge,
> But soon this defect their sage noddles supply'd,
> For they cut a snug ditch to run close by its side.
> Like the man who, contriving a hole through his wall,
> To admit his two cats, the one great, t'other small,
> Where a great hole was made for great puss to pass through,
> Had a little hole cut for his little cat, too.'[16]

Joseph Hill, who was to survey the route of the London & Southampton Ports Junctions Canal in 1796, was appointed surveyor in August 1795, 'the Committee to have exclusive use of his services' for which he was to receive £400 a year. His woefully inaccurate and happily vague estimate for the whole line totalled £48,929.16.6d.*[17]

Five contractors were involved, Thomas Jinkins, a stone-mason ex-the Kington, Leominster & Stourport, was responsible for work on the Southampton arm and Edward Gee, carpenter, the bulk of the Salisbury line. The others of widely differing habitats, John Laurence of Romsey, Thomas Green of Birmingham and John Brown of Wolverhampton, built aqueducts, locks and bridges on the Salisbury line, leaving Gee the 'navvying'. Problems arose on the Southampton line with Jinkins reporting he was in trouble with water on the 3 November 1796, while in the following March the Committee gave him permission to 'cut and cover' at his own expense! Matters then rested until 26 December 1797 – no Bank holidays then! – when the Committee investigated what was happening, calling in John Rennie in January 1798 to survey the work. He

* For details of this estimate see my *The Canals of Britain* (B T Batsford, 1973).

promptly lambasted both Hill and Jinkins:

> 'In respect to the work already done, it is by no means com-
> plete, those parts that are likely to stand are ill framed and
> seem to have been done with little care or judgement . . . In
> joining the different lengths of Arching together they do not
> in many places agree, i.e. sometimes one length is sunk more
> than another . . . At the West end of the tunnel a part of the
> sheeting for about 16 or 17 yards in length has entirely risen
> up and the tunnel has sunk about a foot. The whole of this
> length must be taken out and done anew . . . The Bricks I
> have examined are unsound, there is too much sand in the
> clay . . . The sand that has been used for the mortar is
> perfectly unfit for the purpose, being little better than clay
> . . . An agent or superintendent skilled in works of this sort
> should be procured, with an adequate salary, and his whole
> attention directed to it, not only to see the works are properly
> executed, but that no improper materials be used . . .'[18]

and on 28 March an awful warning was put out:

> '. . . it appears to the Committee by Mr. Rennie's Report in
> his Survey of the Tunnel that the work has been injudiciously
> done and the Materials not of that Quality for such Work
> and that the Contractor has not gone on with the work in the
> way the Committee had a right to expect . . .'

Spitefully, the Committee then directed that Jinkins must put
matters right at his own expense, which having no money
wherewith to pay men or buy materials he obviously could not.
In August, the Committee having taken over utilizing 'direct
labour' they were so financially embarrassed that they had to
admit the navvies were owed a month's money and not very
happy. By December 1798 work had almost stopped, with both
contractors and men laid off, and following a dispute with the
former over who had done what, and its cost, Rennie, Jessop
and Dadford were requested to arbitrate. In the following
April, though, John Savery, a banker of Bristol, and an
influential member of the Committee, wrote to the Company
Clerk, Thomas Ridding:

> '. . . it seems to me very unaccountable that the committee

should be so blind to their own and the Subscribers Interest as to suffer the work, by being neglected in Consequence of their disputes and distress, to run to ruin, and decay; by which a very considerable increas'd expence must be incurr'd. At any rate, the Canal must be finish'd . . . Then if Hill is prov'd to be a Rogue I'll acknowledge myself deceiv'd indeed, and shall perhaps blame my own credulity, but until that is the case, I can never take assertion for Fact. . . .'

John Rennie's final report on the canal received on 17 May 1799, was scathing

'. . . charges for extras along the old Town Ditch and the new Pond are exorbitant in the extreme, these charges amount to at least three times the worth of the actual work performed . . . the extras on the Lock under the Gaol and at Northam pumping water there, etc., are equally extraordinary, this must either have arisen from the most gross inattention on the part of the Contractor or deficiency in the plans pursued . . . the Contractors being confined to their Houses to avoid the sheriff's officers who were then in search of them . . .'

meant little was being done in the way of work. Hill was sacked and replaced by George Jones, a protegée of Rennie's, although Rennie himself was writing to the Committee on 3 February 1801 : 'When is Mr. Jessop and myself to look for payment of our Bill for the arbitration business on the Salisbury and Southampton Canal – besides the Arbitration there is a considerable sum due to me for the former surveys and Reports.' Hill, himself, after a spell in the King's Bench prison in 1800, disappears from the scene in November 1802, when he was bankrupt. Jinkins went back to Gloucester, but even the contractors appointed by Jones (one old and one new) Messrs. Brawn and Small, had to write to the Clerk and explain '. . . wee are sorry to be under the Disagrable nessaty of leaving the Country . . .''.

Finally, on 14 June 1804, George Jones issued a writ against the company for his pay!

By contrast with this unholy shambles Thomas Telford was,

save for a few odd exceptions, well served throughout his career. John Simpson 'a treasure of talents and integrity', was first employed as a mason on the work of Montford Bridge, 1790–1792, and re-appeared for work on the Pontcysyllte aqueduct, initially as partner with James Varley the original contractor, but later, after Varley's departure, as sole contractor responsible for the piers. In turn he employed John Wilson, a Cumberland man, who then remained in Telford's entourage. An earlier colleague, and youthful friend of Telford's, John Davidson, first appears as 'Superintendant' at Montford Bridge, and in a similar position at Pontcysyllte, where the company, upon their engineer's recommendation, built him a cottage. Telford was a Freemason but it may have been coincidence that 'Wizard' Hazledine, of similar habits, was to become yet another 'tied' man. Hazledine had by 1799[17] a furnace in blast at Plas Kynaston only a stone's throw from the line of the canal and was, naturally enough, given the contracts for the iron works of Chirk and Pontcysyllte. Later, too, he was to supply the iron rails for the tramroad from Pontcysyllte Basin and Ruabon Brook, and the ironwork for the famous Beeston Lock on the Chester Canal. Simpson, Wilson and Davidson together with another Scot, John Mitchell, next appear (aside from working with Telford on his Scottish roads) in connection with the Caledonian Canal. Davidson as resident engineer from Clachnaharry to Loch Ness, John Simpson as sole contractor for the entire length, Wilson as foreman mason, and Mitchell as Telford's personal assistant. Davidson died in 1818, but was succeeded by his son; Simpson in 1816, a loss that may well have delayed the works, for he alone could control the Welsh masons he brought with him from the Ellesmere Canal. Wilson and Hazledine both played their part in the building of the Gotha Canal and the Menai Bridge, and Wilson was finally to contract for work on the Birmingham & Liverpool Junction, from Nantwich to the top of Tyrley Locks, employing no less than 1,600 men, and even before this was finished he took on a further contract to complete the line from Church Eaton to Autherley, employing over 700 men there. Like Telford he was not to see the canal completed, for he died on 9 January 1831, leaving the remaining work to his sons; a training that was to stand them in good stead in the railway age.

A tangle typical of that which any self respecting contractor could find himself in occurred to Thomas Dadford senior and to Thomas Sheasby during the building of the Glamorganshire. Unfortunately for them they picked on the wrong bunch of proprietors, in as much as the great ironmasters, the Crawshays of Cyfarthfa, the Hills of Plymouth, Guest of Dowlais, Homfray, etc., were among the number who accepted a contract from the two Thos. Dadfords (father and son) and Thomas Sheasby on 30 June 1790, to build the canal for £48,288; the contractors disgorging a bond of £10,000 (by no means a small sum!) as a surety for their workmanship. No engineer was appointed, but the canal was opened on 10 February 1794. Dealing with the Crawshays directly, it was not really surprising that, when in 1795 the two remaining partners (Thomas Dadford junior having withdrawn) refused to repair a breach in the bank and threatened to withdraw their men unless more money was paid, they were put in prison for non-payment of their bond as part of £17,000 the proprietors thought they had been overcharged. As it happened the contractors were more or less in the right, for Robert Whitworth, the arbitrator, found only £1,512 of the £17,000 should be disgorged by them.

A weakness inherent in the circumstances of any small contractor was that, relying on payment upon work done in order to finance the next stage, and this work being measured in cubic yards, they would tend to work in 'penny packets'. A letter from Samuel Gregson, Secretary of the Lancaster Canal Company, on 5 June 1793, to the contractors Pinkerton & Murray bears this out:

> 'Mr. Murray is wanting to begin upon the New lot, but the Com^e have refused to give him liberty at present because he may employ a greater number of Men on the present Lot, & the Land on the New Lot is not agreed for. The com^e have great complaints that the work is not finished off as they go along, and a number of more hands might be employed without rambling over the Country and creating Damage unnecessarily.'[19]

While this seemed to have little effect, for on 14 December of the same year

8   Hydraulically operated cranes at Ellesmere Port on the
Shropshire Union Canal, about 1900. *(Courtesy of the Waterways
Research Centre)*
9   Dressed narrow boat *Redshank* of the Willow Wren Canal
Carrying Company Ltd at a Rally of Boats on the Oxford Canal at
Banbury in 1953. *(Courtesy of L A Edwards)*

10 Severn and Canal Carrying Company's motor boats and butties by Llanthony Warehouse on the River Severn at Gloucester Docks about 1930. *(Courtesy of The Water Folk)*

11 A pair of A Wander Ltd 'Ovaltine' boats carrying coal to King's Langley on the Grand Union Canal, about 1935. The notice on the derelict building reads 'Canal accommodation and fuel supplies'. *(Courtesy of The Water Folk)*

'. . . The Com^e are sorry that they have reason to observe that the General tendency of your Management is to get the works hurried on without regard to the convenience of the public, the loss of the land occupiers or the advantage of the Company. You seldom provide the necessary accommodations before you begin to make the Bridges, and in the excavation you place your men in so many various places without either finishing as you proceed or making your fences wall & posts & railing – that the whole Country is laid open to damage. This grievance which has already caused so much trouble and expence is so very obvious & so much owing to your neglect that the Company will no longer suffer it . . . The not fulfilling the promises you make & want of attention in yourselves, your Agents & workmen to the direction of the Company agent, are evils there is great reason to complain of . . .'[19]

On the other hand, sometimes a contractor would only take on a relatively small, but hard job, as Charles Jones, described as a mason and miner of Manchester, did when he accepted the contract to dig the Sapperton Tunnel on the Thames & Severn, on 7 October 1783.

'A proposal to make the Tunnel Through Sapperton hill and Haley Wood 15 feet wide and 16 feet high at £8-8-0 per yard – and the undertaker to Sink all the Shafts as may be wanted in the whole Tunnel – the Co to find Timber and Carpenter's work for making Gins Senters as maney as may be wanted to Compleat the Tunnel in the Time as may be fixed by the Committees Engineer and the Co to finde all Barrowes and planks and Ropes and Bricks and Basketts to Compleate all the works Through Hill.'[20]

Under this agreement, sealed the following day, he promised to complete the work by 1 January 1788. All told he was eventually to cut about 100 yards at the Sapperton end and 1,400 yards at Coates, out of a total length of 3,817 yards. In March 1874, due to the nature of the soil, Josiah Clowes, the engineer, certified that it was necessary to widen and deepen the excavation by $2\frac{1}{2}$ feet, so as to allow room for layers of clay and brickwork; and on 5 April, Jones, rather stupidly, signed an agreement under which he accepted this was an 'incident to the Contract' and forgetting the old Northern saying: 'See all, hear all, say nowt, Eat all, sup all, pay nowt, and if tha ivver does owt fer nowt do it for thisen!,' agreed that no extra payment could be claimed. In due course, after his sacking, Jones undertook Chancery Proceedings against the Company, claiming various expenses, and stating that the Committee of the Thames & Severn Canal Company had made him drunk before he signed the agreement. But it seems that Mr Jones was fond of the bottle, being jailed occasionally! Writing to the Superintendant of Works, he says,

'Mr. Smith, Sir, This is to Let you Know that I left Glouster [Jail] the last night about half-past Six O'clock – I gave Single Bale and Then Spasol Baile – Dirickly – To the Ashon – so Know I Shall be advised by you what more to Do . . . for Prue and him has Tould Mr. Gabson all the Dambs Lyles that Could be fromed by men, and for want of Being Better Informed he believed Them – I have Been Thrue the works This Day and we want Lime at Both ends – please to Send Sum as Soon as posoble you Can, from Sir your must Humbl Servt. Chas. Jones. Coates, Janry 23th.'[20]

This was in 1785, but previous to this his son George Jones had threatened to murder the Canal Company's Manager:

'and in consequence of which, the said George Jones was obliged to leave the neighbourhood; and he and his father give a joint undertaking, that he shall forthwith leave the works, and not come within 20 miles of any part of the Canal for 5 years, or molest, directly or indirectly the Manager, during his lifetime, or any of the Canal Company's servants.'[20]

The last mention we find of Jones Senior is in 1788 when he was detained in Gloucester Gaol for ten weeks on charges ranging from being drunk and disorderly, to debt. A contractor's lot was not a happy one.

One of the most abused, overworked and little recorded groups of men involved in canal life were the Secretaries or Chief Clerks (often one and the same). Their job was, on the one hand to fend off the proprietors who wanted their canal finished, in running order and paying, and on the other hand to find enough money – primarily by means of calls on shares – to pay the engineer, the contractors, to buy land, to pay wayleaves and so on, and when the canal was in running order, funds wherewith to pay both his staff and workmen. Necessarily, the tense used must be 'was', as when canals grow into a nationalized body the Secretary has to be a professional, living in an ivory tower, rather remote from the run-of-the-mill canal details and he no longer answers to a (human) 'Company of Proprietors', but instead, the usual faceless, amorphous Treasury.

The types of problems he had to deal with typified the efficiency or otherwise of the company that employed him. For example, in October 1802, the Committee of the Manchester, Bolton & Bury Canal: 'Ordered that the Clerk to the Company do immediately arrest the Little Bolton Colliery Company for all Arrears of Tonnage &c. unless the same is discharged on Notice being given.'[21] How do you arrest a colliery company? On the other hand another letter to the clerk on 7 October 1835, leaves one in no doubt as to the action the clerk should take: 'Sir, I want more warehouse room at Bolton for the purpose of storing more Goods than what I have room for at present. I should wish to have that part of the Warehouse that is on the road side that the packet stops on, the bottom room, and it will join that part of the Warehouse that I have at the present time.'[22]

On the Southampton & Salisbury Canal the clerk, in February 1805, gave what must have been the oddest progress report ever:

'The Southampton & Salisbury Canal is not going on at all at present but rather backwards as the Works are going very fast to Decay'[23] but that was not really to be wondered at when he had been receiving letters which read, for instance, 'Dr. Mackie's Compliments to Mr. Ridding – he declines risking any more of his property on the undertaking of the Southampton and Salisbury Canal.'[22]

Most, but not all, Clerks were either solicitors or attorneys. It is a little incongruous to find Bowsher & Broderip, Solicitors of Bath, calling for persons to contract for 'cutting, embanking, puddling and compleating the Somerset Coal Canal', matters which can hardly be reconcilable with whatever solicitors normally do.

John Meredith, Clerk to the Birmingham Canal, also doubled up as attorney, as can be seen from this notice of 4 June 1767, headed 'Birmingham Navigation':

'At a numerous Meeting held this day, Mr. Brindley produced a Plan and Estimate of making a navigable canal from the Town to the Staffordshire and Worcestershire Canal, through the principal Coal Works . . . and gave it as his opinion that the best [route] was from near New-Hall, over Birmingham Heath, to or near the following Places, viz., Smethwick, Oldbury, Tipton Green, Bilston, and from thence to the Staffordshire and Worcestershire Canal, with Branches to different Coal Works between the respective places. As the Undertaking seems of great Importance, it is agreed that there be a Meeting appointed at this place, on Friday next the 12th Inst., at Four o'Clock in the Afternoon of the same Day, in order to open a Subscription to raise a Fund for the Expence of obtaining a Law, and completing the Work, which it is supposed will not exceed the Sum of £30,000 including all Expences. In the mean time Mr. Brindley's Plan, Estimate, and Opinion, and some Calculations of the Coal likely to pass may be seen at Mr. Meredith's, Attorney at Law. It is expected that a Committee for the Conduct of this Undertaking will be chuse at the said Meeting.'[24]

Later, on 10 July:

'Whereas several numerous public Meetings have been held at the Swan Inn, to consider of a Plan for making a navigable Canal through the principal Coal Fields in this Neighbourhood by Smethwick, Oldbury, Tipton Green, and Bilston, in the Counties of Salop and Stafford to join the Canal now making between the Trent and Severn, at Addersly, near Wolverhampton, Mr. James Brindley having made a Survey of it, estimated that the Expence would not exceed the Sum of £50,000 and on Friday the 12th Day of June last . . . a Subscription was opened to apply to Parliament for Powers to make such a Canal, and for compleating the same. There is already £35,000 subscribed; the Subscription Deeds will continue open at Mr. Meredith's, Attorney at Law, Birmingham, until the 26th of July Inst. unless the whole sum of £50,000 be sooner subscribed.'[25]

On 6 November 1769, when works were almost complete:

'It is with pleasure we congratulate the Public on the probability of Coal being brought by Water near this Town in a few Days; and that the Canal Company have not only resolved to sell the same this Winter at their Wharf for Fourpence Half-penny per Hundred, long weight of 120 lb., but to fix the Price of their Delivery in every Street thereof; and in order for the better accommodating of the Poor, they have determined to establish Coal-Yards in different Parts of the Town, as soon as possible, where it will be sold in Quantities so small as Half Hundreds, or less.'[26]

The Committee furthermore said they hoped that the price of coals would drop after the winter and that they only wanted a 5 per cent dividend.[27] Undoubtedly Meredith earned the £100 per annum the Company paid him, for from 1769 to 1771 a running battle was waged between the Company's Chairman, William Bentley, and one of the Committee, Samuel Garbett, who, wrongly, thought he had been accused of taking undue priority with his demands for coal to serve his brass foundry. Meredith was in the middle. On 4 December 1769:

'That upon examining into the Particulars of a Misunderstanding which happened in the Committee between Messrs. Garbett and Bentley, it appeared, that Mr. Garbett did not intend to insinuate Mr. Bentley's having wilfully mispent any of the Company's Money, but always thought that he did his best; and (taking the whole of Mr. Bentley's Conduct into Consideration) that the Public were under obligations to him. It likewise appeared that Mr. Garbett did frequently request for the Poor to be supplied with Coal, in Preference to any Person whatsoever . . .'[28]

One promise was kept, for on 14 May 1770 following: 'The Birmingham Boat Company take this Method to inform the

Birmingham & Warwick Junction Canal.

Notice is hereby given, that the Birmingham and Warwick Junction Canal, leading from the Warwick and Birmingham Canal, to the Tame Valley Canal, at Salford Bridge, will be Opened for the use of the Public, on WEDNESDAY Morning, the 14th February instant.

CHARLES LLOYD,
Clerk to the Company.

*Navigation Office, Birmingham,
1st February, 1844.*

*Notice of the opening of the Birmingham and Warwick Junction
(Courtesy of the Waterways Museum, Stoke Bruerne)*

Public, that this Day begin selling Coal at Four-pence per Hundred Weight (six Score to the Hundred) on the Wharf at Birmingham aforesaid, where Teams may depend on a constant supply.'[29] Immediately prior to this 'impartiality' took a hand in the matter:

> 'To the Inhabitants of Birmingham. I am sorry to observe, that whenever any one steps forth from the Canvass of common Life, with real Intentions to serve this Town, he is sure to create himself Enemies, and be subject to the gross Affronts of Envy, Jealousy, and lucrative Individuals; . . . but this I must say, that I am surprised that the Birmingham Canal Committee, should think that the Inhabitants

cannot see other Motives for their selling Coal at 4 per Cent (which they boast so much of) than merely serving the Town and Country . . .'[30]

In 1770, Garbett, having left the Committee, was endeavouring to find other outlets for his energy:

'We hear that the Country is surveying from the Coventry Canal by Coleshill, Castle Bromwich, Aston, Perry, Hamstead, and West Bromwich, to the Coal Pits near Wednesbury and Bilston, and to the Lime Pits near Walsall, and we are informed that a Canal in that Tract would very much reduce the Price of Coal and Lime in the Eastern Parts of Warwickshire, and the adjoining Counties; and that a Cut therefrom to Birmingham would occasion the Price of Corn to be cheaper than by Land Carriage. And if Attention should be given by Gentlemen of the Country it is supposed that any Scheme of Combination (in the Article of Coal or otherwise) to take improper Advantage of the Public, may in a great degree be prevented'[31]

and on 19 November of that year put out a notice:

'There will be a Meeting at the Swan Inn, in Dudley, on Friday Morning next, the 23rd of this Instant November, at Ten o'Clock in the Forenoon, to examine into the Manner with which the Birmingham Canal Company have conducted some of their Operations, and to collect an Account of such Hardships and Inconveniences as may appear to be redressed by Parliament . . .'[32]

At which meeting the innumerable complaints of malpractice by the proprietors were reiterated, complaints substantiated by others:

'. . . subscribers are always looking after their private gain instead of the improvement of the Navigation; this is the Case at present upon the Birmingham Canal, for it is cramp'd in many particulars on account of the Expence, although att this time tho' only just finished, every £100 share sells for £170. If this additional value had been expended upon the Canal instead of falling into private pocketts, it would have been much more noble than it is.'[33]

71

Meredith in answer could only reiterate:

'To the Public – The Committee, from a Conviction that they have not intentionally done any Thing unbecoming the Characters of honest Men, either individually or in their collective Capacity, would have rested perfectly easy under their past Conduct . . . regardless of the invidious Insinuations suggested against them in several anonymous Publications that have appeared in the public Papers– but as the Author of these Papers has at Length assumed his real Signature, they think it necessary only, to repeat to the Public their past Assurances of giving the most speedy Redress to all real Grievances, and of endeavouring to procure the most essential Accommodations to the Public.'[34]

In between times Meredith had other worries to deal with, advertizing for such items as '. . . a Number of Carts and Horses, for the Delivery of Coals in this Town; and Horses and Men without Carts, the Company being already furnished with some of the latter'. Trespass was then as common as now and, once again, the Clerk had to try, at least, to placate everyone:

'The Proprietors having had frequent Complaints made to them, by different Land-Carriers, of People trespassing on their Grounds adjoining the said Canal; and the Banks of the same being greatly injured by People taking Dogs with them, and throwing Sticks and other Things into the Canal; It is requested as a Favour, that no Person in future will attempt to trespass on any Lands adjoining the said Canal, or take any Dogs with them; otherwise the Proprietors will, for their own Interest as well as that of the Public, be obliged to take Notice of the same.'[35]

When he was sure of his ground he breathed fire and brimstone, not, however, without appealing to the very human pecuniary interest: 'by the Act of Parliament for executing the above Navigation . . . it is enacted "That if any Person or Persons shall wilfully, maliciously, and to the Prejudice of the said Navigation, break, throw down, damage or destroy any Banks or other Works . . . such Person or Persons so offending, shall be adjudged guilty of Felony . . ."'[26] for which the offender could be transported 'to some of his Majesty's Plantations in

America' for seven years. 'And whereas' says Meredith:

> 'the Works of the Said Navigation (Particularly the Culverts) have, at different Times, been much injured by some malicious Person or Persons . . . and it being of great Consequence that an Example should be made of such Offenders, to prevent, in Future, a Mischief in which the Public is so materially interested, the Proprietors hereby give Notice, that any Person or Persons who will give information of the Offender or Offenders who have been guilty of damaging the said Works, so that they may be convicted thereof, shall receive a Reward of Twenty Guineas and if more than one Person hath been concerned in such offence, and will impeach his Accomplice or Accomplices, so that he or they may be convicted, such Person so impeaching, shall, upon Conviction of his Accomplice, be pardoned, and receive the like Reward of Twenty Guineas, by applying to the Navigation Office, in Birmingham . . .'[26]

Similarly, Edward Hains, Clerk for the Stroudwater, advertized in 1795:

> 'Whereas some time in the Night of Tuesday the 27th of January last, some evil-disposed persons Cut away and Destroyed some Part of the BANK of the said Canal in Pool-Field, near Framiload; whoever will discover the offender or offenders, and give information thereof, shall upon conviction receive a Reward of TEN GUINEAS.'[36]

Half price in Gloucestershire! What a pity they got rid of that law, at least youths with airguns who shoot at boatmen, lock-keepers and the like and wilfully damage canals nowadays (for which they are rarely charged for reasons of policy, it seems) would think twice.

In one issue alone, of a local newspaper,[37] no less than nine advertisements concerning canals were placed by their respective Clerks including the Gloucester & Berkeley who had 'Twenty Shares to be SOLD, upon which a deposit of two and a half per cent, hath been paid', the Brecknock & Abergavenny Canal whose second General Assembly of the Company of Proprietors was 'to be holden at the Angel Inn, in the town of

Abergavenny, on Thursday the 17th day of October at twelve o'clock in the forenoon' while 'Any Person wanting a quantity of TURF or SOIL for MANURE, may be supplied therewith, from the Canal cutting across the Ham, at 1s. 6d. per cart load, or 3s. per waggon load for Turf, and 6d. per cart load, or 1s. per waggon load for Soil, by applying at the Navigation Office'. On the Herefordshire & Gloucestershire Canal the half yearly general meeting of the Company of Proprietors was to be held at the New Inn, in the city of Hereford on Thursday, 17 October at eleven 'in the forenoon' while the Monmouthshire Canal Navigation of 'Pont-pool' ordered that the several proprietors of subscribers to the said canal navigation pay the further sum of 'TEN POUNDS per cent, of their respective shares . . . into the hands of Messrs. Lewis, Stoughton and Co., the Treasurers, at their Bank, in Chepstow, on Tuesday the 22nd day of October next'.

Although never rated as high as an engineer, and far less well-known, there is no doubt the Clerk was a vital skein in the tangled threads of canal life, not the least when telling the shareholders just where the money had gone!

> *'Croydon,*
> *3d June,* 1803
>
> *SIR,*
> *I enclose a copy of the Resolutions of the* GENERAL ASSEMBLY *of* PROPRIETORS *of the* CROYDON CANAL, *held there this day; and am ordered by the Committee, for the further satisfaction of the Proprietors, to add the following statement of the whole expenditure to the present time.*

	£	s.	d.
Paid the Contractor for excavating and forming the Canal locks and reservoirs	13,538	17	7
the Contractor for brickmaking and brickwork	5,090	0	0
sundry persons for compensations	617	4	1
on account of land	450	0	0
Note.—Several of the Proprietors of shares being also owners of land have retained their calls in part payment for their land.			
for carpenters' work	831	6	1
for timber	118	8	9
for barge building	128	14	7

for steam engine	420	0	0
sundry expences, viz. obtaining the act, the various surveys, Chief and Resident Engineers, Solicitor, and Clerk, rent of offices, printing, valuations, boring and sinking shafts, and various other incidental expences	6,296	2	3
	£27,490	13	4

Which expenditure appears from the accounts submitted to the General Assemblies, to have arisen in the four several years during which the works have been carrying on as under, viz.

	£	s.	d.
In the year ending June 1802...............	4,416	6	1
....................1803...............	5,699	16	9
....................1804...............	5,034	14	0
....................1805...............	12,339	16	6
	£27,490	13	4

The following is the General State of the Company's fund.

	£	s.	d.
Expended as above	27,490	13	4
Balance in the hands of the Treasurer 1,852 6 8			
Which includes a sum received for timber sold by the company 80 0 0			
	1,772	6	8
Arrears on the several calls	8,237	0	0
The uncalled part of the capital (£50,000) viz. £25 per cent	12,500	0	0
	£50,000	0	0

The above Statement of the progressive expenditure, and the large amount of the arrears, must evince the necessity of the punctual payment of the future Calls, and of the Committee's taking the steps sanctioned by the General Assembly for the immediate recovery of the arrears.

> *I am, SIR,*
> *Your obedient Servant,*
> *PATRICK DRUMMOND,*
> *Clerk of the Croydon Canal Company.*'

Homeward bound

5 *Success and Failure*

The Thames & Severn and Wilts & Berks Canals had quite a
lot in common apart from location and ampersanded names.
Initially, at least, they shared the same engineer, Robert
Whitworth an ex-pupil of James Brindley, and they both relied
on other waterways for their outlets; the Thames & Severn
upon the Stroudwater and the River Thames; the Wilts &
Berks upon the River Thames and the Kennet & Avon Canal.
They were interconnected via the North Wilts Canal and
perforce should have worked together. Physically they differed
in as much as the Thames & Severn was a presumptuous and
wide waterway, complete with a tunnel described as a 'curious
perforation . . . with a handsome free-stone front' opening 'into
a subterraneous passage, between three and four thousand
yards in length, but so perfectly strait, as to afford a view of the
opening at the other extremity, which appears like a distant
star',[1] and typically, the proprietors even succeeded in per-
suading King George III to visit the works. Unlike similar
circumstances today, he did not hand out OBEs all round, but
expressed '. . . a desire to view the tunnel at Sapperton, in the
praise of which fame has been so lavish'.[4] From their opening
in 1789 this company stated its intentions:

'Gloucester, Nov. 19. This day was effected the greatest object of internal navigation in this Kingdom. The Severn was united to the Thames, by an intermediate canal [from] Stroud, through the vale of Chalford [to where] it joined the Thames near Lechlade. A boat, with the union flag at her masthead, passed laden for the first time to St. John's bridge, below Lechlade, in the presence of great numbers of people, who were assembled on the occasion; and who answered a salute of twelve pieces of cannon from Buscott Park by loud huzzas. A dinner was given at five of the principal inns at Lechlade, and the day ended with ringing of bells, a bonfire, and a ball . . .'[2]

The Wilts & Berks, however, was a narrow, meandering, amiable sort of waterway and the best they could hope was that '. . . it will open up an easy, cheap and expeditious Communication betwixt those rich vales of the White Horse and North Wilts with the two great marts of London and Bristol; from which, bad roads have hitherto secluded them',[5] but their opening ceremony at Abingdon in 1810 was, seemingly, a good excuse for a glorious beanfast.

'At half past two o'clock a body of the Proprietors passed the last lock into the Thames amidst the loud huzzas of multitudes to witness the spectacle. The party then left the canal and proceeded to the Council Chamber . . . [where they] partook of a splendid dinner prepared for the occasion . . . The day was spent with great conviviality and harmony, enlivened by many appropriate toasts and songs, and the Company, highly gratified, separated at a late hour.'[3]

Two years later rumours were circulating that all was not well with the Wilts & Berks and the Chairman hastened to state:

'At the present juncture, many circumstances not at all concerned with the future prospects of the Concern combine to depreciate the price of all property of that description which has not had its value ascertained by a matured income; but the Committee have no reason whatever to abate in the expectation they have heretofore formed of the ultimate advantage of the undertaking.'

For trade they relied to a certain extent on coal from the Somerset fields coming to them via the Somerset Coal Canal and the Kennet & Avon Canal, and later, on completion of the North Wilts, from the Forest of Dean, but more would have been gained if a rather intriguing 'might-have-been', the Western Junction Canal, proposed in 1810 had been built. This was projected to run from Marsworth on the Grand Junction (now Grand Union) Canal to Abingdon on the Wilts & Berks, a realistic plan, as it would have by-passed the Thames and opened up a connection with points North, both as an outlet for coal and for industrial imports 'to the benefit of both Landowner and Manufacturer'.

Another plan, for a canal from Bristol to the Wilts & Berks near Froxham, passing through the Gloucester coalfield, resulting from a meeting held at the Angel Inn, Chippenham, was well and truly up in the clouds.

If both lines had been finished a route would have been opened between Bristol and London, requiring a mere four days' journey, with a toll of between £1.80 and £1.85 per ton 'entirely free from the delays and difficulties inseparable from River navigation'.

Later, in 1818, Thomas Telford was asked to give his great name to the Western Junction project, which he did in July 1819, claiming it would cost £198,735, but when the Wilts & Berks Manager was asked why he was so disinterested in the Western Junction he replied:

'You are no doubt aware that the Grand Junction as the price of their consent to allow the communication at Aylesbury demand a compensation for coal and iron passing into their canal – should such a tax on the trade be conceded it would be entirely subversive to the ideas of profits from these articles. But Lord Shaftesbury sets his face against compensation clauses at all, and although his Lordship is not invincible, he is at all times a most formidable adversary. The Oxford Canal Company and Old Father Thames, you of course must have made up your mind to fight, they are adversaries with whom there can be no compromise.'[6]

In the meantime, business on the Thames & Severn continued,

mainly only to Brimscombe Port for the summit was so porous that

'. . . across the limestone rocks, all the skill of the engineer, supported by even lavish expenditure, often fails to prevent the water from running away as fast as it enters. Such canals, if they happen to have their "summit level" (as the Thames and Severn Canal at Salperton [sic] Tunnel) in these rocks, are like the buckets of the Danaids, and with the water goes the profit. In vain the Thames, raised from its source by a mighty engine, is poured into such a thirsty canal, the flood passes into the gaping rocks below, in spite of renewed puddling and continual repairs.'[7]

In 1793 Robert Mylne – the erstwhile engineer of the Gloucester & Berkeley Canal (later sacked for inattention) had not only been critical but downright spiteful on the subject of water supplies:

'. . . I have no doubt, if Mr. Whitworth had himself executed his own Plan of the Thames and Severn Canal, he would have had the Foresight, to have tried the Canal in different Portions of it at a Time, and not left it, till the whole Work was finished, and no adequate Provisions had been previously settled for its consumption. He would not have made Locks, near the Summit Level, 12 Feet high, when he had laid it down as a Principle, to make none more than 6 Feet: – but so much for, and this indeed comes of, Proprietors and busy men becoming Engineers, self-made and handling Subjects of the most dangerous Kind.'[8]

However, be that as it may, the inhabitants of Wiltshire were well enough served with coal to their great advantage. It came from Somerset via the Somerset Coal Canal and the Kennet & Avon Canal; from Gloucester via the Thames & Severn Canal or the Wilts & Berks Canal; from the Forest of Dean similarly; and in 1827 to the near apoplexy of the Wilts & Berks proprietors, Staffordshire coal, transported via the Oxford Canal, was on sale at Wantage. Railways saw the end of the Wilts & Berks and in 1909 it was said that:

'It was largely used within living memory for the transport

of coal, corn, building and road making materials. Now it is absolutely unused and its banks are dilapidated. The Company which owns it makes a small revenue, insufficient to meet expenses, by the sale of water. The stagnant condition of this canal makes it offensive to the people of Abingdon and Swindon and a desire has been expressed in these towns to close it altogether and fill in the bed. The closing is, however, opposed by the landowners for certain reasons, including the fact that their tenants obtain water from it for their cattle.'[9]

It was abandoned in 1914 and for an epilogue we can but quote:

> 'The old canal, from bank to bank,
> Is filled with reeds and rushes rank;
> And down this line of living green,
> March memories of what has been.
>
> The painted barges came from town,
> And busy life flowed up and down,
> But there is nothing left to show
> Where those old barges used to go.
>
> Progress is always marching on;
> The old canal is dead and gone,
> But still we seem to hear it say,
> "I, too, was Progress – yesterday".'[10]

The Thames & Severn, on the other hand, although weakened by the impact of railways and its own inherent failings, was to receive a new lease of life. In 1883 Mr J. H. Taunton, Engineer of the Thames & Severn Canal Navigation succinctly claimed:

> 'As to the paragraph in the Report about the disuse of barges on the Canal, this has not arisen from any want of capacity in the Thames and Severn Navigation, but because the Upper Thames has ceased to be navigable. Such vessels may still traverse the Canal, and do so, but no barge has passed from it down the Thames to Oxford since March, 1855.'[11]

But after purchase by the GWR formal closure was proposed. Suddenly the advantages of a canal became obvious, as we see

12 Tub boats on the Shropshire Canal near Madeley before 1900, with the Madeley Court Furnaces in the background. *(Courtesy of W K V Gale)*

13 S U R and C Company's boat 387, *Ruth*, on private hire on the Shropshire Union Canal about 1925. *(Courtesy of the Waterways Research Centre)*

14   View of Trevor Boatyard from the 'Gateway to Leisure' on the Welsh Section of the Shropshire Union Canal, in 1966

when a deputation including many notables visited the Board of Trade on 10 January 1894, to protest against the proposed closure. For the capitalist Mr P. J. Evans, representing the Stroud Chamber of Commerce, said:

'That the upper reaches of the Thames and Severn Canal had for some time been in a very bad condition. This matter affected a very large number of traders and manufacturers. For some interests it was a matter almost of life and death. Many people in the Stroud Valley had actually built works and established businesses which were dependant on the Canal. It was almost incredible that in the face of Acts of Parliament intended to prevent Railway Companies strangling Canals that a Railway Company should have possession of this Canal and have the audacity to propose to close it,'[12]

For the consumer, Mr Edmund W. Cripps (of Cirencester), said:

'That if the Great Western Railway Company had its way in the matter a great blow would be inflicted upon the agricultural district of that part of the country. It had been almost impossible to get a cargo of corn along the Canal through the disgraceful way in which it had been kept. In that part of the country there was an area of something like 15 miles long by ten miles broad where there was no Railway, and if the Canal were closed that area would be absolutely deprived of its communication'; and, heresy! Mr. Adams of Gloucester, said: 'In many cases their customers preferred to get the goods by Canal, because they were received in better condition than when sent by Railway.'[12]

But the main reason, aside from the purely physical ones, why any waterway should be closed is that insufficient people use it. The canal was taken over by a trust who carried out some works but by October, 1899, 'The canal was opened for traffic on 15th March last, but the Committee regret to state that the summit level did not prove watertight, and owing to this cause it was only found possible to work the traffic beyond Chalford for a period of about three months, no boats having been able to pass through the summit level since June'[13] so they called in the famous Mr George Jebb, engineer of the Shropshire Union

Canal (upon whom both the waterways and mantle of Telford had fallen) and he estimated an expenditure of £3,696 per mile as necessary to put the whole in order. In 1900 the ownership of the canal was transferred to the Gloucester County Council, possibly the only time a county council has been so venturesome but 'the Committee thereupon decided to appoint an Engineer to undertake the management of the works required'. Such was the paucity of canal engineers that 'Mr. Jebb was consulted but could not recommend anyone'.

However, one was found, and the work duly carried out, as we see from a newspaper report of 26 March 1904:

'The Re-opened Thames and Severn Canal. Staffordshire to Cirencester by Water. CRUISE OF THE COAL BARGE "STAUNCH" . . . the good barge "Staunch" . . . has been traversing the same classic waterway, and on Tuesday last she made the port of Cirencester with a cargo of some 37 tons of Staffordshire coal – the first consignment of water-borne coal that has reached the town for . . . many years . . . Captain Joseph Hewer . . . has been in the boat business all his life . . . When business of the Thames and Severn Canal fell off, owing to its increasingly dilapidated condition and the consequent difficulty of navigation, he betook himself to New Swindon, and for 12 or 15 years he had four boats regularly plying between that place and Bristol. But three years ago the Wilts and Berks canal also became unnavigable, and although Captain Hewer had plenty of work – Messrs. Butt and Skurray, the millers, were willing to keep him regularly employed – he had to seek other occupation, and though he did not actually burn his boats, he broke up two, sold a third, and retained the fourth, appropriately named the "Staunch". Naturally he looks back with regret to the interruption of his old calling – "I should have been a hundred pounds better off today if the Wilts and Berks Canal had kept going" – [but] seeing that his boat was becoming more and more hopelessly stranded, he fifteen months ago headed her for the Thames and Severn Canal via Latton, attracted thither by the restoration works in progress. [After ten months laid up] she carried some gravel from Cerney to Cirencester for Messrs. Gegg and Co., and some hundred tons of road stone from Siddington to Cerney Wick, and a month ago she entered on her Staffordshire voyage. Sailing "light" to Gloucester, she there took up a load of timber baulks which she carried to Old Hill, near Dudley, and then went some 25 miles further on to the Hednesford Colliery, Staffordshire, to embark Messrs. Gegg and Co's load of coal . . . [from the collieries to Cirencester] the 120 miles were covered in five and a half working days, divided by the following stopping places: 1st day, Birmingham; 2nd day, Hanbury Wharf near Droitwich; 3rd day, Tewkesbury; 4th day, Dudbridge, Stroud, where the "Staunch" lay up for the Sunday; 5th day, Tunnel House, Coates; 6th day (10 o'clock) Cirencester Wharf . . . [Sapperton] tunnel nearly $2\frac{1}{2}$ miles in length, was got through in $3\frac{1}{4}$ hours, the boat being propelled by means of tunnel sticks manipulated by Captain Hewer and his "mate" Richard Bentley. The canal was found to be in capital order throughout, including the tunnel, and at no point was there the slightest difficulty with the heavily loaded boat drawing 3 feet 7 inches of water . . . As regards the commercial aspects of the undertaking, Captain Hewer accepted the charter at the same rate as that charged by the railway companies, viz. 7s. 6d. per ton, so that assuming his load to be 37 tons his freight would come to £13.17.6d. The tolls he had to pay to the several navigations traversed amounted to between £5 and £6, and the balance is what is available for labour, horse and other expenses, use of boat, &c. What is needed, of course, to make the venture successful is the development of a traffic in round timber to pay for the outwards voyage.

We believe Mr. E. N. Edmonds has had a cargo of corn carried to Kempsford; Mr. G. Durnell, of Watermoor, has had several cargos of timber; and last Sunday a boat with 21 tons of road stone, carrier Mr. Barnes, reached Kempsford from the Gloucester end. Mr. P. J. Trouncer, of Chester Lodge, has this week placed an electric launch upon the canal.'[14]

The word 'heroic' has been applied to the venture by the county council which, incidentally, cost £25,832, but still plagued by water shortage and dwindling trade the last barge passed over the summit on 11 May 1911, the bulk of the canal being closed in 1927.

It is interesting to note that among canals that may eventually be restored the Thames & Severn stands high, the scenery along the line is superb and given capital there would still seem to be some demand for commercial boats.

From what was really a main line of canal development we pass to a 'backwater' navigation. None of this type was intended to be small but, as with many later railways, what started off as a grandiose scheme often petered out when faced with the hard realities of raising money, finding a good engineer and obtaining, let alone retaining, skilled labour, all of which were commodities hard to locate.

The Portsmouth & Arundel Canal was part of a rather ramshackle collection of waterways that ran from London via the Thames, River Wey, Wey & Arun Junction Canal, Arun Navigation and the Portsmouth & Arundel Canal to Portsmouth Harbour and Chichester. The first relevant Act was passed in 1817,[15] based on a plan surveyed (under the direction of John Rennie) by Netlam and Francis Giles in 1815. Permitted to raise £126,000 – very close to the estimate of £125,490[16] – a fair percentage came from the deep pocket of George O'Brien Wyndham, 3rd Earl of Egremont of whom Cobbett said: 'Lord Egremont bears an excellent character. Everything that I have ever heard of him makes me believe that he is worthy of this princely estate.'[17] He had a vested interest in seeing the canal succeed, for of the capital issued for the connecting Wey & Arun Junction Navigation – which stood to benefit by through traffic – he held about one-twelfth. At the opening of this waterway in 1816 the junketings had spoken of great things to come[18] but, so poor was the trade, the nominal value of its shares had fallen from £110 to £50 by 1820. Small wonder then that Egremont was keen to open up another artery, the one (Portsmouth & Arundel) he hoped would pour trade into the other (Wey & Arun Junction). In a circular dated 5 August 1817, the Committee of Management of the Portsmouth & Arundel made what was perhaps one of the most optimistic and misleading statements ever issued:

'. . . we are strongly of opinion that there is every reasonable expectation of a very abundant and satisfactory interest on the capital to be expended, even in time of peace; but to those persons whose chief object in becoming subscribers might be future advantage to their children, the Committee submit the consideration of the inevitable and greatly increased value that must attend Shares in this undertaking, whenever the country might be again in a state of warfare.'[19]

The canal never paid a dividend, and through traffic ceased in 1840.

That, however, was well in the future. On the 2 June 1823, the *Sussex Weekly Advertiser* wrote of the opening which

'took place this day se'nnight . . . A procession was formed of vessels of various descriptions decorated with gay streamers and colours, which had previously assembled at Ford, near the entrance of the Canal; and at about half-past eleven the flotilla began to glide upon its bosom, preceded by a boat with a band of music. The Earl of Egremont's pleasure barge . . . [was] followed by those of the Mayors of Arundel and Guildford . . . and by six others . . . filled with gay parties of Ladies and Gentlemen, and attended by another band of music; the rear was brought up by eight barges laden with goods of various descriptions (one of which had previously arrived at Ford, from London, in three days) all bound for Chichester. The loveliness of the day heightened the rich and varied charms of the highly cultivated country, through which the acquatic procession passed. At Hunston Common, a schooner, of 80 tons burthen, and five sloops, joined, and shortly afterwards the whole line entered the basin of the Canal at Chichester, amidst the firing of cannon, and cheers of an immense body of spectators, who had assembled to greet their arrival . . . At five o'clock, upwards of 70 gentlemen, friends and promoters of the undertaking, sat down to an excellent dinner at the Swan Inn, Chichester, the Earl of Egremont in the Chair, to whose patronage and exertions the public are principally indebted for this truly national and long-wished for undertaking.'

It was claimed enthusiastically that

'This canal . . . forms a short means of conveyance by water

85

from the Metropolis to the British Channel, whereby the
tedious and often dangerous passage through the Downs, can
be avoided, enabling the Merchant to forward his goods
from London to either of the Ports westward of Arundel,
with nearly as much despatch as usually attends the common
road waggons, incurring, in no case, so much as one-third of
the expence, and in several cases not even one-sixth. Similar
despatch and economy will attend this channel of communication with Guernsey and Jersey as well as with the opposite
French coast, and consequently (by means of the River
Seine) with Paris.'[20]

The journey should, if the three rivers were neither flooded nor
dry, and if the Wey & Arun Junction had enough water on its
summit and if . . . have taken no more than four days to
London. By 1830, in an effort to increase trade, rates from
Portsmouth to London came down to 52½p per ton, rather less
than half the £1.12½ originally quoted. This reduction had
some effect.

> 'The trade on the extensive line of canal from the River
> Thames to Portsmouth is now becoming very brisk. The
> barges are going regularly and well loaded. About twenty
> tons of marble ex Asia, 84, from the Mediterranean, for his
> Majesty at Windsor, and above forty tons of gold and silver
> for the Bank of England have, with other goods, been sent
> by this conveyance from this port within a week.'[21]

The latter traffic was fairly extensive, soldiers acting as
Marines – or Turnpike Sailors – en route. What ruined this
grand scheme? Depression in agriculture primarily, following
the Napoleonic wars; steam-packet boats and, finally, the
railways. A requiem can be gleaned from a letter from the
Portsmouth & Arundel Company addressed to the Wey &
Arun Junction:

> . . . my calculations, though well founded, have been
> baffled by awkward circumstances . . . I therefore would for
> the present, merely advert to the temporary stoppage of your
> Canal, to the various floods which have occasioned detention
> of goods – to the interruptions at the Tunnel – to the im-
> positions of the Commanders of Barges and generally to

many vexatious circumstances which have taken place, commenced by parties not practically acquainted with its details. . . ."[22]

The canal building era lasted from, roughly, 1760 to 1830. Of the canals which were opened later, the Birmingham & Liverpool Junction and the Chard are examples. However, in the main era there were failures, planned, if not built, as a result of the canal mania. And what a superb idiocy this mania was. It has been said that when the British go mad they do so thoroughly and in no way is this better illustrated. At Bristol in 1792 a meeting was held to promote a canal, the Bristol & Severn, to run from Bristol to Gloucester. This meeting was 'enthusiastically supported by influential persons, and a very large sum was subscribed by those present, who struggled violently with each other in their rush to the subscription book'.[23]

On 12 December of the same year, hearing that shares in what was to be the Kennet & Avon Canal were to be allocated at Devizes, the populations of Bristol and Bath, lemming-like, galloped, rode, hobbled or crawled their way to Devizes, and such was the commotion that the local magistrates very nearly read the Riot Act. But no-one knew anything and when at length the Town Clerk took the chair at a meeting he

> 'desired to know, for what purpose the Meeting was called and declar'd, if no Gentleman came forward to avow the advertisement, he would adjourn the Meeting. After some time a proposal was made by some Person, to cut a canal from Bristol, by Devizes to Salisbury, but this was considered as a mere Pretence to amuse the Meeting, who considered themselves drawn together for no purpose, and there was a general cry of "Newbury", "Newbury".'[24] [eastern terminus of the Kennet & Avon].

Incredibly, these people then subscribed to the 'mere pretence' of a canal. Cornelius Vapid Esq., went so far as to write a poem on the matter:

> 'Forth rush'd the mob – but where alas! to go –
> They did not find, 'till now, they did not know.
> Where is the Canal? each ask'd the other – where?

Another cries, "Tis doing at the Bear";
Swift as a hound, they run towards the place,
But find, alas! it was a bugbear chase!
Some scratch their heads, not knowing what to do,
Whilst others raving, travel to and fro;
CANALS were mention'd, but without a scheme,
Nor where should run, or how obtain, the stream;
and most of them, who to DEVIZES went,
Knew but should run from Wiltshire into Kent.'

I suppose that after their labours to get to Devizes the artisans, tailors, boozers and sailors felt they ought to buy something:

'From the statements of the late Mr Lucas of Devizes, it appears, that a day having been appointed in which the public were to be allowed the luxury of subscription, a tent was erected in the Market-place for the transaction of business, at one end of which the victims were permitted to enter, and to emerge at the other. No-one was to have more than five shares, but on each of these shares eight shillings deposit had to be paid for advertising and other preliminary expenses; so that the sum paid down was in the most cases £2. As the crowd were sucked in at one end of the tent and discharged at the other, they were received at the door of exit by parties waiting, either to offer premiums, or to take nominal ownership. Hence many amusing scenes occurred. Some who bought for others, refused to surrender their shares. Many a common fellow having mustered £2 by loan or otherwise, found himself worth £5 or £10 soon after emerging from the tent: and this barter continued all through the day, even after the subscription books were closed.'[25]

Other routes which might have been built during this and later manias included the fantastic Wilden & Kings Bromley, surveyed by Brindley, which was – redolant of today – to have had fords instead of bridges.

In the Midlands, Lord Dudley and Ward proposed a still-water navigation terminating at Stourbridge.

'. . . from the Severn river at Diglis below Worcester city to the Stourbridge canal at that place, passing Bromsgrove, its proposed length was 26 miles with 772 feet of lockage by 128 locks, some tunnels and other large works were necessary; a bill for this canal passed the commons, but was rejected by the house of lords.'[26]

and

'. . . Mr. Roe conceived the idea of opening a communication between Liverpool and Macclesfield by a canal, which should pass through the level below Kerridge hills and thence through Poynton. A Bill was brought into the House of Commons to empower Mr. Roe to realise his plans, and passed there; but it was thrown out of the House of Lords by the influence of the Duke of Bridgewater, whose navigation had been opened for the conveyance of goods but a short time before.'[27]

From London, apart from Rennie's proposed ship canal to Portsmouth (comparable to the Suez) and the 'Weald of Kent' we also have the London & Waltham Abbey for which the advantages were claimed to be 'Health . . . "the first and greatest"'; fresh milk . . . 'which is now of very bad quality' would then have been brought twice a day from cows fed in meadow lands, butcher's meat would be fresher and corn, malt and flour could be moved much easier; and the London & Cambridge Junction[28] whose Act forbade the taking from 'streams, which feed that valuable conduit in the market place of Cambridge, called Hobson's Conduit, from which great part of the town and university obtain water . . . .'.

The Trent & Mersey was opened in 1777 but in 1796 Mr Robert Whitworth was employed to survey the line of the Grand Commercial Canal (Nantwich to the Ashby-de-la-Zouch Canal). 'The objects of this proposed canal were, the forming of a communication for larger boats (40 tons) than the Trent and Mersey is calculated for, except below Burton, and contributing towards the wished for passage of large boats between Liverpool, Manchester, Chester, London, &c.'[26]

One rather 'nice' project of 1796, supported by a detailed and explanatory pamphlet printed in 1804, was that for a Grand Circular Canal. John Hibbard, the proposer, suggested a waterway from 'The Thames and Isis, near Oxford, to London, to proceed upon the level, without locks, by the most convenient places pointing to the New River Aqueduct at Islington, from thence to proceed without locks to cross the country, also cross the Ouse, near Biggleswade; at most convenient places to cross the rivers Trent, &c. to proceed near York, Edinborough [sic] and Inverness; and circuit Britain, near Glasgow, Carlisle, Chester and Worcester on such level, to near Oxford . . .'[29] which would 'produce an immense revenue to the state, and be a great privilege to the subject'.

In 1793 a canal was proposed from the intended Montgomeryshire Canal at Garthmill [now Garthmyl] to join the 'Leominster canal at or near the Leme aqueduct, passing through Montgomery, Chirbury, Bishops Castle, Hopesay, Onibury, Ludlow and Dirty Middleton'.[30] This was rejected as too expensive and a modified scheme was adopted (from Leominster to Lydham Heath) at a cost of £73,000, but with the proviso that no part of the work was to be started until after the conclusion of the Napoleonic war; the war finished but the canal never started. Perhaps it was as well, for the connecting Kington, Leominster & Stourport navigation petered out incomplete.

> 'But think not Politics alone,
> Can in large free trading town
> At this time fam'd for SPECULATION,
> Engross the public conversation.
> O'er cheering cups, as things fall out,
> and false alarms are spread out,
> Some grave appear, some gay, some sad,
> And some are NAVIGATION mad.'[31]

In 1793 Denys Rolle had written to the Salisbury & Southampton Company as follows:

> 'I beg leave to offer a sentiment to obviate objections rais'd against Canals mentioned in Parliament only as to the taking off the Hands in time of Harvest destroying the Cultivation of the Land. From the Immense Numbers of Canals now coming on and the not only absence of a Multitude of the Labouring Class abroad in the War but the vast suppos'd Diminution that there will arise from the Destruction in it,

a great Scarcity of Hands for the Cultivation will be found at the End whenever it may be. The neighbouring Kingdom has furnish'd yearly many Hands for the Harvest from Chester to Dover, many were employ'd in the Canals in the North. Some came with the Engineers to the Canal at Cirencester I saw and some with them to Basingstoke. I have recommended therefore in Devonshire where several Canals are propos'd to even solicit or encourage a supply from Ireland where it might lessen the constant annual Emigration to America and reform a dissolute Wild and Barbarous Class by Industrious Labour. That they exceed in strength our Class employ'd now on the canals is observ'd and get their 3 shillings to the others gaining two. . . .'[32]

Schemes for cutting across the toe of England proliferated, but failed. In 1769 Robert Whitworth trotted his horse between the River Exe at Exeter via Tiverton, Taunton and Glastonbury, to Uphill in Somerset but 'This project was condemned on account of its cutting up rich meadows, interferring with mills and incurring the necessity of transhipment of seaborne cargoes.'[33] Later, in 1822, William Summers under the guidance of James Green and at the behest of Lord Rolle of Torrington, surveyed the land between the Bridgwater & Taunton Canal via Chard and Axminster to Beer, '. . . but this plan was never seriously pursued'. Thomas Telford, in 1834, estimated the cost of a 200-ton canal from Seaton to Stolford at £1,712,844, promising a dividend of 12 per cent. From these, and others, emerged just four waterways – the Bridgwater & Taunton, which replaced the extant River Tone Navigation, resulted from proposals for a Bristol & Taunton Canal Navigation. Although the subscribers were confident enough to promise £571,800,[28] when real cash was required it could not be found.

The Chard, under the guidance of James Green, opened in 1842 and closed in 1867 – too little, too late – and the proprietors lost £132,000 in the process. The failure of the Grand Western was only equalled by that of the Dorset & Somerset. Planned to run from Bath to Frome – with a branch to the collieries – and thence via Sturminster Newton to Poole. Traffics were on offer – for instance potters' clay from Dorset, which currently went around the coast to Bristol, and thence via the Severn and the Staffs & Worcs to the Potteries. Coal was almost unobtainable in Dorset, so that was to be the back-carriage and

> 'Exclusive of the articles of coal, corn, etc., which would be conveyed by this canal, the salterns of Lymington, which have for many years ceased to work, would be revived and the county of Somerset be supplied with salt at a much cheaper rate and of a quality superior to the Droitwich. The Purbeck, and Portland stone, would be conveyed at an easy expence, and the timber of the forest of Selwood would in return be taken to Portsmouth. In short, the advantages of such a canal are so manifold that a recapitulation thereof would take up more time than at present I can bestow.'[31]

The first meeting took place on 10 January 1793 at Wincanton, but on 7 February 1793, following some argument as to the final line it was resolved that

> 'before any positive determination respecting the line of the Canal be fixed on, some eminent surveyor or surveyors, engineers or other persons, be appointed to take the necessary levels and make proper calculations and estimates of the expences likely to be incurred, as well as of the tonnage likely to arise on the lines respectively proposed, and to report the same to a committee to be appointed by this meeting . . .'

A deposit of £1.05 was to be paid on each £100 share to cover these primary expenses. And people paid. Robert Whitworth (of the Thames & Severn) agreed to carry out the survey, reporting in September 1793 that the whole would cost £183,587. By 13 August 1795, it was finally agreed to join the Kennet & Avon Canal at Widbrook; William Bennet was appointed engineer and £3 per £100 share collected. When the Act was obtained, 24 March 1796, subscriptions totalled £79,200 to meet Bennet's estimate of £146,018 for the whole line. Although £27,000 was subscribed by the 'landed gentry' many small people also paid up. On 12 September 1796: 'We hear that the Dorset and Somerset Canal advances very rapidly in its progress, and that the public will soon begin to experience the benefits that must arise from this undertaking; part of it near the collieries is already completed, and a barge was launched there on Monday'[35] but ominously a year later the Clerk to the Dorset & Somerset wrote:

'Dear Sir, I beg leave to acquaint you that the Company of Proprietors of the Dorset and Somerset Canal do not consider themselves as liable to refund any of the Deposits which they have received from persons becoming Subscribers to that Concern and afterwards declining their Subscriptions . . . I am happy in saying that the Work is very rapidly proceeding and in a very satisfactory manner.'[36]

And people not only would not, but could not pay, preferring instead to sacrifice the payments made. Despite the successful trial of Mr Fussell's lift on 6 and 13 October 1806, and possibly remembering a survey by John Rennie in 1799 which made gloomy prognostications about a tunnel being built:

'. . . but as there is great reason to believe that the ground is very unsound and of course liable to sink I should hesitate much in Recommending a Tunnel here, the ground adjacent round is also underworked and perhaps is liable to give way as under the Tunnel, yet whatever failures happen in the open cutting can easily be repaired. But were a failure to happen in the Tunnel I scarcely know how it could be repaired . . .'[37]

having paid up their £100 shares, the shareholders baulked at paying any more. Calls of amounts between £3 and £10 were spread over five years – £20 per annum, far more than a tinker, tailor, soldier or sailor could ever find, so small wonder only £58,000 of the promised £79,200 had ever come. True they might have been greedy, but

'Every prospect of remuneration to the subscribers seemed almost certain from the conveyance of coals alone in a district where this article of domestic utility and comfort could be obtained by land carriage, from these collieries . . . only at a high price. By some injudicious management the subscriptions were expended, before the work was near completion; the further progress was suspended; and, after a useless expenditure of a large sum of money, the whole was abandoned'[38]

The epitaph of the canal came on the 19 September 1825,

'The shares of the Dorset and Somerset Canal scarcely bear nominal prices at this time, and are literally worth nothing, unless by public exertion. They have sold for less than £5 per share, although they originally cost £100. In fact the Company can do nothing without a new subscription',

which of course the widow, the labourer and other poor people could not face; finding the £100 had placed many in the workhouse.

Early container traffic

6 *Carriers to All Parts*

Canal carriers occupied a position totally unlike that of railway companies. By law, the bulk of companies were not initially allowed to own their own boats for fear this would lead to a monopolistic position, but instead they had to accept any boats that presented themselves. Having stated this it must be admitted that, as on the railways, both trade and carriers had to conform to certain restrictions. The first was often stipulated in the Canal Company's Act and was designed to avoid trade being strangled at birth, and to preserve water supplies. On the Swansea Canal 'No Boat under Fifteen Tons to pass any Lock when the Water does not flow over the Waste Weir; nor any Boat under Ten Tons to pass when it does so flow, without leave or paying the Tonnage respectively';[1] on the Thames & Severn Canal 'Vessels of less than Six Tons to pay a lock Due of Sixpence at each Lock, for Waste of Water, and in addition to pay for Six Tons of Lading'[1] and more succinctly on the Dudley 'Boats under Fifteen Tons not to pass Locks without leave'. Further regulations stated that fractions of a mile would count as a quarter, half or three-quarters; tonnage would count similarly. None of these rules should apply to empty boats returning, or going to fetch goods, although on occasion they were so treated. 'Boats returning with a back Lading of Oil-cake, Malt-dust, Pigeon Dung or any other Kind of Manure, which have passed up or down the River immediately before, and paid the Tolls or Rates on their Cargoes, shall be exempted from Tonnage Rate on such Manure.'[1] To compensate for this though, only certain tolls could be charged, either for the whole length (Dudley – coal 2½p for 2½ miles), or by mileage (Coals on the Glamorganshire cost 1p per mile; Grand Surrey 2p per mile; Louth 1½p but 'A Chaldron of Coals containing Forty eight Winchester Bushels to be estimated as one Ton'). Again using the Dudley as an example, it will be seen that drawbacks were often given by force of law rather than by agreement:

	d.
Coal, Coke and Iron-Stone, which shall have paid Tonnage to the Birmingham Canal	3 per Ton
For the same Articles, for which no Rates shall have been paid to the said Canal, and which shall pass through any part of the Dudley Tunnel	3 per Ton
For the same Articles which pass between the South End of the Tunnel and the present Dudley Canal	3 per Ton
For the same Goods got or raised within a Mile of the Birmingham and Fazeley Canal, and which shall pass into the said Birmingham Canal	½ per Ton
Lime and Lime-stone which shall pass out of the South End of the Tunnel	4½ per Ton
For the same which shall pass into the Birmingham Canal	½ per Ton
For all Stone, Timber and other Goods	6 per Ton

These and similar drawbacks were of vital importance to both the company and the public. Two similar mileages would carry quite different tolls, thus:

From	To	Mileage	Load	Toll
Coombs Wood Tube Works	Autherley	13¼	Spelter	11.625d (4.843p)
,, ,,	Berkeley Street	13½	,,	16.35d (6.812p)

The former was through traffic, bound for the Shropshire Union Canal, the latter only local. The alternative form of drawback was that granted to a factory, coal-haulier or whatever, who promised to shift a given tonnage per annum. This latter was often granted as an incentive to keep goods off of the rail. On the Birmingham Canal Navigations coal traffic from the Fly Colliery Basin to the Stourbridge Canal was normally charged 7.35d (3.06p) per ton for the 5¼ miles, but for companies like Pearson or Matty the rate was 6d. (2.5p). Today, with inflation galloping on, this difference may not seem much but at a time when a loaf of bread would remain constant at, say, 2p, for a decade or more, in quantities of 5,000 or 10,000 tons per annum it could represent the difference between life and death for the carrier.

Certain items stipulated by the House of Commons in their collective wisdom could pass either free of tolls or pay a very reduced rate. Still on the Dudley:

'Lime and Lime-stone to pay only one-third of the Rates; but Paving stones, Gravel, Sand, and other Materials for the repair of Roads, (except Lime-stone), Dung, Soil, Marl, and all Sorts of Manure for the Improvements only of Lands belonging to Persons whose Lands may be taken for this Canal is exempt, provided they do not pass a Lock, except at such times as when the Water flows over the Lock Weir'[1]

Incidentally, on this waterway 'Six Score Pounds Avoidupois shall be deemed a Hundred Weight' while on the Market Weighton Canal the rate was calculated at 2/- (10p) per Chaldron for coals 'each Chaldron containing Thirty Two Bushels'. Ah! the glories of decimalization!

Let us also look at some of the items that were carried on canals in their heyday. Coal, iron, salt, salt rock, lime-stone, chalk, crates of pottery, or 'black glass', window and plate glass, timber, flint, bricks, stone, clay, copper and brass (these latter often carrying a high toll), tin, bark (tree), dog's-bones (Minus Bark?), corn, grain, tar, vitriol (punitive tolls on this), peat, milk, 'Cattle, Sheep and Other Beasts', night-soil and so on, almost *ad infinitum*. For some of the more unlikely loads the precise quantities were defined. Five quarters of wheat, rye, peas and tares (cattle food) were to be regarded as a ton, six though of barley, eight of malt, ten of bran but only eight of flour, howbeit each quarter could hold five bushels. To further confuse matters each of the items above might well have separate rates, with different poundages allowed for, say, coal (120 lb) and iron (112 lb). On the Regent's Canal which included, *inter alia*, 'Things' as a toll-carrying item, 24 separate tolls existed depending on the place of loading, the goods, and place of discharge. Having thoroughly confused the public, their tollkeepers and the carriers, clauses might inhibit the canal company from making too much money. On the Leicester Navigation:

> When this Company shall receive what will produce a Nett Income of £5 per Cent. per Annum, then the additional Rates are to be taken off Coals which pass on the Leicester-shire and Northamptonshire Union Canal beyond Ayleston Mill. Coals passing through the Oakham Canal are also exempt from the additional Tolls,'

while on the Glamorganshire the proprietors were limited on an 8 per cent dividend per annum. However, in the latter case, although disallowed from carrying directly (i.e. as the Canal Company) the proprietors, including such notables as Richard Crawshay and Thomas Guest, carried on their own account. When they had made the requisite 8 per cent a toll free period would be declared.

Other fees were also stipulated by Parliament, mostly referring to warehousing and wharfage. Obviously, having loaded the goods they had to be discharged somewhere; again the ability to control all the land along the canal might give the canal company that most abhorred thing, a monopoly, so the rates were again tied. But they varied enormously from the 3d per ton for all goods remaining not more than 48 hours on the

Carlisle, to 2d per ton per day on the Forth & Clyde, although they have a 24 hour period of grace. The Glamorganshire offered various permutations:

> 'Coal, Lime, Lime-stone, Clay, Iron, Iron-stone, Timber, Stone, Brick, Tile, Slate or Gravel . . . 1d per Ton. Any other Goods . . . 3d per Ton. The above Rates are payable if they remain upon the Wharfs for the Space of Six Days, except for Coal, Iron and Lime-stone, which may continue at the above Rate Six Calendar Months; and Timber, Clay, Lime, Iron-stone, Stone, Brick, Tile, Slate, or Gravel, may remain Thirty Days.'[1]

Concessions were built in, as on the Coventry, where the company were obliged to erect a crane at Tamworth, no charge was made for its use. On the majority of waterways His Majesty's ships, men and stores could do more or less as they liked without charge. On a few, even the rates for the use of the towpath were listed, an interesting commentary on the habits of farmers. The Croydon charged 2d (0.83p) for every horse, mare, gelding, mule or ass 'except such as are drawing any Boat or Vessel'; 1/8d (8.3p) a score for 'a drove of Oxen or Neat Cattle' and a ½d (0.21p) for swine, sheep or lambs. The normal goods to pass free of toll were, as shown above, manures in one form or another (whether sea-sand, dung or night-soils) but even here there were exceptions, one being on the Tavistock Canal 'Ores may be carried to the Dressing Floor, or the Waste or Rubbish of Mines or Lodes be removed to proper Places in any part of the Canal free of Toll'. This may well have been (if unconsciously) for environmental purposes.

It is an accepted fact that laws are made to be broken, whether it be by the income-tax dodger, or merely the owner of a television set without a licence, and 150 years ago the same principle applied, even on the Duke of Bridgewater's canal.

> 'There yet remains another exaction on the part of the Duke to be pointed out. All goods which pass up from Liverpool to Runcorn, to enter the Trent and Mersey navigation, pay above twice the freight which they ought, owing to the Trustees of the Duke having monopolised nearly the whole of the land and warehouses at Runcorn. At the present

moment, they charge 5s. per ton on grain, while bye-carriers, in abundance, would be found to contract at 2s. But, if a bye-carrier arrive, the owner of the goods, who thought to save a few shillings a ton, finds that he has not only to pay the 2s but also the 5s; for say the Trustees, what will you do with the goods? Ours are the only warehouses, and your goods shall not be landed without your paying us as much as if we had carried them ourselves. Pay us the 5s. and your goods shall be received and forwarded.'[2]

How so? The company that operated the wharves – other than those directly owned by the canal company – was a mere puppet in the hands of the Duke of Bridgewater's Trustees.

It will be understood, therefore, that arranging for a load of unusual goods to go anywhere unusual was a rather hit-or-miss affair. The carriers added to the complication as three, or even four classes of boats were in operation, rather like Continental railways of today. First, was the express packet: not too common, but capable of carrying small parcels in addition to passengers, at a rate simply defined as 'if you want it there quickly, you pay more'. Next were the 'fly' boats, travelling, in theory at least, both day and night, with a 75 per cent chance that, according to destination, the goods would leave and arrive at a certain day and time. As an extension to this, delivery could probably be arranged to a given address. Third class transport was the orthodox boat moving solely by day, taking four or five days to reach London from Birmingham; goods were taken at a proportionately lower rate. Finally, there was the heavy goods boat, more often than not, bereft of cabin, but carrying a heavy tonnage to and fro; on some routes at least, the precursor of today's 'merry-go-round' trains.

Canal packet-boats had quite a long life. The first purely passenger boats appeared on the Duke of Bridgewater's canal. The boats were, we are told, pleasant, tidy and clean, carrying two or three classes of passenger, the fares from Runcorn to Manchester being (in 1772) 5p, 7½p, and 12½p, with '. . . each [boat] provided with a coffee house . . .' from which could be got wine and other refreshments. Between 80 and 120 passengers were carried, leaving Runcorn at 08.30, arriving Manchester at 18.00 hours. In the reverse direction they left

Manchester at 08.00, meeting the Liverpool coach near Warrington at 13.00, the Chester coach near Frodsham at 14.30, giving arrival at Runcorn as 16.30, in all 8½ hours. The journey was patchy, for some way 'basking in the sunshine, and gliding through a continuous panorama of cows, cottages, and green fields, the latter gaily sparkling with daisies', but nearing Manchester 'the water of the canal is as black as the Styx, and absolutely pestiferous, from the gas and refuse of the manufactories with which it is impregnated'.[3] The horses, to maintain the speed of the journey, were maltreated:

'The boat was towed at the rate of about five miles an hour by a couple of clumsy cart-horses, driven beyond their natural pace, and working under all possible disadvantages; for half the strength of one horse was continually exerted to prevent itself from being dragged into the canal by the other. It has frequently been observed that to break a horse no other art is necessary than to conquer his temper; and those acquainted with the good qualities of the animal need not be told that a light hand on the bridle is, in point of fact, rather an appeal to his moral than his physical nature. Servants and postboys are above these considerations; and, in the present case, the two small boys, who rode each on one of these unfortunate horses, exhibited an utter insensibility to that lively state of muscle which is the result of a well-tutored mouth. They whipped and kicked as if sitting across a tree. . . ."[3]

If the horses suffered it is a matter of conjecture how those on the Glasgow, Paisley & Ardrossan survived in the 1830s:

'The ordinary speed for the conveyance of passengers on the Ardrossan Canal has, for nearly 2 years, been from nine to ten miles an hour; and, although there are fourteen journeys along the canal per day, at this rapid speed, its banks have sustained no injury. The boats are 70 feet in length, about 5 feet 6 inches broad, and, but for the extreme narrowness of the canal, might be made broader. They carry easily from 70 to 80 passengers; and when required, can and have carried upwards of 110 passengers. The entire cost of a boat and fittings is about £125. The hulls are formed of light iron plates and ribs and the covering is of wood and light oiled cloth. They are more airy, light, and comfortable than any coach. They permit the passengers to move about from the outer to the inner cabin, and the fares per mile are one penny in the first, and three farthings in the second cabin. The passengers are all carried under cover, having the privilege also of an uncovered space. These boats are drawn by 2 horses (the prices of which may be from £50 to £60 per pair), in stages of 4 miles in length, which are done in from 22 to 25 minutes, including stoppages to let out and take in passengers, each set of horses doing 3 or 4 stages alternatively each day. In fact, the boats are drawn through this narrow and shallow canal, at a velocity which many celebrated engineers had demonstrated, and which the public believed to be impossible.

The entire amount of the whole expenses of attendants and horses, and of running one of these boats 4 trips of 12 miles each (the length of the canal) or 48 miles daily, including interest on the capital, and 20 per cent. laid aside annually for replacement of the boats, or loss on the capital therein vested, and a considerable sum laid aside for accidents and replacement of the horses, is £700 some odd shillings; or, taking the number of working days to be 312 annually, something under £2.2s.4d. per day, or about 11d. per mile. The actual cost of carrying from 80 to 100 persons a distance of 30 miles (the length of the Liverpool railway), at a velocity of nearly 10 miles an hour, on the Paisley Canal, one of the most curved, narrow, and shallow in Britain, is therefore just £1.7s.6d. sterling. Such are the facts, and, incredible as they may appear, they are facts which no one who inquires can possibly doubt.'4

In 1832 alone 148,561 passengers were carried, rising to 373,290 in 1835, proving, if nothing else, just how vital a service this had become. Virtually every canal had a similar service, though travelling at nowhere near this speed. Thus, from Preston to Kendal, although a longer journey than by land '. . . this natural disadvantage is compensated by the ease and rapidity with which passengers are conveyed by the quick passage-boats, in a sufficient degree to raise an effective

Carriers to All Parts

Late Register No. *16 7 22*

Date when Gauged, Weighed, and Measured. *16 . 11 . 00*

Tipton Station.

B.C.N. Register, No. *17525*

Owner *Rowley Regis* Address *Rowley Regis*

Cabin Herd Boat. Name *Lily* No.

Extreme Length *41.0* Extreme Width *70*

Stowage „ *49.2* Stowage „ *68 2*

Draught when Light *10 40* Draught when Laden with *25* Tons *45.34*

Articles on Board when Weighed *3 Beams*
Rudder
Air Case

Tons.	Dry Inches	Difference	Tons.	Dry Inches	Difference	Tons.	Dry Inches	Difference	ALTERATIONS	
									Cwts. DATE.	
Light.	38.10	106	21	16 85		42				
1	37 04		22	15 08		43	*Deduct* 6			
2	35 98		23	14 91		44				
3	34 92		24	13 94	97	45				
4	33 86	102	25	12 97		46				
5	32 84		26	12 00		47				
6	31 82		27	11 03		48				
7	30 80		28	10 06	99	49				
8	29 98	1 01	29	9 07		50				
9	28 97		30	5 08		51				
10	27 96		31	7 09		52				
11	26 95		32	6 10	99	53				
12	25 94	100	33	5 11		54				
13	24 94		34	4 12		55				
14	23 94		35	3 13			37 94			
15	22 94		36	2 14	99		16			
16	21 94	95	37	1 15			38 10			
17	20 96		38	16						
18	19 95		39							
19	18 80		40							
20	17 82	97	41							

Boat gauging register (Courtesy of the Waterways Research Centre)

opposition against the coaches; and reasonably, for no sort of locomotion can possibly be more agreeable.'[3] That the boatmen worked without supervision is hardly surprising as – unlike today – the cost of such an overseer had to be allowed for in the fares, but of course it did leave the system open to abuse in the collection of fares.

> 'That every person passing in any boat between Wigan and Liverpool, or any other part of the line, shall pay for every two miles or under, one half-penny; each passenger to be allowed fourteen pounds weight of baggage; and in case any boatman shall neglect to give a just account of the numbers of passengers he shall at any time carry on his boat, with distance each passenger shall have passed, he shall forfeit the sum of ten shillings.'[5]

Comparatively, for travelling was until relatively recent times, a rich man's occupation, canal boats truly had the edge on road traffic and, surprisingly, even rail. Thus, to take a family of two adults and three children from Manchester to London in 1844, by boat, including 'provisions', cost £3.70 and took 5 days; the coach took 2 days costing £6.10; while by rail, though admittedly the journey was completed in one day, it cost £4.15. What the nature of the provisions were then can only be guessed at, but one hopes they were better than those found on a Pickford's boat in the 1830s:

> '. . . we left . . . in high glee and marched to London and proceeded to our destination by canal in Pickfords boats which travelled night and day and the distance between London and Chester (200 miles) was performed generally in five days, this of course was before the general introduction of railways, we got along very comfortable in these boats, they were covered in with tarpaulings and a quantity of straw in the bottom. The only inconvenience attending them they did not halt for meals so that we had to do the best we could in that respect, our meals generally consisted of bread and raw bacon which was generally taken while walking on the banks of the canal and washed down with an occasional glass of ale in passing, for we seldom had time to sit down unless we happened to be in the neighbourhood of Locks which

somewhat delayed the boats. After five days of this dog like kind of life, a bite and a run, we arrived at a place called Preston Brook, a small village within 14 miles of Chester and the nearest point to the canals. Here we disembarked and the Detachment proceeded to Chester.'[6]

Shorthaul traffic, so-called market boats, were not forgotten and a special *Glasgow Packet* was run on the Glasgow, Paisley & Ardrossan Canal, 'Every Wednesday at 9 in the morning' for those going to the Market. Further South, Thomas Monk ran his famous *Euphrates Packet* from 'Mr. Jos[h]. Aston's Factory Bridge, Tipton' in 1820 to 'Mr. R[d]. Heathcote's Waggon & Horses, Friday Bridge, Birmingham' at a cost of $7\frac{1}{2}$ or 5 pence. On Tuesdays, Wednesdays and Fridays the boat was available for private hire. Despite shortening of the route and changes in the points of departure, railway competition virtually eliminated the service in the 1840s, but not before Monk had reduced the running time from Wolverhampton to Birmingham to two hours ten minutes. It was mentioned as still running in 1851. He was a shrewd man and it would be interesting to know his thoughts on 15 September 1830, when a party was organized by 'Squire Downing and others to witness the opening of the Liverpool and Manchester Railway. Special permission was given to enable the packet to pass over the Bridgewater Canal without paying tolls'.

One long-lived packet boat service was that which operated on the Manchester, Bolton & Bury Canal. Among the byelaws of the company was one that ruled: 'If any Boat navigating the Canal do not drop its Line and give the inner Side to the Packet Boat in passing the Manager of such Boat shall forfeit 10s.' From Bolton to Manchester the first class single fare was $7\frac{1}{2}$p, return $12\frac{1}{2}$p and the boats, rather unusually, ran on Sundays. We find, in 1834, that prayers must have been interrupted at Christ Church, Salford: 'Mr. Ritson [Treasurer] directs that the Packet Steerer ceases to blow his horn when passing the church near Windsor Bridge on Sunday evening as it annoys the congregation.'

The three hour journey must have been pleasant enough in summer, as a voyageur (a child) tells us:

'Our trunks were carried to the boat by the two maidservants; and after a grand flourish on a horn and a loud "Gee" from the captain, we set off; two horses pulled at the rope, and we went on our way at a speed of three miles an hour.

The boat was covered, and had seats and a table inside; but if the weather were fine, it was pleasant to sit in the fore-part outside and watch the water sink from the banks of the canal, and the water-lilies and rushes bend their heads as we passed, and then to see the swelling wave that followed us, rushing on and filling all up again. This sail in the early morning was a pure and perfect enjoyment. It was gratifying to think that we were five miles away before the people at home had breakfasted . . . Presently we came to a lock in the canal. We sailed slowly into a long, deep, dark trap, with solid wooden gates at each end. The sides were of stone – massive, mossy and dripping. The gates were closed behind us, and the sluices were opened. Then began such a turmoil in the water beneath us, such a heaving, roaring, foaming and tumbling, as if some huge monsters were imprisoned in the water, and were churning and lashing in their rage to get free. Imperceptibly, we rose and rose into the open day, the gates were thrown back, and we glided through in gentle contrast to the hubbub we had so lately witnessed.'[7]

Parcels were also carried, small ones at 2½p each, large at 2½p per half-hundredweight (60 lbs then). The service died in 1838, as the Manchester, Bolton & Bury had sold itself to a railway; there was then no point in competing.

In later days boats ran occasionally, carrying parties of orphans, church congregations and similar groups on outings; these were normally ordinary boats dressed up for the purpose. One exception commenced in April 1919 when a trial run was made from Aston Station to the Dunlop Rubber Company's works at Bromford, 2¼ miles 'a district which is not, unfortunately, fed by a tram service'. Due to the aftermath of war no buses could be bought and by February 1920 'it was . . . necessary to run no less than five boats, each with a seating capacity of approximately 100, some of the boats making several journeys a day. At the present time [1924] over 5,000 passengers per week are being carried to and from the works.'[8]

Hooke's Detachable Motor (a primitive form of outboard) was used but:

> 'The boats now in use are of the ordinary light build of canal boats with sharp bows, and drawing less than 1 foot of water when light. They are housed in with timber, have glass sides, and the necessary gangways for boarding and alighting. They are fitted with electric light, and are heated with hot-water pipes. The inside is fitted with seats, and is warm and comfortable in all weathers.'[8]

Interestingly, and possibly still applicable today, 'each boat, as fitted up, cost slightly more than half that of an ordinary motor omnibus, although its seating capacity is three times as great'.[8] They were not, however, financially self-supporting as they ran only at the commencement and the end of shifts and '. . . as soon as the trams or other means of transport are available the boats can be reverted to the carrying of goods, and the loss on capital expenditure will be very slight'.[8]

The second class of carrier, the so-called 'fly' was interchangeable with the third, in as much as after the 1830s the larger carriers always claimed to operate 24-hours of the day, albeit with certain reservations, and subject to the exigencies of trade. Again, with certain exceptions, it must be understood that the bulk of carriers were very small; two, three or four men, perhaps a father and sons going into partnership and agreeing to run to some sort of timetable, and using common booking arrangements and wharves. Beyond this they were rarely a 'company' as we understand the word. Similarly, while they might depart from their base every day, or every other day, and ply to a given point, they could and would stop and discharge or load at any intermediate point, with detrimental effects on their timekeeping. A list of carriers all operating 'fly' services from Worcester in 1820[9] includes Danks & Co., whose agent (at about 5 per cent commission) was James Wall and who operated daily to Birmingham from Diglis (Public) Wharf. James Bromley on the other hand operated from his own warehouse, though only on Mondays, Wednesdays and Fridays and 'arrives in Birmingham the succeeding days'. He discharged at N. & G. Wheatcroft's warehouse and offered on-carriage on their boats, leaving Birmingham Tuesdays,

Thursdays and Saturdays for Derby, Nottingham, Leicester, Loughborough and the intermediate places. If the goods were booked to Buckland Hollow, Wheatcroft's base on the Cromford Canal, waggons were utilized daily to Chesterfield, Sheffield, Doncaster, York and 'all parts of the North'. This kind of service was comparable to the rail, save only in two respects. Speed – it took about a week to get goods to Chesterfield, and being 'fly' boats of relatively light build and loading, probably not in excess of 12 tons, when that boat was full another could not be hitched on. Then the excess goods might wait, or be taken on a standard boat, thus missing their onward carriage.

> WORTHINGTON & CO's Fly Boats, from James Bromley's Warehouse, Lowesmoor, to BIRMINGHAM, WOLVERHAMPTON, STAFFORD, the POTTERIES, CONGLETON, WARRINGTON, LIVERPOOL, MANCHESTER, and the intermediate places, from whence goods are forwarded, by respectable carriers, to all parts of CHESHIRE, North WALES, WESTMORLAND, CUMBERLAND, and parts of SCOTLAND adjacent. – Agent G. Wood

The 'respectable carriers' were, of course, by road, once more negating the value of canal transport, and to a man who waited eight days in 1826 for goods to travel 9 miles from the canal company's wharf at Chester, it showed the geographical limitations of water transport all too cruelly. Some further examples of timing are relevant here. Glass, a fragile cargo which was best suited to the gentle ride of a canal boat, took 4 days from Birmingham to London; a similar cargo 7 days from London to Bristol. Overall, the average speed maintained 24 hours a day was of the order of $2\frac{1}{2}$–3 m.p.h., and the carrier might charge 1.5p–1.75p per ton per mile. By way of contrast, the normal day-boats would take 10 days London to Bristol, at a charge of roughly 1p per ton per mile.

Although there were geographical limitations to the operations of canal carriers, nevertheless the points to which they could offer services were even more widespread than might be gathered from a mere canal map. The table following shows the places served from Birmingham in 1830, or at least the destinations advertised; the frequency of service to 'intermediate' places would be higher, if goods were offered and space was available; but services to Hull, the west of England, Wales, etc., were determined by tide and traffic.

Fly Boat Services ex. Birmingham, 1830

	Boats per week
Altringham	3
Ashby Canal	9
Ashton	3
Barnsley	3
Bath and the west	4
Black Country	32
Boston and district	3
Brecon and South Wales	9
Bristol	31
Burton	12
Cambridge	3
Cheltenham and district	12
Chester	9
Chesterfield	6
Coventry	14
Cromford	3
Derby	15
Doncaster	3
Fazeley	23
Fradley	2
Gainsborough	20
Gloucester	20
Grantham	6
Halifax	3
Hereford and district	3
Hillmorton	2
Huddersfield	3
Hull	14
Lancaster Canal (to Kendal etc.)	3
Leeds	6
Leek	12

	Boats per week
Leicester	18
Liverpool	25
London (by canal)	15
,, (coastwise)	3
Loughborough	9
Louth	3
Macclesfield	15
Manchester	23
Market Harborough	9
Market Raisen	3
Melton Mowbray	6
Monmouthshire	3
Nantwich	3
Northampton	9
Northwich	6
Nottingham	24
Oldham	6
Oxford	6
Retford	3
Sleaford	3
Shardlow	20
Sheffield	9
Shrewsbury and district	6
South Wales	7
Staffordshire Potteries	27
Stockport	15
Stourbridge	14
Stourport	15
Stratford	14
Swansea	3
Tewkesbury and district	7
Wakefield	3
Walsall	8
Wellingborough	6
West of England, all parts	9
Wigan	6
Worcester	31
Uttoxeter	5
York	3

'From Liverpool goods are forwarded to Glasgow, Greenock, Ireland and the Isle of Man by regular steam packet.'

****

One carrier, G. R. Bird & Son, offered a service to Somersetshire, Gloucestershire, Herefordshire, Worcestershire, Shropshire, Staffordshire, Northamptonshire, Bedfordshire, Buckinghamshire, Berkshire, Hampshire, Hertfordshire and Middlesex, & Warwickshire.

****

'The smacks arrive at Swansea,' says James Bromley, 'and the boats at the Worcester Warehouse, Birmingham, delivering and receiving to and from Swansea, Neath . . . Caermarthen and all adjacent towns.'

****

Messrs. Simpson, Hyde and New, '. . . whose fly-boats . . . are met at Gainsborough by Hyde and Company's Vessels, which sail regularly twice a week laden or not to and from Hull . . .'.

****

Mr. Smith & Son operated daily to Gainsborough from whence goods were forwarded 'by Henry Smith's Steam Vessels, to Hull in one day'.

****

Messrs. Worthington & Company offered a 'regular Service' to Manchester, 'from whence goods are regularly and expeditiously forwarded by respectable Carriers . . . to all Parts of North Wales . . . and to Parts of Westmorland, Cumberland and parts of Scotland adjacent "thereto".'

If the ordinary boats were included it would be safe to assume the movements would be at least quadrupled, while day boats skittered to and fro like water-fleas, a very minimum of 4,000 boats on the move in any one week.

Obviously traffic demands had led, even by 1820, to special-ized types of boats coming into use:

Crocket and Salkeid operating ex Birmingham stressed that 'No other firm conveys goods all the way to Liverpool by their own vessels', offering less chance of pilferage en route. Messrs. Crowley, Leyland and Hicklin were adamant that 'wines and spirits are conveyed in boats secured by Locks' as well they might be for woe betide the unsuspecting customer who used an ordinary boat.

'A short time since, a steerer employed upon the canal between Birmingham and Wolverhampton was detected under circumstances which left no doubt upon the minds of those who heard the case that he had been pursuing a regular course of systematic pillage of wines and spirits. On his arrival at the latter place upon the day in question, he was observed to be the worse for liquor, and on unloading his boat a cask of wine was found to be in bad condition and leaking. The circumstances of the leaking cask of wine and the drunken steerer, were supposed to be more than a mere casual coincidence, and an investigation took place. In his cabin were found several vessels, – jugs, bottles ; and, if the circumstances are correctly remembered, – a bucket either filled or partially filled with wine, together with hammers, plugs, gimblets, and a small pump, fitted with a narrow tube for insertion into a hole made with the gimblet. The worst part of this practice is, that the deficiency so occasioned, is usually supplied with an equal quantity of water – thus, not only is a portion stolen, but the remainder is deteriorated. The man in question, as soon as he heard that suspicions were entertained of him and a search was about to take place, went direct to the stable in which his horse was put up, took him out, mounted his back, and rode away, and all the exertions of his employers and the police have hitherto been unsuccessful in tracing him out. Similar instances might be multiplied to any extent.'[10]

Similar services were operated wherever there was justifica-tion. From Leeds to Selby in 1822 fly-boats left every evening (Sundays excepted) arriving there'. . . in 12 hours and deliver their cargoes on board a steam-packet which sails every

15   An unusual houseboat on what is possibly the Brecon and Abergavenny Canal, about 1914. *(Courtesy of the National Museum of Wales)*

16   The zoo bus on Regents Canal. *(Courtesy of the British Waterways Board)*

17   A girl steering a boat on the Grand Union Canal, about 1944.
(Courtesy of the Geographical Magazine)

18   Children playing in an empty narrow boat during the 1950s.
(Courtesy of M Webb)

EXPEDITIOUS AND DAILY
CANAL CONVEYANCE,

Between London and Liverpool. Manchester, Newark,
Nottingham, Mansfield, Leicester, Birmingham, Derby,
Gainsborough, and Burton-upon-Trent.

German Wheatcroft and Son,
GENERAL CARRIERS,
126, London Wall, & No. 4 Wharf, Paddington, LONDON.

Duke's Dock, Liverpool: Piccadilly, Manchester: Brown
and Ragsdale's Wharf, Newark: Three Cranes Wharf,
Nottingham; Crescent Wharf, Birmingham; Portland Wharf,
Mansfield: Thames Street, Leicester: Cock-pit Hill Derby;
Bond End, Burton-upon-Trent: Gainsborough,
W. HOWARD, AGENT.
Buckland Hollow and Cromford, Derbyshire.
All Business Communications are requested to be addressed
to their Offices as above.

Goods are Forwarded by their Conveyances to the un-
dermentioned places, (in capitals) and those which follow by
responsible Carriers:—
LONDON, BIRKHAMPSTED, Chesham, BOXMOOR, St. Albans,
LEIGHTON BUZZARD, Dunstable, Luton, Hitchen, Woburn,
FENNY STRATFORD, Amphill, Bedford, Biggleswade, Wins-
low, LINFORD WHARF, Newport Pagnell, Olney, Cosgrove,
Stoney Stratford, Buckingham, BLISWORTH, Northampton,
Towcester, BUCKBY WHARF, Daventry, LEICESTER, Market
Harborough, Kettering, Hinckley, Melton, Oakham, Up-
pingham, Stamford, Lutterworth, Colsterworth, Buckmins-
ter, LOUGHBOROUGH, Kegworth, NOTTINGHAM, Bingham,
Southwell, MANSFIELD, Sutton-in-Ashfield, Worksop, Ret-
ford, NEWARK, Lincoln, GAINSBOROUGH, Hull SHARDLOW,
BURTON-UPON-TRENT, Ashby, Tutbury, Uttoxeter, DERBY,
ILKESTONE, RIPLEY, ALFRETON, BUCKLAND HOLLOW,
CHESTERFIELD, CRICH, BELPER, CROMFORD, Wirksworth,
Ashbourn, Bakewell, Winster, Buxton, Longnor, Tideswell,
Castleton, WHALEY, CHAPEL-EN-LE-FRITH, Dishley, Hazle-
grove, STOCKPORT, Macclesfield, ASHTON, Staley Bridge,
MANCHESTER, Bury, Bolton, Rochdale, Todmorden, Old-
ham, Blackburn, Halifax, Preston, Garstang, Lancaster,
Kirby Lonsdale, Kendal, St. Helens, Warrington, STOCK-
TON QUAY, Ormskirk, Wigan, Prescot, PRESTON BROOK,
Runcorn, Liverpool, BIRMINGHAM, Worcester, Gloucester,
and Bristol.

Advertisement (Courtesy of the Waterways Research Centre)

113

morning and lands packages at Hull the same evening', while to Liverpool, the Union Canal Company offered 'services three times a week' having '40 vessels engaged' and arriving in 4 days. York, Gainsborough, Nottingham and Manchester (via the Rochdale Canal), Bradford, Hull and London had at least one boat a day. From Dewsbury, Widow Welsh, an indomitable old lady, the relict of a boatman, together with her sons, offered daily services to and from Leeds and York, and every evening Manchester. Doncaster to Barnsley was a weekly sailing, returning on Fridays; Huddersfield to Manchester (Widow Welsh again) a 24-hour journey, operated daily. Ripon to Hull, twice weekly, was run by Martin Keddy & Co. 'in one bottom'. On lesser used canals, the Pocklington for exa ple, which only handled 5,000 or so tons a year, a weekly service from Hull sufficed; a true 'fly' boat, it bore the name *Union Packet* and completed the round trip in the week. One of the largest carriers to operate a round-the-clock, time-tabled service was the firm Thomas Pickford & Co., who once seeing the growth of the canal network was quick to adapt its already extant road haulage system to that of water transport. Initially in 1786, Mathew Pickford, in charge of operations within the family concern, absorbed the carrying trade of Hugh Henshall & Co. from Manchester via the Bridgewater and Trent & Mersey canals to Shardlow, and routed goods from there to London via waggons. His move to Rugeley later the same year was a logical step to reduce road haulage, but two years later he negotiated warehouse accommodation at Braunston on the Oxford Canal, utilizing this as the point of transhipment. Thereafter, progress was steady if not spectacular; Blisworth on the Grand Junction Canal came into use in 1796, although as the tunnel through Blisworth Hill was not opened until 1805 most goods for London still went by road. An extension of the tramroad, crossing the line of the tunnel and connecting the two halves of the canal, was made, at Pickfords' behest, to their wharf in May 1801, which suggests that some, at least, of their traffic was transhipped. After completion of the tunnel, trade was steady from Lancashire to London, by water throughout. Derby (1801), Birmingham (1803), Leicester (1814), Worcester (1815) and Bristol (1829) were added to the destinations. The number of boats rose steadily to meet the traffic from 10 in 1795,

83 in 1821, 90 in 1830, to 116 in 1838, although boats were often hired to make good any shortfall in their own. Obviously, the number of horses in use also rose; 398 being bought in 1838 alone. The firm of Pickford were indeed 'fly', for, using the argument that an increase in their trade necessarily meant an increase in revenue for the canal companies, they were able to obtain warehousing facilities at relatively low cost, thereby reducing capital outlay. Although they brought their administration block cum warehouse complex at City Road Basin, Paddington, almost outright (as an incentive to move there the canal company made them a gift of £5,000 towards it), normal practice was to arrange a lease for 21 years or so at an annual charge of 7½ per cent of the building costs. Special arrangements – beneficial to all concerned – were made with the canal companies for either through tolls, or tolls calculated on the passage of a given number of boats carrying an average tonnage per year. Notwithstanding these arrangements, superb chaos could be arrived at quite easily by both carrier and his servant, the boatman, and the canal company's servant, the toll-collector. Pickfords put this in a nutshell when they wrote to the Oxford Canal Company in March 1832:

> '. . . the canal accounts are now becoming so complex that it is difficult to know where we stand – some things being charged different rates, according as they are coming up or going down – and in some cases where a reduction is made, part of the goods are charged the reduced rate and part the full rate in the tonnage accounts leaving a portion to be obtained by way of over-charges, and again some allowances are made from statements furnished by us and some from accounts rendered by other canal co's. . . .'[11]

Though already in difficulty due to frost: 'Pickford and Co. beg to inform the Public that in consequence of the frost, and the scarcity of water in the canal, goods cannot be forwarded whilst the present state of the weather continues. Caravans are usual to and from Manchester, Liverpool, Macclesfield, Derby, Leicester, Nottingham, etc,'[12] and maintenance stoppages: 'Pickford & Co. beg to inform the public that a stoppage will take place on the Canals on the 2nd of June next at day-break, and continue for the week . . . Caravans daily as usual'[12] when road, coastal and steam transports threatened to write 'finis' to the fly-boats, Pickfords were still adaptable enough to change to rail transport, abandoning the main waterway to Manchester (the Macclesfield) in 1841, the Coventry and Oxford routes in 1845 and 1846 respectively, the Worcester and Birmingham in 1847, and finally changing almost entirely to rail in 1850 when horses, boats and warehouses were disposed of. Such was the rivalry between carriers that they were commemorated in verse, typically:

> 'Crowley and Hickling, mind your eye,
> For fear bold Pickford should come by.'[12]

The passing of the true fly-boats was a matter of much regret; a writer in 1890, speaking of his youth, expressed it thus:

'Among the prominent and more obtrusive establishments of the time were the canal wharves, situated on the right hand side of the Tipton Road, a little lower down from this brook. The first was that of Messrs. J. Whitehouse and Sons, carried on by them for many years, and their head office being at the top of the Birmingham Road, at Dudley, was a great convenience to the grocers and other retail traders in Dudley, as by enquiry there they could obtain early information as to whether their goods had arrived or were on the way, and when they were likely to reach the Tipton Wharf, whence they could be carted by the company, or by the owners, to their destination. This wharf and receiving establishment passed into the hands of the Grand Junction Canal Company about the year 1850; they carried on the business there for some years and then removed it to their new premises at Dudley Port, which had been built for the purpose. The Tipton warehouses became dilapidated through mining operations till they had to be cleared off, and then the ground was worked for minerals underneath. The next wharves and carrying establishments were those of the old firm of Pickford and Co., and then those of Crowley & Co., and some others. The carriers conveyed by canal the chief of the goods and merchandise for the grocers, drapers, and other shopkeepers from London, Liverpool, and Manchester, and also from the Potteries, from Nottingham,

Leicester, Northampton and Stafford for all the retail traders in Dudley and the district. They also carried the various local products and manufactures to those centres, and all the places on the way, fifty years ago and long before any railway had penetrated or was thought of in this vicinity.

When the railways had been made, and the companies had established their usurping business with the assistance of the principal common carriers like Messrs. Pickford and Co. and Crowley and Co. who became agents of the railways; the other and lesser carriers gradually withdrew their fly-boats from the canals in favour of the railways . . .'[13]

It is not true to say, as is often the case by crocodile-tear-shedding writers, that when the railways arrived, the canals died. True, the system contracted, but given an asset in which you have sunk money but find you cannot sell, what is to be done? In today's terms, consider a car: inflation means its second-hand value has fallen to uneconomic level, so it is not expedient to sell it even if it is possible. Logically, you go to the garage, have odd jobs done to it and hang on; maybe buying those bits and bobs that will make it better. So it was with independent canals; tolls were cut and night-working became the order of the day. Some carriers changed to the use of family boats throughout, but one result of this was the almost total extinction of the lightweight fly-boat, save in exceptional cases.

In 1845 canal companies were given the right to carry on their own account; this is therefore a convenient point at which to introduce the third – 'heavy' – class of boat.

The standard, or heavy-goods, vessel served a rather different class of customer than the fly-boats. The craft were heavier, on narrow canals 20–25 tons was normal, operated at a reduced fee, and were slower in as much as they did not necessarily operate at night. Most, but not all, were cabin boats, the crew, whether all male or family, lived on board for the duration of the trip, at least after the 1830s. Prior to this they still stayed with the boats but, officially, spent the night at lodging houses. Until recently one of these was still standing at The Summit, Rochdale Canal, and appears to have had two dormitories each holding six or more men, a kitchen and, in latter days, some primordial form of sanitation. Little has been written about canal lodging houses; boatmen, if not illiterate, were disinclined to writing, considering it a waste of good beer-drinking time, and the self-styled 'philanthropists' were too busy mumbling about the abhorred family boats to know or care aught about such places. However, unless they were exceptionally clean, bugs would be normal: 'It was' as a friend told me, 'rather fun making them pop with your fingernails,' bed-linen, if supplied was both bug-ridden and unwashed; the straw 'donkey' (mattress) holding both a kick and a bite. Food may have been available, if not, a charge would be made for coals when using the range. In view of these conditions it is hardly surprising that the boatman would sooner stop at a hostelry for the night, and conveniently these pubs came neatly at the end of a reasonable day's working. Not that these were always that good; a splendid story current among boatmen of the time tells how a flea went into such a canalside hostelry and drank a glass of whisky, and another, and another, until it was closing time. It then staggered up the stairs, jumped in the air and fell flat on its face. 'Dammit' it said, getting up, 'who's moved my boatman?'. The London–Birmingham route was split in three, four or five sections, with recognized overnight stops: Cowroast, Stoke Bruerne, Braunston, Itchington, Warwick, all had good pubs and stabling. The run from Oldbury to Ellesmere Port was a $3\frac{1}{2}$ day affair with stops at Wheaton Aston, Cheswardine and Chester. The goods carried were not the light-weight stuff of the fly-boats, but coke and coal for outlying villages, iron-ore for the furnaces, potters clay, chemicals, timber – a traffic often overlooked nowadays but not in 1795 as the following advertisement shows.

'Glocestershire. Oak and Elm Timber.
To be SOLD by AUCTION. by Mr. READ.
On FRIDAY the 13th of February inst., between the hours of three and four in the afternoon, at the BELL INN, FRAMPTON-UPON-SEVERN, 350 Capital ELM TIMBER TREES and 178 Good OAK TIMBER TREES, all marked and numbered with white lead and oil, situate in the PARISH of EASTINGTON, and adjoining the Turnpike Roads leading from GLOCESTER to BATH, BRISTOL,

FRAMPTON, &c. distant from the RIVER SEVERN about TWO MILES, and all within ONE MILE Of STROUDWATER CANAL, and very near the line of the GLOCESTER and BERKELEY CANAL . . . Dinner to be on the table precisely at two o'clock.'[14]

On some waterways the trade available would not justify the operation of fly-boats; for the extra cost of nightworking through locks for which a supplementary toll could be payable to canal companies outweighed the advantages. To combat this it was not unknown for a heavy boat to start literally at break of day ('half past 4 o'clock a.m.') and work until dark, perhaps making use of an eight or ten mile pound for the final three hours. The limitation of this kind of work was simply that of the horses' endurance. While the larger companies could have spare animals available at the end of eight or nine hours work, the one man business could rarely afford the extra corn, let alone the animal – Pickfords valued theirs at an average of £5 each in 1838. When times were hard – say after a long frost – a boatman would have to use a Tommy Shop wherein goods were supplied 'on tick', resulting in him getting poor value for high prices. This treatment was usual in South Wales but was also meted out elsewhere. As times got harder it could happen that one boat and one horse owner could not even afford to pay the bill at the stables and his credit, which was shrewdly calculated on the profit he might make on a round-trip, would run out. The only course of action left, and this did happen, was for the man to bow-haul his boat on a journey that might stretch from Wolverhampton to Preston Brook, or Tyseley to Paddington. The boat was assuredly heavy. It is interesting to note, however, that although 'Number Ones' were never to regain their numerical strength once the canal companies began carrying on their own account, nevertheless a very few were to see out the end of commercial carrying on narrow canals.

Prior to 1830 we had this twin service of fly and heavy boats operating to the same places; one light and fast, one slow but carrying more; the traffic generated by ever improving services was strangling both waterway and carrier, resulting in the larger carriers absorbing many of their weaker brethren. Part

Advertisement (Courtesy of Waddingtons of Swinton)

of the strangling process was the fault of the canal companies, the wealthier ones were complacent, the poorer had often expended their funds and incurred enormous debts and literally had no cash for maintenance let alone improvements. The more traffic, the greater the wear and tear on banks, locks, bridges even, and most particularly on warehouses. Once adequate to cope with the trade, these were often jammed tight with goods, to such an extent that on the Birmingham Canal Navigations boats were used to cope with the overflow. Not only did this cause utter confusion among all concerned; clerks unable to say where anything was (or even if it was), boatmen unable to discharge, old hand operated cranes leisurely lifting items out and putting the wrong ones in, and perishables rotting, but what a magnificent opportunity it was for the pilferer. And for that matter the arsonist, for this was the time of the Chartists, when feelings were running high; when the have-nots, unable to have it, burnt it so that no-one had it. A not untypical incident took place in the Black Country:

> 'On Monday morning, April 28th, 1800, a Dudley mob sought to enlist the Tipton colliers on their side in an attack on the baker's shops, but were dissuaded by Mr. Amphlett and other local magistrates from immediately carrying out their purposes. In the afternoon, however, they found their way to Nine Locks, Brierly Hill, and there took possession of two canal boats, laden with grain for Birmingham. When the Dudley volunteer cavalry put in an appearance they were assailed with bricks, stones, bull-dogs, &c. Then the Riot Act was read . . . the tumult was quelled after one rioter had been killed and many wounded.'[13]

Warehouse fires were commonplace, Pickfords suffered a particular disastrous one in their City Basin warehouse, Regents Canal, in February 1824, when it was said that they had contained 'the greater portion of the produce of the Northern part of England'.[15]

Typical of the notices which appeared was the following:

> 'Whereas on Wednesday Night the 25th of October last, or early on Thursday Morning, a Pack of Irish Linen was cut open, and five Pieces of Yard-wide, directed to Mr. John

Francis, of Bewdley, marked No. 4, and D A S G, was taken out. Whoever will discover the Person or Persons that committed the said Robbery, so that he or they may be convicted for the same, shall receive Five Guineas Reward by applying to the Owner James Wilson, of Shrewsbury. And if more than one were concerned, and will discover the others, he shall receive the above Reward, and Endeavours used for a Pardon. – The above Pack was opened and the Goods taken out near the Welch Bridge, Shrewsbury, from on board a Vessel belonging to Owner Field.'[16]

The thefts were often trivial in themselves, but cumulatively they took their toll. Various Acts were passed to reduce the losses; one of which[17] pointed out the obvious: that felonies were often committed on board a boat and as that boat was moving it could pass through several counties and the criminal could not be brought to trial unless it was established in which county the crime took place. Therefore:

'. . . be it enacted . . . That from and after the passing of this Act, in any Indictment for any Felony committed on board any Barge, Boat, Trow, or other Vessel whatever, employed or used in carrying or conveying Goods, Wares and Merchandize, or in which any such Goods, Wares, or Merchandize shall be, in or upon any Canal, Navigable River or Inland Navigation, in any Part of the United Kingdom of Great Britain and Ireland, it shall be sufficient to allege that such Felony was committed, within any County or City through any Part whereof such Boat, Barge, Trow, or other Vessel shall have passed in the Course of the Voyage or Journey during which such Felony shall have been committed. . . .''

The penalty was succinct: 'Person or Persons who shall be convicted . . . shall be subject to all such Pains of Death,' as would be the case if they had been landsmen. By 1840, the sensible move of appointing constables to patrol the banks had been mooted and was agreed that year.[18] Penalties were surprisingly light, resisting arrest: £10 fine or two months' imprisonment, with or without hard labour,

'. . . every Person who shall be found upon any such Canal

or River, or in or upon any Lock, Dock, Warehouse, Wharf, Quay, or Bank thereof, or on board of any Boat or Vessel lying or being in any such Canal or River, or in any Lock or Dock, thereunto belonging, having in his Possession or under his Control any Tube or other Instrument for the Purpose of unlawfully obtaining any Wine, Spirits, or other Liquors or Goods, or having in his Possession any Skin, Bladder, or other Utensil for the Purpose of unlawfully secreting or carrying away any such Wine, Spirits, or other Liquors or Goods, and any Person who shall attempt unlawfully to obtain such Wine, Spirit, or other Liquor or Goods, shall for every such Offence be liable to a Penalty not more than Five Pounds, or, in the Discretion of the Magistrate before whom he shall be convicted, may be imprisoned as aforesaid, with or without Hard Labour, for any Time not more than One Calendar Month.'

A similar sentence applied if you were caught in the act.

Applicable, if only for the number of convictions it brought, was clause 10:

'. . . it shall be lawful for any such Constable to take into Custody, without a Warrant, any loose, idle, and disorderly Person who he shall find disturbing the public Peace, or whom he shall have good Cause to suspect of having committed or being about to commit any Felony, Misdemeanor, or Breach of the Peace, or other Offence contrary to the Provisions of this Act, and, every Person whom he shall find, between Sunset and the Hour of Eight in the Morning, lying or loitering in or upon any Towing Path, or in or upon any Wharf, Bridge, Railway, Quay, Landing Place, Lock, Dock, or upon the Bank of any such Canal or River, and not giving a satisfactory Account of himself.'

Obviously these laws had to be enforced and near Cassio Park:

'. . . a watchman's cottage belonging to the Canal Company, whose occupation is partly to prevent the navigators from committing depredations in their passage through the park; for which purpose a vista is cut through the plantations, so that a view of the boats may be distinctly had, during their passing from hence to the fisherman's cottage at the opposite extremity of the park, and vice versa. This dwelling resembles those erected by the Earl of Essex, and has innumerable flowers and flowering shrubs surrounding it.'[19]

This both helped to keep an eye on the boat – and its crew – and at the same time met the demand from the landowner that a suitable cottage be built. Interestingly, in a chronicle of 1819 we have examples of the use of female labour. Stoke Bruerne at that date presented a very different picture to that of today.

'Every object that encountered our sight, as we passed to the village . . . appeared of the picturesque; the team retiring from the glebe, had its rustic mate and tired plough boy, with all their paraphanalia, seated on the leading horses; the navigation attendants and their cattle were bustling to pass the lock; the freighted boats presented a motly group of passengers on their decks; while a number of female attendants on the canal horses, reminded me of those hardy Cambrian lasses I have so often seen following their laborious avocations.'[20]

Further up the canal, at Blisworth Tunnel, a spectator's beady eye saw both women, and a method of passing the tunnel which must obviously have been practised despite the fact it was – and is – forbidden, for fear of damage to the clay puddle forming the bottom of the canal.

'Several barges were now preparing to enter the excavation; the men throwing off their upper garments and lighting up their lanthorn, gave the helm for steerage to the women, one or two females generally attending each boat; when ready they loose the tow-rope of the horses, and apply themselves to the poles, with which they sturdily shove the boats through the dark channel. On the top of the hill, just above the navigation, there is a small shed erected for the attendants and cattle that have come over from Blisworth, and are to await the arrival of their proprietor's barges passing through the tunnel from that village.'[19]

Other boat types have proliferated, according to the size of the canal and the demands of its traffic. The towering hay-barge working from perhaps Norfolk to Chiswick, or from Leighton Baudesert [Buzzard]

'"a market town" which had "... a considerable traffic from its neighbourhood for hay, and milch cows, to supply the metropolis; the hay is conveyed in barges up to eighty tons burden; and the channel of the canal is always kept of sufficient depth for craft of that tonnage"[19] or the flats of the Mersey & Irwell; these by contrast with an East Coast "stumpie" (one man and one boy) needing a two-man crew on the river and three when they ventured "outside"; or the coal boats of Newcastle which often turned up on the Thames; all were the equivalent of our lorries. To bring the trade that was carried by "heavy" boats into focus we can hardly do better than quote the traffics carried on the Grand Junction Canal in 1831. "The staple goods of Manchester, Stourbridge, Birmingham and Wolverhampton – cheese, salt, lime, stone, timber, corn, paper, bricks, etc. – are conveyed by it to town, whilst in return groceries, tallow, cotton, tin, manure and raw materials for the manufacturing districts are constantly passing upon it."[1]

But the real backbone of canal trade was coal, followed by iron (finished products, the ore and the limestone used as flux). Without doubt the long distance boats had the greater social impact, nevertheless, without dayboats industry must necessarily have strangled. And without a special breed of men to man these dayboats Britain would never have achieved her greatness. Without these 'sullen, stinking waters' how would we ever have developed that industry that still props us up today. The normal dayboat of the Midlands is a box-like structure, sharpened at both ends, but they are not, as is commonly believed, identical at both ends; on an open boat the lowest platform is the fore-end, by 4 inches. Their work was arduous and the boatman – who worked solely with the aid of a boy or a 'mate', – a mate who might be here today and gone the next – had to know every pit, every factory, every wharf on the Birmingham Canal Navigations, said to have numbered over 2,000. Carrying normally a 40-ton load he worked through all weathers, shovelled coal in, shovelled it out, manhandled two-cwt sacks of castings, barrowed in ashes and 'threw' them out; this latter traffic almost as vital as the coal he took in. He legged his way through tunnels (Lappal 3,295 yards; Dudley 3,172; Wast Hill 2,726 were three), 'mauled' (bowhauled) his boat up and down locks, locks that were not the pretty ones of today, but locks covered in oil, like glass in the frost and the 'old 'oman's frypan' in spring. Sweltered his way along the main line in the heat of summer with the fumes of brass and iron works beating down upon him and his boat. And how little he was noticed save such comments as that upon a boatman employed in Dudley Tunnel, 'The steersman of the boat, even to his very garb, is the exact counterpart of Charon' and this from a man of the cloth![20]

Day boatmen undoubtedly drank hard, but worked hard. A further traffic that was handled by day boats was that of night-soil. Anyone who keeps a horse will know well enough its output per diem in manure; imagine, if you will, this multiplied by 1,000, 2,000 or 10,000; for with all traffic horse-drawn these would be the figures for any city. Add to this the habits of the citizens in Bradford:

'. . . dungheaps are found in several parts in the streets and open privies are seen in many directions . . . The chief sewerage . . . is in open channels . . . the flow is tardy and the whole soil is saturated with sewage water. The main sewers are discharged either into the brook or into the terminus or basin of a canal which runs into the lower part of the town. The water of this basin is often so charged with decaying matter, that in hot weather bubbles of sulphurated hydrogen are continually rising to the surface, and so much is the atmosphere loaded with that gas, that watch-cases and other materials of silver become black in the pockets of the workmen employed near the canal'[21] and Wigan, 'These streets were unsewered, unpaved; every few yards a pool of stagnant water, and heaps of accumulated filth of every description'[22] or Dudley where there were 'Large quantities of dung and manure, liquid and solid, from stables'.[23] Similarly in neighbouring Wolverhampton '. . . is a dunghill – yet it is too large to be called a dunghill. I do not misstate its size when I say it contains a hundred cubic yards of impure filth, collected from all parts of the town.' Another prize spot was Manchester, '. . . the sewers are all in a most wretched state, and quite inadequate to carry off the surface water, not to mention the slops thrown down by the inhabitants . . . The privies are in a most disgraceful state, inaccessible from filth, and too few for the accommodation of the number of people – the average number being two to two hundred and fifty people.'[24]

It will be apparent how much the night-soil man could do to alleviate the position. At its simplest the muck was collected into one heap – 'The bones are always sold to the Jews and they send them away in barges . . . [to be] used for manure' – and the older the 'filth' the more valuable, in some cases it was sold by the cartload and had to be dug from the middle! The usual position of the heap, however, was alongside the canal from whence it was loaded – with shovels – into boats, and taken away to be sold to farmers as manure; if the farmer were some distance away it might well be transhipped en route. There was in London a class of men named 'Bunters' (Oh Lord Peter Wimsey!) who with the aid of a bit of candle and the co-operation of the boatman, would sift through the material during the night for rags, bones or valuables which could be sold the following morning.

Rivalry between carriers could be taken to extremes

As this was the trade that was not to be affected by railways, but by other social changes, it is worth following the story to the end. One of the greatest of all night-soil operators was William Perry, known in his time as 'The Tipton Slasher'. Born on the cut bank at Tipton in 1819, and following in the footsteps of his father, he became a boatman on the Birmingham Canal Navigations and after gaining a name for himself by bashing other boatmen in the course of his work, he came under the wing of Lord Dudley, as a prize-fighter. Perry himself was said to have had a kindly expression and not to look as though he had been thumped too hard too often. Most distinctive of all was the shape of his legs, for as a result of a boating accident one was bent so far inward as to give him, from the waist down, the shape of a letter 'K'. The Tipton Slasher was unusually tall for a boatman, being 6 feet $0\frac{1}{2}$ inch and weighing 14 stone in his prime. His first professional fight took place in 1835 when he beat Bob Gogherty in seven rounds. Thereafter his fighting career continued with various ups and downs.

In 1843 he fought Tass Parker and although 67 rounds were fought in 85 minutes the result was inconclusive as Parker resorted 'to that system of dropping which we have always held to be unmanly and unEnglishlike'. In February 1844 they battled for 133 rounds in 152 minutes, and in 1846 the last fight for £100 took place between these two men – the 'Tipton Slasher' won after 23 rounds in 27 minutes. The money he picked up was considerable – bearing in mind the sport was illegal – 1850 = £100; in 1856 = £150. This last, however, was his swan-song for the following year he was broken-winded, handicapped by his damaged leg, thinner at 12 stone 10 pounds and suffering eye-trouble, and he lost to Tom Sayers. After this '. . . he slowly, but gradually, reverted to his former position in the social scale . . . when he saw that pugalism would avail him no longer as a means of livelihood he went back to his original occupation as a boatman'. Interestingly, he combined his night-soil boating with the occupation of publican, but was forced in 1881 to enter Wolverhampton Workhouse. However, he was granted an annuity by his admirers which was sufficient to keep him in beer and baccy. It is not impossible that at some time William Perry may have carried for the Birmingham Corporation. They had five wharves at Montague

19　Children playing by, possibly, the Glamorganshire Canal, in the 1920s. *(Courtesy of the National Museum of Wales)*

20　Queen Victoria visiting the Bridgewater Canal on 18 October 1851. *(Courtesy of the Waterways Research Centre)*

21 A husband and wife team at Braunston on the Grand Union Canal, in 1963. *(Courtesy of M Webb)*

Street, Shadwell Street, Rotton Park Street, Newtown Row and Holliday Street, the first known to this day as 'Muck Turn'; all had unprintable nicknames. At the first three there was provision for burning dry refuse, the balance travelling in boats, the overall tonnage was quite high:[25]

	Refuse collected (TONS)	Burned in furnaces (TONS)	Shifted by boat (TONS)
1890	155,252	45,825	109,427
1893	191,940	81,493	110,447
1896	199,588	93,703	105,885
1899	205,545	95,618	109,927

In 1895 the Corporation congratulated themselves on making an average annual profit of £545 for 'poudrette'; a manure made from powdered night-soil. The hours of employees were reduced in 1896 from $59\frac{1}{2}$ to 48, a year later wages of carters were raised to £1.25 a week, roughly the equivalent of the boatman's rate. This traffic continued until relatively recent times, as did that of ordinary household refuse, the latter being worked until the late 1960s.

The efficient railway

7 *Something old,*
Something new

The 'natural break' in canal history is generally taken to be 1830, the opening date of the Liverpool & Manchester Railway, but in fact it was the next decade that brought down the curtain. By 1850 most of the changes to the network had taken place and the remaining companies, carriers, boatmen, maintenance men and their customers had to face up to the realities of the situation. In 1848 a pamphlet[1] summarized the condition of canals and their likely future, stating that 'active influences' had for some time past been at work, and were still in operation on the part of the railway companies to bring about amalgamation of railways with canals. Many of these latter, who had for some time stood as independent rivals, were swallowed up by the railway companies; while others had been reduced to such a helpless condition that they too were discussing what on the face of it was a logical move – submitting to the same treatment. It had become 'quite a rage' amongst railway companies to endeavour to buy up the canals running in opposition to them.

The pamphlet then states quite bluntly – once again raising

the bête noire of the Victorians – that the railways want a monopoly. 'The London and North Western Railway Company have, it is well known, thrown the carriers off their lines, monopolizing the whole of the traffic themselves,' thus ensuring that the carriers were only left to carry goods to and from the railways. 'The Canal companies, thus disturbed of a considerable portion of their traffic, and embarrassed with the remainder owing to the difficulty of providing at short notice, efficient substitutes in the room of their most important traders, are thrown into dismay,' as well they might be, for bereft of companies like Pickfords and Crowleys they could no longer offer a sensible system of carriers. The railways were, of course, quick to seize upon the vacuum and, reducing rates, further weakened the canals. They then sat back and waited for the overtures that, inevitably, were to come, seemingly, voluntarily from the canal companies, who in the circumstances had to be content with 'cut-price' offers and were thus 'in danger of falling, a bargain, into the hands of the railway companies, to complete the establishment of the most powerful and unassailable monopoly, which the commercial materials of the kingdom could combine to furnish'.

During a battle for traffics the canal 'fly-boat' rate dropped to £1.61½ per ton from Birmingham to London. The railways came down to £1.87½ – allowing for the saving in time – a more than competitive rate, but all their goods traffic was divided into different classes. Not surprisingly after a company had a rail siding installed their traffic soon moved into another, the fifth class, at £2.75 per ton.

The differing approaches to payment were shown:

'The [canal] carriers allowed their customers, invariably three, and frequently six months' credit; or, for cash at the end of three months, 2½ per cent discount, and were not always very particular to a trifle of reduction. The railways require prompt monthly payments, made in hard cash, allow no discount whatever and not a farthing of reduction. The carriers allowed their customers to warehouse their goods without charge, till it suited their convenience to consign them to their destination. The railways insist on their being immediately forwarded or removed, or impose a charge for warehousing. Returned empties were always conveyed free by the carriers. The London and North Western Company has laid a charge upon them of 3d. per cwt. under 50 miles – 6d. above 50 miles and not exceeding 100, and 9d. for any distance over 100 miles. This payment they require in advance; and if the packages are not immediately removed by the consignee on arrival at their destination, they are either destroyed or sold.'

Needless to say, this was passed on to the customer.

Railways always look efficient, whereas the canal:

'on the contrary, is not calculated to deceive anybody. Beside the railway it appears the embodiment of quiet, plodding, undisguised, sluggishness . . . There is certainly nothing fast about a canal. It seldom changes or improves; and when it does so, it is only by imperceptible degrees. It is apparently the same yesterday, today, and for ever; perpetuating its primitive arrangements to all time and under all circumstances . . . The arrival of boats at any given point upon canals, and their departure therefrom, takes place at all hours, according to the numerous circumstances which are allowed to affect the speed of their transit.'

But there was an answer to the railways – modernize the canals, and let there be harmony among carriers. One writer suggested the formation of a 'Merchants and Manufacturers Carrying Union' for 'UNION is power – division is weakness'. The railway companies [he said] comprise a number of individuals united to gain money, let the users of all transport combine and meet them as a united body. Under the Union:

'The whole carrying operations of the kingdom will be linked into one general system, under the control and influence of those who feed it with their traffic. There will be one universally recognised medium of conveyance existing everywhere – the "Union Carrier". Lists of rates will be published and placed gratuitously in the hands of the patrons of the "Union" by which they will be enabled at a glance to determine the rate to any particular place. A general understanding will be promoted throughout the system by which efficiency will be ensured, and the annoying delays, losses, overcharges, and other errors which characterise the present carrying operations of the kingdom, will be as much as possible avoided and correct.'

This was not nationalization but rationalization.

Unfortunately the Union remained a dream, the railways and canals in the main continuing as they were. Rates went up, the customer paid more, the canal companies cut their losses and manpower. If railway-controlled some of those owned by the GWR or its satellites were deliberately run down, while the LNWR nursed theirs where it suited them. The older, independent waterways, such as the Weaver, Mersey, Aire & Calder, whose usage was a matter of habit, as well as being due to the bulk of the load, continued as hitherto. Figures, if not entirely accurate, put out by the Board of Trade and drawn from official statistics show the almost unbelievable tonnage that still moved on waterways, but the greatest quantity, probably 75 per cent, was shorthaul.

Canal	Independent Canal or Railway	1848	1868	1888	1905
Aberdare	I	159,653	93,542	102,805	Closed
Aire & Calder	I	1,335,783	1,747,251	2,210,692	2,810,988
Birmingham Canal Navigations	R	4,696,192	6,982,773	7,713,047	7,546,453
Bude	I	52,501	53,103	30,611	Closed
Coventry	I	520,000*	427,808	451,521	425,774
Rivers Kennet, Avon and Kennet & Avon Canal	R	360,610	210,567	135,802	63,979

* Approx.

Canal	Independent Canal or Railway	1848	1868	1888	1905
Regents	I	1,097,711	1,633,098	1,672,959	1,045,184
Somerset Coal	I	131,001	140,112	22,044	Closed
Stourbridge	I	332,207	301,673	321,128	334,933
Stratford	R	143,740	95,439	48,818	34,323
Thames & Severn	I	58,600	51,407	34,542	16,904

Who and what goods used canals? This may be answered easily by looking at a series of letters published in 1901.[2] From Newport, Monmouthshire (Gwent) a coal merchant writes to the Manager of the Stroudwater Navigation: 'Some friends of ours will probably be sending some coal of the Channel ports to Swindon, via Gloucester, or Sharpness and the Canal. Can you quote us for transit by the Canal, and state if your charge includes wharfage, stowage, &c.?.' From a sawmills merchant at Stonehouse, Gloucestershire, regarding the almost moribund Thames & Severn:

'In reply to your letter respecting delays in traffic upon canals between our mills and Lechlade, London, &c., we have been very greatly inconvenienced by our not receiving timber from Lechlade, Swindon and Cirencester Wharves, owing to the state of the canal between Stroud and Cirencester. We have also had orders for several barge loads of stuff for Cirencester for months past, but cannot send owing to this cause. We may say that at other times the timber has laid on wharves for months, and we were unable to get it home.'

A cider and perry merchant, claimed the loss was not only to him, but to the quaffers of his nectars:

'We do business in Cirencester, and all towns up to London. We could send, if this Canal [the Thames & Severn] were

open, all our goods to those places by water. As it is we are
bound to send them by rail. We also get at least 500 and
sometimes 1,000 tons of cider per annum from London. It
would make a difference not only to us, but to our customers,
to whom we could sell cheaper. As an instance of this, the
rate from Stonehouse to Swindon, under 30 miles, is more
than what it has cost us to get cider from Boston to London.
Our agent in Swindon bought a barge and commenced to
fetch the goods from here to Swindon; he was able to do it at
two-fifths of the Railway charge, and did it successfully for a
time; but the last cargo of about 12 tons he got bunged up
in the summit and had to cart it into Swindon.'

A brickworks, too, was affected, having in the spring of 1892
received an order for a boatload of special bricks as a sample.
Being found satisfactory, they then had an order from the Wilts
& Berks Canal Company for 50,000 of the same type. These
were got ready, but due to the waterless state of the Thames &
Severn Canal could not be sent.

Workman, of the Steam Saw Mills, Woodchester, burned
his fingers:

'At the present time we have a quantity of timber on wharves
between Cirencester and Swindon which has been lying
there since last March, and we have repeatedly wanted it for
use; but, from the above-named cause [lack of water] we
have not been able to get it, and if we have to go to the
expense of hauling it home, we had better never have bought
the timber.'

Another canal company, too, were in a bit of bother for The
Wilts & Berks, aside from not getting their bricks, had a
quantity of round timber, of converted wood, and also rags in
bales, awaiting transport – some of the rags, indeed, had been
lying about for some six months.

Seemingly, canal carriage could still be competitive with
rail, albeit only in certain circumstances:

'I have suffered considerable inconvenience and loss, owing
to the waterway of the Thames & Severn Canal not being
navigable. I have frequently purchased timber near to this
Canal, relying on being able to have it home by water; but

I have eventually had to haul it some miles to a railway station, at an extra expense for hauling equal to the water carriage home. For instance, I have had timber lying on the wharf at Cirencester for twelve months, which I have had to haul home at a cost of double the water carriage. I have also had timber at Cricklade which I have had to haul to Purton Station, incurring a cost of 5¼d. per foot; whereas the water carriage home from Cricklade would have been 2¾d.'

The County Surveyor to the Gloucester County Council was not only concerned about materials, but the effect of the canal's closure upon employment within the county:

'There are some 70 miles of main road that require some 4000 tons of road-stone annually for their maintenance. This would all be taken up this Canal, but, owing to its neglected state, this stone is now sent by rail. During the past two years 2212 tons have been sent round via Oxford and Witney, to Fairford and Lechlade: all of this would have gone up this Canal. In addition to this, about 4192 tons have been sent to Cirencester by rail and hauled some six miles by traction engine, that should have gone to Kempsford – a distance of about three miles – the loss to the ratepayers being several hundred pounds. Early in the year I contracted with the Penmaenmaur Stone Company to deliver into boats at the Junction of the Stroud with the Gloucester and Berkeley Canal, 250 tons of road-stone to be delivered in September. The stone duly arrived, but it was impossible to get it to Kempsford, and it had to be taken on to Frampton and discharged on the wharf, and is still there, subject to charges for wharfage. The loss to the ratepayers on this cargo will not be less than £20. Basalt for road repairs can be obtained from the Executors of the late C. Parnell, Wicklow, from the Penmaenmaur Co. and the Cornish coast, at an average cost in the Gloucester and Berkeley canal of 9/5 per ton. Stone of a similar quality costs at Lechlade 13/3, at Fairford 13/3, and at Cirencester 11/10 per ton free on rail; and as stone of this quality can only be obtained from one locality by rail, it practically creates a monopoly, destroys competition, and raises the cost of these roads to the ratepayer. When the large bridges over the Thames at Lechlade and Kempsford were under repair, I had to haul material many miles by road and import stone from another county, whereas, if the Canal had been available, the material could have been delivered direct on the works, and stone quarried in Gloucestershire used, thus keeping the cash in the County. In 1891 I paved the town of Lechlade. 189 tons of material were sent by rail there. All this would have gone by the Canal at a much less cost.'

James Smart, a carrier on the Thames & Severn, had many offers of trade in 1893, including two boat loads of wheat from Bristol to Lechlade, another from Sharpness, 50 quarters of Barley from Faringdon to Lechlade, 100 sacks ex Lechlade, 35 quarters from Burford (Oxon), 120 quarters from Kempsford: all to Gloucester. He also received many requests for quotations, stone from Chalford to Swindon – in boatloads; rags from Swindon to Stroud, as well as timber. None of this could be carried – to the benefit of the GWR and a loss to the public. Paying more for bread, more on the rates, more for furniture and timber products, they were probably inclined to wish they, too, had a Manchester Ship Canal, which could compete with carriage by rail.

This waterway (formerly opened in 1894) had a long history most of which centered on the clashing economic interests of the citizens of Liverpool and the cotton-spinners of Manchester, who were charged stiff tolls, for their goods, in and out.

The eventual waterway resulted from a meeting called in 1882 by Daniel Adamson. The objectives in building the waterway were:

'Cheaper Carriage and Expanding Trade to break the tyranny of the Railroad "rings" which handicapped industry; and to bring about a new era of prosperity to the toiling millions of Lancashire & Yorkshire.'[3]

The late 1870s and early 1880s had produced for Manchester the beginnings of a slump: empty factories, empty houses, empty bellies. Trade was stultified by the policies of the burghers of Liverpool towards canal carriage and the effects of the opening of the London and North Western Railway. In the prospectus of the Liverpool and Manchester Railway, January 1825, it was declared:

'that we must not limit our consideration to the immediate accommodation of the mercantile classes . . . or even the still more important saving to the consumers of coals . . . we must contemplate the important affect upon the commerce of the nation created by such facilities . . . it becomes a question of serious importance whether this country . . . shall now pause in the career of improvement.'

This argument was reiterated by the projectors of the Manchester Ship Canal and still holds true today when we contemplate modernization schemes put forward. Within the reach of the projected canal was three-quarters of the British cotton trade and 'the greater portion of the Woollen, Glass, Chemicals, Pottery, Salt, Coal, Iron and Machinery Trades'. The chances of trade expanding without a new waterway were limited, for:

'. . . no effort is made towards cheapening transport, and that, as a result, and notwithstanding the heavy volume of trade upon our lines, we have the highest railway charges of any leading country, – without any of the compensating advantages from water carriage – is no more than we should expect from such an unqualified monopoly as we have given to our railway companies.'

The railways claimed to be caught in a cleft stick, the London and North Western Railway proving, on paper at least, that the rates left very little profit. For example between Liverpool and Manchester, after paying terminal and collecting charges, only 8.75p was left, for the $31\frac{1}{2}$ miles of carriage, out of the 45.83p paid for cotton. However, when the Ship Canal Act was passed the rate dropped to 40p! They also claimed in 1880 that manufactures were carried at a rate averaging 9p per ton when they actually cost the railway 11p. One doubts such philanthropy. Nevertheless a comparative statement shows the advantages of water transport:[4]

Commodity	Cost via Liverpool and cart to Manchester	Via Ship Canal to Manchester	Saving by Canal 1896	
			Actual	%
	(ALL FIGURES IN DECIMAL PENCE)			
Cotton	68.33	31.25	37.08	54.27
Apples	76.25	25.00	51.25	67.21
Iron Ore	34.58	5.00	29.58	85.54
Tea	93.33	36.25	57.08	61.16
Sugar in bags	60.83	23.75	37.08	60.96
Paper	75.00	26.25	48.75	65.00
Timber, Deals, Battens and Boards	44.58	15.00	29.58	66.35
Timber, Furniture Wood, Mahogany, &c.	61.67	20.00	41.67	67.57
Wool	81.67	31.25	50.42	61.74

Three specific examples may be quoted to show how the Manchester Ship Canal could affect not only the trade of Manchester but that of towns some miles away. Ashton-under-Lyne is 41 miles from Liverpool and 7 from Manchester. The total cost of carriage of cotton via Liverpool was 85p per ton; via Manchester this dropped to 55p. Todmorden is 49 miles from Liverpool and 20 from Manchester. Total cost per ton via Liverpool was £1.01; via the Manchester Ship Canal 70p. Oldham, then using about 160,000 tons of cotton a year and crowded with cotton mills and machinery works, is situated 6 miles from Manchester, but the rate dropped from 88p to 55p. Tonnage shifted rose rapidly from 925,659 tons in 1894 to 3,060,516 by 1900.

The goods imported, apart from the obvious cotton, included grain, timber, paper, pig-iron, oil (100,000 tons in 1900 by tanker); cement and green fruits, both at roughly 28,000 tons, while other foodstuffs totalled 115,000 tons in 1900 alone. To add to this we have nearly 100,000 head of live animals, and in terms of such bulk it is obvious that prices must have fallen in the markets to the benefit not only of cotton-mill owners but also their operatives.

The progress of the Manchester Ship Canal had been slow. The first bill was presented to Parliament on 15 January 1883, a second on 21 December 1883 and a third on 16 December 1884. Such was the opposition that it did not receive its royal assent until 6 August 1885, the whole legal struggle having cost about £672,000. The contract for the works was let to T. A. Walker on 8 June 1887, who was to die on 25 November 1889, after which the works were taken over by the company and labour employed direct. On 3 August 1887, the whole of the Duke of Bridgewater's canal and dock system was bought, for the sum of £1,710,000, as it was essential to utilize the Mersey & Irwell Navigation as part of the line of the Manchester Ship Canal. This purchase was not from the trustees of the Duke of Bridgewater but from a limited company controlled by Sir Edward Watkin of the Great Central Railway, and W. P. Price, Chairman of the Midland Railway Company, who had bought the canals from the Duke's trustees on 3 July 1872, for the sum of £1,120,000. During the building, the company had to purchase 4,600 acres of land at a cost of £1,287,205.

An army of nearly 17,000 navvies 'were grouped into communities at several points, and resided, many of them with their wives and families, in timber-built settlements, almost suggestive at a first glance of early times in a new country', together with a good number of machines they excavated over fifty-one million cubic yards of soil (roughly half the Suez Canal), used seventy million bricks, one-and-a-quarter million cubic yards of concrete, 120,000 tons of coal per annum and '173 locomotives working a rolling stock of 6,300 [7 ton] waggons', over a glorified 'spaghetti-junction' of 30 miles of railway.

These cold statistics give little idea of the struggles of the navvies and their engineer, Sir E. Leader-Williams. The main problem in utilizing the river bed was that the water had to be absorbed into the works where, to use Leader-Williams' own words 'great difficulty and expense arose from the necessity of keeping open a channel for the flood and ordinary waters of these rivers which were intersected in thirty places'. The spring tides upon the river were so powerful that in November 1890, 13 miles of the canal were prematurely filled, and in December 1891 another flood filled 10 miles of cutting.

'The damage caused to the slopes of the cuttings was great, and the plant was much damaged, while the delay of the work, and the cost of pumping out the water by additional pumps, was serious. The affect of the rush of flood-water down the cuttings was to set the trains of earth waggons in motion at high-speed, when, on reaching a block they piled up on each other in similar manner to the result of a collision on a railway.'

Problems arose with the railway bridges near Irlam, the Cheshire Line's viaduct suffered from settlement, causing cracks in the high arches, which were removed and replaced by girders. Brindley's original 'castle-in-the-air', the Barton aqueduct, was demolished and replaced by the present swing bridge-cum-aqueduct. Mainly because of these delays, the cost proved to be well over the estimate of £6,309,536, but certain improvements were made as work progressed, ultimately giving a figure as of 1 January 1898, of:

Construction of works	£10,258,696	3	2
Purchase of canals and navigations	1,785,334	6	5
Purchase of lands and compensation	1,233,006	14	9
Engineering and surveying	162,717	2	5
Interest on share and loan capital	1,170,733	13	4
Parliamentary expenses	175,922	1	7
General expenses	396,260	7	9
	£15,182,670	9	5

It can be claimed with justice that at least £10 million of this money ultimately benefited the ordinary person; the million or so in interest no doubt enriched the moneylenders.

The final word on the Manchester Ship Canal could well come from a speech given by C. W. MacAra, President of the Manchester Cotton Association, on 17 November 1900.

'. . . whatever else may be necessary for the maintenance of our position, the strictly economical charges for transit of raw material and merchandise by land and sea is one of vital importance. All enterprise that has for its aim the reduction of what I fear must be characterised as somewhat excessive railway rates and freights ought to be welcomed by the whole community, and no effort should be spared to defeat combinations formed for the purpose of maintaining these charges, which must of necessity seriously weaken our power of successful competition with our foreign rivals, who are not so handicapped. Indeed I consider a great responsibility with all who either through a short-sighted or selfish policy, interfere with the expansion of a great national industry.'

Despite these happenings in Manchester, carriers on other waterways just jogged along, often still maintaining a service the railways could, or would, not provide. Typical of these was Mr George Jobbins who operated a market boat on the Monmouthshire & Brecon Canals, trading with a partner, Henry Davies of Brecon, as Jones & Co. The business had run from 1794, Mr Jobbins purchasing it in March 1892. He operated one boat from Newport to Crumlin on Mondays and Thursdays, although in conjunction with Davies there was a through boat to Brecon on Mondays. The goods carried were truly 'market', as his loading sheets show:[5]

| | 19 October 1896 | | 21 October 1897 | 20 October 1898 | |
| | *Weight* | | *Weight* | *Weight* | |
Destination	*(cwt)*	*Including*	*(cwt)*	*Including*	*(cwt)*	*Including*
Risca	9¼	2 posts			2½	meal
		1 gate				seal oil
		12 4″				taper
		pipes				wick
		1 chimney-				
		pot				
		1 pair				
		shafts				
		1 barrel				
		petro-				
		leum				

Destination	19 October 1896 Weight (cwt)	Including	21 October 1897 Weight (cwt)	Including	20 October 1898 Weight (cwt)	Including
Cross Keys	67¼	meal 1 bag lime petroleum corn 'last minute'	54	21 boards match 1 door 1 bed 10 bags potatoes 3 sacks leather 6 barrels petrol	37½	petroleum composts maize potatoes
Pontywain	12¼	meal corn			59½	leather flour potatoes
Cwmcarne	51	meal	24¾	meal	42	potatoes swedes 3 firkins butter 10 boxes cheese petroleum
Warrens Bridge			3	20 boards 7 rafters		
Engine Bridge			5	slabs		
Abercarn			102¼	soda corn sulphur turps sugar peas 10 boxes cheese potatoes parsnips onions lime	126¾	meals butter bacon sugar apples 5 sacks bakers pride petroleum potatoes swedes

The tolls he received for this service were poor: on 20 October 1898, cash taken was £2.34½ with about another 75p on account. All items were manhandled on and off; many of the items were fragile, else they would not go by canal. Tonnages on the whole were poor, more redolent of fly-boats than latter-day carrying. In the first three months of 1901 he moved a total of 258 tons in 21 trips, there was little seasonal variation.

But the troubles of Jones & Co. had one root cause: the Great Western Railway who, as owners of the canal, considered the company to be a nuisance and did all they could to obstruct them. On 5 April 1892, concerning a proposed increase in tolls, Jones & Co. wrote to Courtney Boyle, the Secretary to the Railway Department of the Board of Trade:

'We beg most respectfully to ask you not to allow any increase in their maximum powers or the traffic on the canal will be entirely dropped, we might point out that the Great Western Railway Company own the railway from Newport to Crumlin and also the canal between the same places therefore goods sent by canal are charged by the Great Western Railway Company the full maximum tolls authorised, these tolls in many instances prevent traffic going by canal because it is cheaper by rail.'[5]

And a month later, regretting their inability to attend a meeting in London to object to the increases they asked that the Board of Trade should not overlook the fact that nearly all the traders on the Welsh valley canals generally owned and worked only one boat and could not therefore afford to go to any great expense, a plea unlikely to disturb the Board of Trade! Later the same year, weather took a hand in their struggle. On 31 December 1892, we find Jones & Co. having to write to the GWR Superintendant at Newport asking that he give instructions to have the canal cleared of ice, as their livelihood was being lost. What must have been the oddest reply in canal annals was sent on the 2 January 1893:

'The liability of clearing the ice from the canal rests with the traders. The Company only find ice-boats.'[5]

Recovering from the shock, on the 5th January, Jones wrote:

22 Washing hung out to dry on the Grand Union Canal below Cassio, in 1949. (*Courtesy of P Garrett*)

23 The gang involved in the New Works on the Grand Union Canal above Knowle Locks in 1934. (*Courtesy of P White*)

24 Looking west from Linlithgow, showing the stop-lock, on the Union Canal during the 1960s. *(Courtesy of D G Russell)*

25 View from Bryn Ceirch Bridge on the Welsh Section of the Shropshire Union Canal in 1967

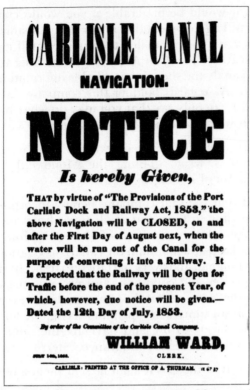

CARLISLE CANAL
NAVIGATION.

NOTICE
Is hereby Given,

THAT by virtue of "The Provisions of the Port Carlisle Dock and Railway Act, 1853," the above Navigation will be CLOSED, on and after the First Day of August next, when the water will be run out of the Canal for the purpose of converting it into a Railway. It is expected that the Railway will be Open for Traffic before the end of the present Year, of which, however, due notice will be given.— Dated the 12th Day of July, 1853.

By order of the Committee of the Carlisle Canal Company.

WILLIAM WARD,
JULY 12th, 1853.   CLERK.

CARLISLE: PRINTED AT THE OFFICE OF A. THURNAM.

Notice of the closure of Carlisle Canal (Courtesy of the Waterways Museum, Stoke Bruerne)

'. . . we are surprised that you should state the clearing of the canal rests with the traders, this appears really absurd, the traders might just as well be asked to supply the water. The advice we have received is that the canal company must keep the canal open and navigable at all times, Section 17, Rail Act 1873, and as this subject is a serious matter to us, we must hold your company responsible for the loss incurred by us during the stoppage.'[5] and also requested special rates for timber, corn, flour, oil and provisions, adding '. . . we understand it was the custom for canal rates to apply on the railway whilst the canal is frozen.'

Oh no, said the GWR, you are entirely wrong; rail rates must be paid and, dustily:

'I think it would be preferable if you would endeavour to state facts. I again repeat that under the companies canal act 1793 they are not compelled to keep the canal navigable in frosty weather. The Rail Act 1873 has nothing whatever to do with canals and shews what reliable information you have obtained. As regards holding this company liable for loss incurred I can only say that you may do what you like, but I think it will be a difficult matter to get any satisfaction.'[5]

Being tough, the canal carrier – whose clients were probably equally irate – wrote quoting the Monmouthshire Canal Company's Act of 13 August 1846

'. . . and that the said company hereby incorporated shall . . . from time to time and at all times from and after the completion of the purchase of the said Monmouthshire Canal, to keep and maintain the canals, navigations, and the works belonging, and every part thereto respectively, in good working order and condition, and preserve the supplies of water to the same, so that the same canals and every part . . . may be at all times kept open and navigable for use of the persons desirous to use and navigate the same, and that without any unnecessary hindrance, interruption or delay,'

and to rub salt in the GWR's tail he sent them a bill:

January 21.	To detention of our boat at Alteryn owing to canal blocked with ice from December 28th '92 to January 20th '93 inclusive. 21 days @ £1 per day	21	0	0
	January 17–19. 2 men and horse assisting to break ice. 3 days.	3	0	0
		£24	0	0

The railway company's reply was succinct:

'I am in receipt of your letter enclosing a claim for £24 against the Great Western Railway Company for detention of a boat during the late frosty weather, and in reply I have to repudiate on the part of the company any such claim.'

Jones & Co. then took the matter up with the Board of Trade, hoping they would act as arbitrators, explaining that not only did the GWR fail to clear the ice, but in the end they (the carrier) had had to send men and horses to break the ice for several days before the boat could run again on 23 January. They also pointed out that the Glamorganshire Canal had been free ten days earlier due to a steamer (probably the *Bute*) being used to break the ice. Courtney Boyle of the Board of Trade wrote in reply to the effect that the Board of Trade had no authority to express any opinion on the matter, ending with unconscious humour 'I am, Gentlemen, Your obedient servant'!

In 1895 another wrangle started when Jones & Co. paid their January account from the railway but 'under protest'. Wharfage had been charged although the traffic had always been carted direct from the boat, little being landed on the canal side as it was both inconvenient and there was the risk of goods being lost or damaged. In any event the customers preferred taking the goods overside as the boatman always assisted in loading the road waggons. The wrong rates per item – in this case bricks – were being claimed and furthermore both the minimum, as well as the actual tolls, had been itemized. The GWR accountant was, however, a decent chap and wrote back that they would '. . . correct our account and have to express my regret that the errors arose', leaving only one problem to be resolved: that Jones & Co. were being charged a minimum 12½p for an empty boat returning, plus tolls on empty barrels, whereas they felt that they should pay either one or the other. The accountant wrote back that '. . . for the present we will allow this to stand over until a new manager is appointed for the canal when we will go into the question more fully with you.' Nine months later Jones & Co. tried the Board of Trade again:

'. . . there is very little excepting returned empties to come back, and these are only handed to us in small lots, at the present time the Great Western Co. are charging us the minimum tolls of 2/6, if we only have 10 cwt of returned empties, the tolls on the same weight when full on the up journey would be 5d., because we should have other traffic in the boat, we think we should therefore be only charged 5d. for the empties back but the Great Western Co. say they are entitled to 2/6d and we must pay it.'⁵

And they replied? As ever:

'I am to state that the Board of Trade have no authority to advise you or to express an opinion,' remaining, however, 'Your obedient servant.'

However, Jones & Co. did win one battle in September 1896, when their boat was sunk due to a hole 'measuring 15″ × 5½″, 3 planks broken, left from bow, starboard side in bottom' being knocked into her after striking tree roots projecting into the canal near Cross Keys, but they were able to muster good evidence – that of a ships' carpenter, W. Whitford, who stated only a year before new bottoms had been put in, '. . . which with ordinary wear and tear should last for 4 or 5 years', and a petition signed (or marked X) from the owners and boatmen of the partnership stating they had often complained about the condition of the canal. Indestrictible goods were salved, but 28 stones of meal, 12 sacks of corn, 7 of bran, 32 of flour, 5 of oats and 1 bag of cement were all refused by the consignees. While Jones were peeved about the damage, they were exceedingly angry over hindrance to their efforts to save the cargo.

'We have also to complain of the way in which your lockmen acted after the boat was sunk, immediately our boatmen found that the boat was sinking they asked the lockmen to let out the water, but they declined to do so until they had instructions from Mr. Butler [Superintendant] if they had let the water out a considerable part of the cargo would have been saved.'⁵

Initially, the rail replied that the matter would be referred 'higher up' but that Jones & Co., could hire a railway boat at 10p a day while their own was being repaired. On 28 September acceptance was held in abeyance for their sheets [cloths for covering boat] were still in use covering the damaged bags lying about on the wharf! However, they did win and the GWR eventually paid up.

Early in 1897 the carrier again wrote complaining, in this case that the boat was held up for lack of water; in November that the towpath at Newport was obstructed by trucks and the horses had to be 'unharnessed' before they could pass, and on 22 February 1902, to the Board of Trade complaining that the canal had been closed since the 7th, and please would they do something about it. This stoppage was caused by a breach in the bank following subsidence due to mining, although immediately prior to this the canal had been closed for twelve days due to ice:

> 'This long stoppage is enough to ruin any trade and we really think you should send one of your representatives to inspect the canal when the water is out and to also see if it is reasonable to keep the water out so long, as we are certain that if repairs had to be done on the railway instead of the canal at the Great Western Railway Company (who are the owners of the canal) there would have been very little stoppage . . .'[5]

The Board of Trade did not bother to reply until 11 March, when they informed Jones & Co. that according to their information the canal had been re-opened 'on the 7th instant'.

What a pickle canal carriers like this were in, for as Jones & Co. said: 'It is impossible for small traders like ourselves to go to the law with a large company like the Great Western Co.' and the only supposedly neutral body, the Board of Trade, stayed on the side of the big battalions. There was no Plaid Cymru to help the Welsh then, but it is a tribute to the doggedness of Mr Jobbins that he stayed in business until 9 January 1915, the 'last week for the Market boat to run on the Monmouthshire Canal after 120 years service. Men joined up and served, sent to France during the great War.'[6] It is still a puzzle how, paying his men (three) £1.10p each and with receipts of only £5 to £6, Mr Jobbins even fed his horse, let alone lived himself. Now he, his boat and (almost) his canal have gone.

Whereas Jones & Co. expired during the First World War, the Shropshire Union Railways & Canal Company survived. In 1903 they had appointed 'a Lady inspector who would be able to visit the Cabins and exert a beneficent influence, especially in seeing that the children attend school',[7] for which service she was paid £1 per week. By 1905 they had almost eliminated bye-traders – carrying the half-a-million or so tons of traffic in their own boats – but in turn they ceased trading on 31 August 1921. Operating mainly from Ellesmere Port to Birmingham (35 hours) and to the Potteries (24 hours), flints, china-stone, clay, earthenware and grain were carried in a form of fly-boat, one operating 24 hours of the day, but carrying 18 to 20 tons, nearly double the pre-1850 load. Traffic in the 1880s was on the ascendant, boats in service increased from 363 in 1884 (189 family, 174 all-male crews) to 450 in 1902, (151 family, 2 all-women, 297 all-male), and by 1920 there were no less than 592, of which 202 were family boats. The hardships endured by these people when they were declared redundant may be imagined, as compensation was only paid to those with 10 years' service or more.

To the east, the carriers Fellows, Morton & Clayton had commenced running steamers on the Grand Junction Canal. Using coke-fuel they could run between Birmingham and London in 52 hours, although transhipping often took place at Braunston, with a great reserve of steam (a full head would last from Itchington Bottom Lock to Braunston, 8½ miles*) and a crew of four it was no problem for them to work round the clock. In this way Fellows, Morton & Clayton could offer their version of a fly-boat service and advertised that their boats ran to a timetable, loaded or otherwise.

Various nicknames have been applied to certain services and/or the boats operating them. Those from London to Braunston were the 'Braunston Rubbing Rags'; the through-boats (many of which carried soap) earned the sobriquet 'Greasy Wheelers'; while 'Mud Heelers' went from London to Coventry – no doubt because of the canals' condition; and London/Leicester men were 'Woolly Backed 'Uns'.

In 1906 a Royal Commission on Canals and Waterways was appointed, and after some five years' deliberation they summarized the position: Canals with a capacity of 30 tons formed only 35 per cent of the total mileage, 40 to 60 tons 58 per cent, and over 60 tons only 7 per cent. While there were 4,053 miles of inland waterway, only 1,184 were railway owned. But of a

---

* A propos of this, captains of the Bolinder semi-diesel engined boats used to claim they did this length with one beat of the diesel!

main line mileage of 2,415, 1,045 miles were railway owned.
For 1905 the profit-and-loss statistics were cold.[8]

Waterways	Tons conveyed (per mile of waterway)	Receipts from tolls (per mile)	Total receipts (per mile)	Expenditure (per mile)	Net revenue (per mile)*
	£	£	£	£	£
Independant	14,300	345	566	403	163
Railway owned	12,100	291	361	281	80
All waterways	13,300	322	477	350	127

* The net revenue includes profits from carrying business earned by the
Aire and Calder – £41,586, and the Leeds & Liverpool – £32,693.

The main canal companies that acted as carriers were the Aire
& Calder, Leeds & Liverpool, Rochdale, Trent, Shropshire
Union, and Manchester Ship Canal; this latter company
operating on the Bridgewater Canals. Traffics on all waterways
were classed as heavy; on 14 waterways, carrying an aggregate
of 21½ million tons, coal formed 45 per cent. Of the 32 million
tons (yes, 32 million tons were carried in 1905) two-thirds were
carried on the following waterways:[8]

Waterway	Mileage	Tonnage conveyed	Average miles travelled by 1 ton	Net revenue £
Birmingham Canal	159	7,546,000	—	91,607
Aire & Calder Nav.	85	2,810,000	21.2	111,511
Leeds & Liverpool	145	2,467,000	19.6	37,629
Grand Junction	189	1,794,000	23.2	51,328
Thames River (above London Bridge to Inglesham)	144	1,395,000	16.7	6,588 (loss)
Trent & Mersey	119	1,137,000	—	15,883
Regents Canal	11	1,045,000	—	52,991
Weaver Navigation	20	1,076,000	13.5	2,247
Sheffield & South Yorkshire Nav.	60	835,000	—	24,005

A supplanter of the horse: a Bolinder engine

On the Birmingham Canal Navigations 6 million out of the $7\frac{1}{2}$ million tons were loaded and discharged on the canal system itself, while on the Aire & Calder:

'This undertaking pays a dividend of $3\frac{1}{4}\%$ to its ordinary shareholders, and its success is largely due to the special advantages it possesses combined with enterprising management. It is in proximity to important coalfields: it has few locks: ample water supply: and moreover a special method of haulage has been adopted upon it. This consists in towing square steel boxes, each capable of holding 40 tons, in trains. A train may consist of 30 such compartments in line, carrying in all some 1,200 tons. Such a train is hauled by a steam tug to Goole, where the boxes are tipped into sea-going vessels. The result is a very low cost of haulage with which it is difficult for a railway to compete.'[8]

On the Grand Junction a total of 1,800,000 tons were moved, 55 per cent of this no further than 12 miles from Paddington, and 'only' 43,000 tons went between London and Birmingham.

'The Commission were of the opinion that experience both in this and in other countries shows that the chief use of water transport to the public is in the conveyance in considerable quantities of goods the weight of which is large in proportion to the value, such as coal, minerals, building and road-making material, timber, and food stuffs, when unloaded in bulk from sea-going ships.'[8]

But,

'A vicious circle has been established. Because the authorities owning waterways are weak, divided and disorganized, they cannot raise funds necessary for improvement, and because they cannot improve them they continue to be weak and to inspire no confidence in the investing public.'

The Commission suggested a central 'Waterway Board' be set up and that (*de facto*) the waterways would be nationalized, with Government loans to modernize the following routes:

Route A   Birmingham and Leicester to London (to the Thames and to Paddington).

Route B   Leicester, Burton and Nottingham to the Humber Estuary.

Route C   Wolverhampton and Birmingham to the Mersey via Stoke-on-Trent.

Route D   Wolverhampton and Birmingham to the Severn Estuary.

Two standards would be offered '100 ton' and '300 ton'. The total costs were estimated at:

Route	Mileage	Total cost
A. Birmingham and Leicester to London with branches '100 ton' standard	348.18	£6,679,031
B. Leicester, Burton and Nottingham to the Humber with branches, '300 ton' standard with 750-ton vessels to Nottingham	'77.10	£4,075,014
C. Wolverhampton and Birmingham to the Mersey with branches, '100 ton' standard with 400-ton vessels on Weaver	156,72	£3,449,513
D. Wolverhampton and Birmingham to the Severn with branches, '100 ton' standard with 600-ton vessels to Stourport, 750-ton vessels to Worcester & 1,200-ton vessels to Gloucester	121.91	£2,549,121
Birmingham Canals	144.86	£764,527
Grand Total	1,048.77	£17,517,206

Unlike the 1947 nationalization scheme the Commission recommended that the proposed Waterway Board should not become carriers of traffic on any waterways, the routes remaining open to any carrier whether a public company, a private trader, a bye-trader, or a railway company. Nothing happened and canals trundled on their way into the chaos of war.

In 1917 the Board of Trade took most canals under their wing, listing the operating carriers in an official publication[9]. The Aire & Calder was shown as having 72, the Rochdale 22, the Birmingham Canal Navigations 44, the Staffs & Worcs 19, the Grand Junction 24 including 9 who only operated barges from the Thames. Near the bottom of the league came the railway owned canals: the Kennet & Avon with 4 carriers, the Stratford 2, the Cromford 3, the Union (Scotland) nil, the Lydney nil, the Glamorganshire 1 and the Shropshire Union 2. The Brecon and Monmouthshire canals, following the extinction of Jones & Co., solely listed the Great Western Railway!

In 1920 came the usual decennial silly suggestions: close the canals and turn them into roads. Once, in 1906, they did this when eliminating the Aberdare, but the arguments against still hold good today. For example where there is a steep flight of locks (21 Hatton, 29 Devizes, 30 Tardebigge) is the rubble used to infill them and the necessary widening of the track economically justified? '. . . or have they any idea of the number of bridges that would have to be taken down and reconstructed? Have they propounded a scheme for dealing with tunnels of 2,000 yards length, and considered the cost? I think not . . .'[10] One writer indeed wondered 'whether it would not be an easier accomplishment to convert 1,000 miles of roads into canals?' As before writers stressed the obvious: '. . . the thing to do with our canals is to use them for the purpose for which they were constructed, namely, to transport goods by water along their length.' Another gentleman not only derided the whole scheme, but raised a query that is topical today: 'Fantastic schemes for their conversion into motor roads are not worthy of consideration, for, apart altogether from the farcical character of such attempts at solving the canal problem, the cost of even an experiment in that direction would be a useful contribution towards the cost of an initial step in the matter of canal improvement, viz. the dredging of our waterways.'[10] How right. For one mile of motorway we could have a clear track now on ten miles of new waterways.

During the 1920s and 1930s overall traffic figures declined; as did the tolls received and the number of boats employed. On the Birmingham Canal Navigations alone, receipts dropped from £272,858 in 1920, to £132,020 in 1930, and £115,359 in 1935.[11] But on 30 October 1935, the Duke of York, on board the wide boat *Progress*, re-opened Hatton locks following their rebuilding under a Government improvement grant – a measure undertaken to relieve unemployment pending the commencement of the Second World War. In 1929 the Grand

Junction, Warwick & Napton and Warwick & Birmingham canals, together with a connecting length of the Oxford Canal became known as the Grand Union Canal, the holding company having previously absorbed the lines to Leicester.

The modernization scheme was unfortunately never finished, for although the locks were widened to take 60-ton barges, the cross-section of the canal was unaltered, as were the bridges, although many improvements (sadly neglected since) were made to the waterway walls. As wide boats proved, after some trial runs, to be impractical many new narrow boats were built, until the operators, the Grand Union Canal Carrying Company, had no less than 186 pair. Together with the Fellows, Morton & Clayton fleet and various bye-traders this meant that about 600 boats were in operation between London and Birmingham. Sadly, the efforts of the GUCC had not by the outbreak of war received the reward they deserved, as the chairman tells us in his annual report for 1939. He prefaces his report with the sober statement that:

'I regret that Mr. Whittington is unable to be present with us today as he has joined the Army. I am sure the stockholders will desire to join the board in wishing him good luck, a safe return, and a successful military career' and continued 'You will, I am sure, support the view held by your board that considering the time through which we are passing the results may be considered as satisfactory. But I have no hesitation in saying that if war had not broken out the accounts would have presented an even better appearance, and the board would have probably recommended some payment being made to the Preference stockholders. As it is we still find it impossible to pay a dividend . . . The tonnage results show a decrease of £4,757 but this has been caused entirely by war conditions under which we are now operating, for up to the first week of hostilities there was an increase of £13,000 in comparison with the same period last year. The extent to which this company and its subsidiaries have been hit may be best understood when I tell you that up to the outbreak of war tonnage passing over the canal amounted to 1,207,344 tons, as against 1,159,568 tons for the same period last year, an increase of 47,776 tons.' The

causes of the company's troubles (aside from the outbreak
of war) were dealt with '. . . the company has been faced
with heavy expenditure in connection with I.R.A. outrages
earlier in the year, and our troubles have been further
accentuated by a serious burst in the canal banks at Weedon
on October 18 . . . This cost us £1,180 in repairs. But
unfortunately it necessitated closing this part of the canal for
10 days, and in consequence some thousands of tons of
traffic were lost. It is to be hoped that both these items may
be considered as non-recurring expenditure . . . Once again
throughout the year the company has suffered from the lack
of skilled boatmen, which seriously handicapped its operations, and in consequence many thousands of tons of goods
were lost. Although the actual traffic booked by the company
amounted to 211,959 tons, an increase of 16,178 tons over
last year, it was only able to carry 166,044 tons in its own
boats, the balance of 45,915 tons being given to other carriers
operating on our canal.' His closing notes showed incredible
prescience: 'What the future has in store for us no one would
attempt to forecast, and I am certainly not going to endeavour to do so. I can, however, say that the management
has a most difficult time ahead. I am convinced that we shall
need stout hearts and courage to meet the future.' How right
he was.'

Salvation Army

8 *Those Magnificent Men*

Bargemasters and boatmen, although unalike in some respects, mainly due to social conditions, nevertheless owe their living to one thing alone: the ability to navigate a boat, whether a 350-ton, 'West Country', or 'Odd'n' barge, 'Joey', 'Narrow' or 'Worser' boat, flat, wherry or tug, along navigable waterways, and accepting this I have not attempted to differentiate between them except in so far as history demands. One of the earliest comments on Thames bargemasters occurs in October 1586 when, in answer to complaints about the condition of the river, the writer gives reasons why the *status quo* should be maintained. Apart from mills being necessary:

> 'The causes of the increased peril of the passage was that the Barges were become of greater burthen: almost double what they used to be; that they laded them beyond reason: that they used partly to unload below the lock and reship again above, even when they used to bring but seven or eight Loads.'[1] and what was more they '... employed people of no skill.'

How little we change, when one of the grumbles against boatmen in the dying days of commercial carrying on narrow canals in the early 1960s was: 'They'm ain't boatmen, thems amachers'. In both cases exterior causes lay at the root of the claim. In the seventeenth century:

'The Locks and Turn-pikes made upon the River Isis, when it was made navigable from Oxford to Bercot to keep up the water and give the vessels an easie descent. For the first whereof, a [flash lock] will suffice, which is made up only of bars of wood called Rimers, which must be all pulled up at [the barge's] arrival before the boat may pass either down or upwards; which with the stream, is not without precipitation; & against it, at many places, not without the help of a Capstan at Land; & sometimes neither of them without imminent Danger.'[2]

a mode of operation that led to many deaths and many maimed bargemasters. This, coupled with delays, '. . . in dry times, barges do sometimes lie aground three weeks, or a month, or more . . .',[2] led to men seeking other occupations while in the mid-twentieth century the lack of water and the poor conditions of locks which resulted in low wage packets caused men to 'go on the bank', for they were paid on the tonnage shifted.

A group of men closely connected with river bargemasters were the men who bow-hauled the barges prior to the building of a horse-towing path. The number of men required could, when a river navigation was in flood or, alternatively, the barge was slurping from one mudbank to another, be in excess of forty:

'The traffic on the upper Thames was in the last century principally conducted by large barges carrying as much as 200 tons each and held against the stream by 12 or 14 horses and 50 or 80 men. These men were usually of the worst possible character and a terror to the whole neighbourhood of the river.'[3]

The figures quoted to a parliamentary committee in 1793[1] for the number of horses required to pull a 70 ton barge upstream on the Thames could be multiplied by a factor of five where man-haulage was used.

From Stadbury to Windsor	10 or 12 horses
Windsor to Amerden Bank	8
To Boulter's	10 or 12
Boulter's to Poulter's Horsing	6
To Hedsor, Spade Oak or Marlow	8
To Henley	5 or 6
Thence to Kennet's Mouth	8
To Geddington (Gatehampton)	10
To Chamberhole (Wallingford)	6
To Benson	7 or 8
To above Abingdon	10 or 11, sometimes 12
From thence we take our own horses	5
Oxford to Lechlade	3 boats to take up 70 tons, 3 horses to each Boat.

On the Severn conditions were identical; with the hauliers wading thigh deep through the water in winter, 'breaking down fences', robbing orchards, stealing chickens, leaving 'women with childer', to be kept by the Parish, and generally committing all kinds of mayhem. 'With regard to the mode of hauling barges, an obvious improvement would be the opening of a good towing path along the river, and the substitution of horses for men in the slavish labour.'⁴ It is not unreasonable to say that due to the hard, unsavoury and irregular nature of the work, no doubt, boredom – as well as hunger – led them to get up to more mischief than they might otherwise have done. In 1607 a Mr Bush developed a 'fearsome machine' which could, it seems, travel both by water and land. This met with much opposition

'. . . having but two men with him, attendants in his company, who were both grievously wounded and hurt in their heads and other places by these riotous persons. For all this, these rude fellows were not satisfied, neither for the abuse offered to himself nor the hurts done to his men, but they manifested their further cankered stomachs and malice, after the hurt men retired into their lodgings for safeguard of their lives, and went into the pinnace where they had left her and with great stones, hooked staves, and other weapons maliciously rent and spoiled her, and beat great holes through her, not forbearing to continue this violence and

26 Henpole Lane Bridge over the Tipton Green and Toll End
Communication Canal, 1972

27 The Stroudwater Canal at Upper Framilode, derelict in 1967,
is now being re-opened.

28 Runcorn Locks on the Locks Branch of the Bridgewater Canal, 1968. Closed in 1966, the Locks are now obliterated.

29 Blackfriars Bridge over Irwell Navigation in Manchester, about 1830. *(Courtesy of the Waterways Research Centre)*

outrage until they thought they had sufficiently torn her for travelling any more, either by land or water . . .'[5]

Some likelihood of change could be foreseen in 1813:

'When the craft proceed upwards against the stream, and have not the advantage of a leading wind, it has been the custom to track them by manual labour, to the number of ten or twelve men, dragging a single barge. Of late years, indeed, horses have been introduced, sometimes solely, at others one, or perhaps two, harnessed to the track rope along with a half a dozen bipeds; this extraordinary melange, however, may soon go out of fashion, as there was a bill before the House last session (1811) for the improvement of the "Severn Horse Towing-Path".'[6]

The first stage of this towpath was completed in August 1812 when there was 'A fête on the occasion of the opening of the Severn Horse Towing Path from Worcester bridge to the Lower Parting'[7] but this was quickly outdated – after centuries of man-haulage – when the butterfly of the future emerged from its chrysalis: '1814 – August 17 – The first steam boat made its appearance below Gloucester, intended for the conveyance of passengers and light goods between Gloucester and Worcester. It made the return voyage to Gloucester in four hours and a half.'[7]

All 'Turnpike Sailors' – that derisory name first applied to wherrymen in East Anglia – whether working boats singly or with the assistance of a boy or in a gang, were males. Women on board were almost unknown and indeed a woman's presence on board was considered unlucky by those who worked 'up the tideway'. My own belief, at least where my own East Anglian men were concerned, is that this only applied if they were married and the wife caught them dallying. There was one class of boatmen, those who operated the little flats carrying 4 or 5 tons of peat, manure, lime and potatoes around the Fens of Lincolnshire, Suffolk, Somerset, the Thames marshes and some parts of Wales, who always had a bad reputation. Camden castigates them thus: 'The inhabitants of this and the rest of the fenny country . . . are a sort of people (much like the place) of brutish, uncivilised tempers, envious of all others, whom they

*Women on board were almost unknown! Vane on the masthead of a wherry
(Courtesy of the Waterways Research Centre)*

call upland men . . .,' but in reality this 'brutishness' was
native taciturnity. Today, when many ex-boatmen work on
maintenance, or as lock-keepers, they are the first to help
anyone in distress but they watch the pitiful struggles of some
'Noddy' boaters who have neither muscle nor wit to use a lock
properly, with a total lack of interest.

On 'narrow' canals, a further group of men necessary to the
canal boatman to help move his boats about, were a contribu-
tory factor in gaining him an ill-name. The Grand Junction
Canal Committee in 1825 recorded a complaint: '. . . of a
nuisance arising from the notoriously bad characters of the
persons who frequent the neighbourhood of the Tunnels upon
the plea of assisting Boats through them',[8] but that wasn't really
surprising when the conditions under which these 'leggers'
laboured are considered.

> 'The Huddersfield Tunnel [Standedge, 5415 yards] is a most
> extraordinary work . . . cut through the middle of a solid
> mountain – the face of the country altogether would seem to

bid defiance to such a work of art. The cost is said to have been £300,000, which brings the expense to £11.5.3½d. per inch; but, notwithstanding the line is regularly worked, the undertaking has failed to reimburse the original proprietors. As the dimensions are too small to admit of two boats passing each other during their passage through, strict regulations are enforced as to the times when they are permitted to enter at either end. Accordingly they adopt intervals of four hours, continually, during day and night; when the towing horses are sent over the hill in [the] charge of a man, who receives sixpence for conducting each horse. The span of the circular aperture is about ten feet; the height not sufficient to allow a man to stand upright in the boat, – those used in this navigation being of a narrow, compact build, suited to the service, and capable of carrying from twelve to twenty tons. The operation of working the boats through is a singular one; and performed by a description of labourers adventitiously hired for the purpose. As there is generally work to be had, a sufficient number of these continually present themselves, who having remained a few days or a week, or as long as it suits them, receive their payment, pursue their march, and choose another occupation . . . It is a hard service, performed in total darkness, and not altogether void of danger, as the roof is composed of loose material, in some parts, continually breaking in. Two hours is the time occupied in legging a boat through, and a legger earns a shilling for a light boat; after twelve tons he receives one shilling and sixpence; and so on.'9

There are a number of other methods of moving a boat, whether in a tunnel or not, including quanting which was extensively practised by keelmen working their craft along the Humber and its contiguous canals. It was and is illegal. These keelmen had their own name, at least until the end of the nineteenth century: Keelbullies, 'though the name bullies is probably derived from an obsolete adjective boolie, i.e. beloved; and is therefore in a good sense rather than bad'.10 There method of working has been described very clearly by a contemporary writer:

'One man on each side of the vessel going towards the prow,

puts down his pole to the bottom, in a position inclined towards the head of the keel, at the same time thrusting against it forcibly with his shoulder, and walking down on the gangway towards the stern as the keel moves under him; by this method the keel gains a tolerably quick and even course on the water. Having walked the whole length of the vessel, they pluck up the great oars, which they call puys, return hastily to the prow, put down the puys again, and thrust as before.'[10]

On some waterways leggers were unnecessary as spikes, chains or rails were attached to sides or roof of the tunnels and the boats were dragged through. The first method was to be found on the Duke of Bridgewater's colliery canals,[11] chains inside Crimson Hill Tunnel (1,707 yards/1,561 metres) on the Chard Canal and rails are still (1975) in situ along the walls of Dunhamstead Tunnel (230 yards/210 metres) on the Worcester & Birmingham Canal.

In normal conditions narrow boats carried two pairs of planks or 'wings', one short and one long as tunnel widths varied. On arrival at a particular tunnel, for example Maida Hill on the Regents Canal, the procedure was for the captain to hire one – or if he could not face the exertion – two men (although he would have to pay for the second out of his own pocket[12]) who would tie the 'wings' to the boat, lie down on an old coat, and by pushing their hobnails against the wall of the tunnel lever themselves and the boat through. A dark, dank and singularly unpleasant way of earning (1920) 5p! In the meantime the captain, or a boy, would lead the horse over the hill.

When man-hauling of boats ceased on the Severn, the Sharpness New Docks Company were obliged to keep 50 pairs of donkeys for use on the river and its connecting canals. It was the custom to keep donkeys always in pairs as, oddly, they grew quite pally. This usage proved satisfactory and always seems wrong because donkeys are normally considered shy of water. A maintenance man[13] relates how:

'On this particular day my father steered the boat through the two tunnels while I took two donkeys over the tunnels. All went well until I got on the top of Shortwood tunnel, there are two clap gates that close the fields from the towing path, I got through one gate with the donkeys alright, but on getting to the second gate I had to go past alongside the donkeys to open the gate, this was when the trouble started. Those donkeys started off at the gallop towards Stoney Hill with me after them, I never got hold of them, still and docile, until they had been as far as Cattespoole House and again up the hill and running as far as the top of Scarfields Hill, Alvechurch. When I finally got to the other end of Shortwood with the donkeys my father was still waiting with the boat, after two hours! Of course I had to do some explaining and tempers were not at the best! . . . We had missed the tow through the Kings Norton [Wast Hill] tunnel so we stopped at Bittell that afternoon. I took the donkeys over the bridge above and stabled them in a shed for the night . . . I had some trouble next morning, the towpath was very narrow in the Bittell cutting and these donkeys, not being used to working together, the one would not get too near the canal water, consequently the other donkey was pushed up the bank, this caused him to lie on the other donkey's back, his legs working in a walking motion on the bank! This did

A typical fenman (Courtesy of the Waterways Research Centre)

not last long before they were stupid and began kicking. I tried working them in single file on this narrow path, but the first donkey kept looking round to see if his mate was coming along. I was glad when we had got out of that cutting. However, we had got to get the tow at the tunnel so I, getting fed up with being so long, thought I would have to get them to travel a bit faster, so I lifted one of the donkey's tails and put a strong stinging nettle under, this did the trick, that donkey slapped his tail down on that nettle and started to move into a fast pace, making the other donkey travel fast with it. We caught the tug alright, however the donkey had his own back on me, when I was taking the harness off them at the Birmingham stables . . . he kicked me well on the backside and I might tell you that was painful for a day or two.'

This minor cruelty would have been abhorred by the 'missionaries' who, to do them justice, did their utmost in encouraging boatmen to treat their animals in a decent manner. While, generally, long distance boatmen regarded their horses – which they often had to buy – as an investment to care for, Birmingham day boatmen lacked such feelings. The Incorporated Seamans and Boatmans Friendly Society finding this to be the case erected a horse shelter at the top of the 'Eight Locks' in Walsall where both man and beast often suffered long delays in 'rain, snow and cold and piercing winds'. Thereafter it was presumed that the horse would be left in the stables while the boatman hied himself off to the Boatman's Rest where he could enjoy a cup of hot cocoa. Later, with some assistance from the Ingram Trust another, similar, shelter was built near the interchange sidings at Riders Green.[14]

George Bate's little speeding up method pales against some stories of the cruelty that went on at times. A discerning man wrote in 1781:

'The boats are nearly alike, constructed to fit the locks, carry about 25 tons, and are each drawn by something like the skeleton of a horse covered with skin; whether he subsists upon the scent of the water, is a doubt; but whether his life is a scene of affliction is not; for the unfeeling driver has no employment but to whip him from one end of the canal to the other . . . We can scarcely view a boat travelling this liquid road without raising opposite sensations – pleased to think of its great benefit to the community and grieved to behold wanton punishment.'[15]

A bored boatman might be found too: 'Now and again he makes a flick at a fly on the horse's "near" ear, thereby hurting his charge considerably more than the insect.'[14]

An occurrence far from a minor cruelty occurred in 1931 when a boatman, Albert, going along quietly, crossed with a day-boat bound for the collieries. The normal whip was a length of braided rawhide, anything from 12–30 feet long with, rarely, a lead tip inserted, but the day-boatman was thrashing his horse with a length of barbed wire. Albert and his mate took the wire from the man, booted him a bit and then used the wire on him. They patched the horse up and left him at the stables, not coming by again until some months later when they found the hostler waiting as the horse had not been collected. "Well," says Albert, "I give he £5 and took 'un for me bruvver".'

Some horses – and their boatmen – had odd quirks. One horse, named Nigger, who used to work on the 'gas-oil' run was normally peaceful, but if anyone walked in front of him and stuck their tongue out 'he 'ould go up on 'is 'ind legs and he'd go at you like, he'd box like 'ell'. Possibly an ex-circus animal, his performance was good enough for the ring.

Not all horses were maltreated however, and well looked after boat horses are reputed to have been long-lived, a few even achieved fame. One horse, the property of the Thames Navigation Company, was reputed to have reached the tremendous age of 52.[16] Another, belonging to the Mersey & Irwell Navigation, 'Old Billy': 'for so he was named, worked all his life on the towing-path of one of the canals adjoining the city, and died on the 27th of November, 1822, at an age, testified beyond all manner of doubt, to have been sixty-two years. Before his demise he attained the honour of forming, decorated with ribands, part of a procession assembled at Manchester to celebrate the coronation of his Majesty King George the Fourth.'[9] If of a macabre nature, you may like to know that the skull of this latter is exhibited in a Manchester museum.

It has been claimed with justice that life is in some respects easier for a motor-boatman than it ever was in horsedrawn days. The horse boatman had his stages where 'bedding and food for man and horse' might be found. If the hostler was good all that had to be done, whatever the time of night, was to take the horse to the stables after removing the harness, clean round the boats, tighten everything up, have dinner and off for a 'jar' (pint or quart) and a game of dominoes. If the hostler was missing, the horses food had to be made up.

'You mixed it with shovels, the recipe was 1½ of chaff, 3 bushels of oats, a stone and a half of bran, plus beans. All put on a clean floor, all tipped out together and you mixed it with a shovel and put it in your own corn bags, you took it to the boat and stacked it in the corn deck. You would fetch a bag out in the morning and put it in a horse-bag, nose-tins we called them for they were tins painted with roses.[17] Among the more intelligent 'cabin' boatmen 'The horse came first – he had to get their living. If they were short of money they would go short of food themselves to buy it for the horse. They were never cruel to their horses, and the horses got wise to the whip – they knew you was on the boat not the path.'[17]

Until the time of severe railway competition every boatman had his home 'on the bank', probably a canalside cottage, which he could go to for, say, two nights a week. If the size of the families was anything to go by, their enforced separation for the other five hardly mattered! Unfortunately, when rates were cut the boatman first took his sons with him and then, logically, his wife. Curiously, this move only seems to have occurred to any extent on the so-called narrow canals, where the type of craft in use – the narrow or 'monkey' boats – had the least suitable cabins.

Thomas Monk, born in 1765, was the son of a barge-builder and we have it on good authority[18] that he was 'the inventor and first builder of the small canal cabin-boat'. He was, seemingly, a 'dynamic man and albeit a hard business man, brooking neither strike nor insolence. Finding wages rising he counteracted this, at least on the Thames and contiguous wide canals, by joining two boats together, thus reducing his crews! Very soon the descriptive nickname of 'monkey boats' (whether derived from the antics of his crews passing over the boats or his own name is uncertain) entered common usage and may still be found today. His habit of sending two butties together down the Thames also gave rise to another name – 'Worser' boats; an elderly lock-keeper once told me this was derived from the fact that the conditions on board were 'worser nor the others'.

While statistics of a cabin's size do not really conjure up any particular picture – 250 cubic feet does not sound unreasonable – we can instead quote the view held by contemporary writers. The outside was noticeable for colour:

'I have noted by this time the strange love of the boatman for pictorial display. He likes the outer shell of his cabin bedaubed in streaks of gay colour. Inside he rejoices in highly illuminated panels, he affects a gay pictorial pail, the top rim of which is embellished by a painted garland of small flowers; the body is enriched by designs of outrageous roses and sunflowers; while the bottom offers a good ground whereupon to depict a gay cavalier or valiant crusader in full armour . . . If our water-faring friend has another weakness it is for knobs – knobs of all kinds, which he screws in everywhere. The dining-table cupboard is a very favourite place. I counted twenty-eight adorning one door; there were fourteen white china ones, six black ones, and eight brass ditto, and the combined effect was dazzling in the extreme.'[19]

While lower down in the country a traveller on the Thames[20] not only commented on the pride taken in the appearance of the boats by the owners but drew attention to the fact that on the outside of the cabins were 'painted two or four landscapes (usually river-scenes) of which they are proud enough'. If they had been paintings of castles, as is now taken to be traditional, surely he would have mentioned this?

Call them water gypsies as Meade did in 1850,[21] but even she had to admit: 'How picturesque is their life from an outsider's point of view! The gaily coloured boat, floating on peaceful waters on a summer's evening, the children picking daisies on the bank, the father smoking his pipe as his eldest son or assistant leads the tired horse away to rest, the wife leaning against the cabin door with her baby in her arms . . .'

Inside, too, colour was to be found, although 'graining' of most wooden surfaces was de rigueur. Usually this was done to hide the dirt; curiously no matter how often and how well white paintwork is washed in a living cabin it soon goes cream, and then a dingy brown.

'And that cosy looking little cabin, is that what it seems? Drop into it, and you find yourself in a home with rather less elbow room than a railway compartment – to be exact, about 250 cubic feet. On your right is a locker forming a seat, on your left a small stove, or, if the boat is new, perhaps a range, polished a beautiful glossy black and the brass rods above it, as well as the ornaments at the side nearest the bow, glistening like burnished gold, for the women, as a rule, keep their domiciles spotless. Beyond the fireplace knobs of cupboards and more lockers, and that is all, with the exception of a clock and a few household articles here and there. The eye has completed its survey of a narrow boat cabin.'[12]

That was a comment by a relatively unbiased writer but unfortunately the bulk of reports were written by do-gooders; who then (and now) were not only impertinent in their questioning but sought solely to find all that was bad, describing cabins as 'the most filthy holes imaginable' ridden with bugs and other vermin 'stinking mud finding its way through the old leaky joints' and emitting 'stenches enough to make a dog sick'.

When a writer settled down to show his dislike of waterways nothing pleased him, neither man, woman or even children; especially if the latter were working:

'The boatman was propped up against the helm, steering, smoking a short black pipe as usual, and his face as grimy almost as that of a sweep. While he was enjoying his tobacco and the sunshine, his wretched-looking, ill-clad, badly shod, and generally unkempt little daughter of some seven or eight summers was painfully trotting along the tow-path driving a couple of donkeys which drew the boat. Thus the real hard work of the boat was shirked by the man of thirty in the prime and vigour of manhood, and turned on to the tiny child.'[19]

For relaxation on the canals there was little choice, on a summer's day it is true that one could sit outside but after a November's day grinding up the locks what could be more

How picturesque is their life!

pleasant than to go to the 'pub'? But even this offended for:

'The canal-side town "public" is a thing to be remembered.
You come on it suddenly, hiding modestly in a dark hole or
corner of a dark wall. Its dirty little windows display weird
and fearful compounds, its sign hints in irregular printing –
"ale, porter, cider, and tobacco", and being "drunk on the
premises". I go – of course at another time without my kind
guides – to inspect the amphibious "public". I find the

grimiest of low-ceilinged taprooms, a truly savage and barbaric "tap" wherein is dispensed the thinnest and flattest beer I have ever yet come across. This is the "bargee's" usual tipple, for rum is only a special drink for great occasions. Greasy wooden "settles" and battered wooden tables furnish the apartment, and there come the "jolly bargemen" to make merry. The walls have two distinct and clearly defined rows of black lines, indicating the presence of greasy backs and heads, and when the boatmen have mustered "harmony" reigns . . . the ballads peculiar to boatmen possess either the humour of the not specially decorous country ditty, or the sentimentality of the Holywell-street "lay" . . . The singer having duly rammed his hands deeply into his breeches pockets, leans his head against the wall, fixes his eyes on the ceiling, assumes a most serious and dismal countenance, and goes to work with the air of a man doing penance for his sins. The choruses are frequent and tremendous. The "armony" is often relieved by a little step dancing, in which, strange to say, the boatman is an adept; the big burly men are wonderfully light of foot, and keep time accurately. The orchestra is usually composed of a fearfully dilapidated old man, operating feebly on the last remains of an ancient fiddle . . .'[35]

But the rather odd thing about this life is that the boat-people stuck to it, generation upon generation. They actually volunteered to be on one of the '25,000 boats ploughing up the decayed animal and vegetable matter at the bottom, and impregnating the air with its stenches, and scattering death and disease along their track without any government supervision or control'. In July 1877 the Home Secretary stated that at the time of the census, 1871, there were about 29,500 persons employed on waterways of which 10,576 were actually on board boats.[37]

This figure was probably an understatement but a writer ruefully admits:

'There must be some Bohemian charm about canal life, for the boatmen seem rarely to leave it. Sons follow in the fathers' steps and espouse daughters of other boatmen, and the children take naturally to the calling as soon as they are able to steer or drive the horse, and strong enough to assist in opening locks. The boatman or "bargee" is to a great extent a social pariah, a water Ishmael. We accept him somehow as a type of savage brutality; in his constantly changing life he makes few friends, save the "mates" on his journeys, for the outer world will have none of him.'[34]

Many popular Victorian misconceptions of canal life were drawn from the canals of the Midlands. Towpaths were almost invariably 'slimy', 'slippery', 'hazardous', covered in 'rich coaly mud'. Nothing was to be seen except grimy, endless brick walls. The water 'putrid', 'foul' and permanently emitting vapours and stenches. The whole of the network based on this one relatively small area was considered to be 'a land of mud, water, and utter desolation, and bridges'.[35] In their endeavours to change all this the 'do-gooders' of the mid-nineteenth century appealed to the patriotism of their readers.

'We shall, as a nation, have something to answer for some day for neglecting to protect the boatwomen and children. We seem to forget that in taking care of the children we are also providing for our own safety. We seem to forget that in taking care of the children we are giving physical stamina to future generations, instead of propagating a race of short, stunted, decrepid, pale, sickly men and women, who become aged at 50 . . . Let us take timely warning, and rescue these miserable women and children from the physical degredation, moral pollution, and unhealthy atmosphere they have to endure in those hot, damp, close, stuffy, filthy and stinking holes called boat cabins.'[19]

Incredibly, even fifty years on, contemporary writers still harped on the same old themes.

'Ah! that picture! The eye, taking in merely the broad details, does not see that the principal figure – the woman at the helm, is often steering, suckling her last born, watching the older children on the cabin floor, lest they come to harm, and paying attention to the pot on the top bar simultaneously . . . Here a meal is in progress on the cabin top, there the family wash is likewise being done in public, and presently you hap on youngsters, engaged in the delicate operations of the toilet in full view of all the world that cares to look . . . Imagine,

PUBLIC HEALTH ACT, 1936

THE HULL AND GOOLE PORT HEALTH AUTHORITY.

Certificate of Registration of Canal Boat.

Registration Number of Boat }   **1411.**

WHEREAS application has been made to us. The Hull and Goole Port Health Authority, acting as the Registration Authority, under the Public Health Act, 1936, to register as a dwelling a canal boat, of which :— The Flixboroug Shipping Co., Ltd., 7, Theodore Gardens, Scunthorpe, Lincs.,

are the owner(s), and which is accustomed or intended to ply on the canal whereon the said district abuts.

AND WHEREAS we have ascertained that the said boat conforms to the conditions of registration prescribed by the Canal Boats Regulations, 1878 to 1931, for the number of persons allowed by the said regulations to dwell therein.

NOW WE the Hull and Goole Port Health Authority, acting as the said Registration Authority, do hereby certify as follows, that is to say :—

1. That the Boat named   "ENID HILDA" whereof The Flixborough Shipping Co., Ltd., of 7, Theodore Gardens, Scunthorpe, Lincs., are the owner(s), has been duly registered as a dwelling.

2. That the place to which the said boat has been registered as belonging, for the purpose of the Elementary Education Acts, is HULL.

3. That the number with which, in pursuance of the statutory provision in that behalf, the said boat is required to be numbered is............1411.........................

4. That the distinctive mark or marks with which we require the said boat to be marked are—Registered HULL. 1411.

5. That, in accordance with the provisions contained in the subjoined Article of an Order of the Local Government Board (Ministry of Health) dated the Twentieth day of March, one thousand eight hundred and seventy-eight,

(TURN OVER

(TURN OVER

Certificate of Registration under the Public Health Act, 1936
(Courtesy of P. L. Smith)

the maximum number of persons for which the said boat is registered as a dwelling
is as follows :—

Otherwise than as a fly boat—

~~In main cabin~~ xxxxxxxxxxxxxxxx ~~persons~~ xxxxxx xxxxxxx xxxxx ~~adults~~ ~~under 12 years of age~~

In fore cabin **two**   Adult persons ~~xxx xx xxxxxxxx xxx children under 12 years of age~~

The Article before referred to is as follows :—

For the purpose of fixing the number, age, and sex of the persons who may
be allowed to dwell in a canal boat, which conforms to the conditions of registration provided by these regulations, and which shall, in pursuance of the statutory
provisions in that behalf, have been registered as a dwelling, the following rules
shall apply :—

(a) Subject to the conditions hereinafter prescribed with respect to the separation of the sexes, the
number of persons who may be allowed to dwell in the boat shall be such that in the cabin or cabins
of the boat there shall be not less than 60 cubic feet of free air space for each person above the age
of 12 years, and not less than 40 cubic feet of free air space for each child under the age of 12.

Provided that, in the case of a boat built prior to the Thirtieth day of June, one thousand
eight hundred and seventy-eight, the free air space for each child under the age of 12 years, shall
be deemed sufficient if it is not less than 30 cubic feet.

Provided also, that in the case of a boat registered as a "fly" boat and worked by shifts, by
four persons above the age of 12 years, there shall not be less than 180 cubic feet of free air space
in any cabin occupied as a sleeping place, by any two of such persons at one and the same time.

(b) A cabin occupied as a sleeping place by a husband and wife shall not, at any time while in such
occupation, be occupied as a sleeping place by any other person of the female sex above the age of
12 years, or by any other person of the male sex above the age of 14 years.

Provided that in the case of a boat built prior to the Thirtieth day of June, one thousand
eight hundred and seventy-eight, a cabin occupied as a sleeping place by a husband and wife may be
occupied by one other person of the male sex above the age of 14 years, subject to the following
conditions :—

(i) That the cabin be not occupied as a sleeping place by any other person than those above
mentioned.

(ii) That the part of the cabin which may be used as a sleeping place by the husband and
wife shall, at all times while in actual use, be effectually separated from the part used as
a sleeping place by the other occupant of the cabin, by means of a sliding or otherwise
movable screen, or partition of wood, or other solid materials, so constructed or placed as
to provide for efficient ventilation.

(c) A cabin occupied as a sleeping place by a person of the male sex above the age of 14 years, shall
not, at any time, be occupied as a sleeping place by a person of the female sex above the age of 12
years, unless she be the wife of the male occupant, or of one of the male occupants, in any case within
the proviso to Rule (b).

Given under the Common Seal of The Hull and Goole Port Health Authority,
acting as the Registration Authority,

this   **18th**   day of   **August**   one thousand
nine hundred and **fifty-five.**

E. A. Bullock

*Clerk of the Hull and Goole Port
Health Authority.*

100/3-55/H.P.L./Q107.

for instance,, washing-day on board a canal boat in mid-winter, with the little home reeking of soapsuds, and the air laden with steam from drying clothes suspended on lines from the roof.'[22]

This last was surely picturesque imagination, as washing was usually carried out in the hold of an empty boat, left with a lock-keeper's missus, or even taken to the bag-wash. Relatively, boat people were fussy about their washing. The existence was arduous, the conditions cramped, pay minimal and facilities poor, but look how many dirty, scruffiily-clad creatures there are about today when washing facilities are available on every corner and unlimited dole can be got for the asking. How many must there have been a century ago? Small wonder a few odd dirty boatmen were to be found.

Because of the cargoes carried workaday clothing was necessarily rough:

'In waterside settlements at different parts of the route dwell the tailors – sometimes feminine – who supply the sleeved plush-fronted waistcoats, the thick blanket-coats, and beloved fur-caps, and the shoemakers who build the mighty hob-nailed lace-up boots.'[19]

Strong, hand-made stuff, that had to be well made, for whole canalside businesses of this nature grew up relying upon the boat traffic for their existence. But even the best could wear out and some unmarried boatmen were sometimes 'not too particular' as witness Abel, who worked for T & S Element around Birmingham until the late 1950s. Working a horse-drawn boat one day the line slackened, dropped under water, and on tightening was found to have a 'dead 'un' draped over it. Seeing the chap had good boots, he took them off the corpse, found they fitted and swopped, throwing the body back in now wearing his (Abel's) old boots.

Poverty was one shadow overhanging the lives of all boat-people – to this extent they did not differ from people on the bank. Accidents were an in-built risk, broken arms, legs; lost eyes; damaged spines and hernias passed almost without comment. During the 1930s one boatman slipped into a lock at Minworth, somehow dragged himself out up the wing wall and crawled to the nearest house for help. He had a fractured spine and, perhaps luckily for him, died soon after. Another recently-dead witness to the harsh side was an old man who lived by the Grand Union. He had two hooks instead of hands as the result of a boating accident in 1931. His pension was 8op a week. It is worth noting that another canal man who retired in 1973 after 49½ years continuous service on the canals receives exactly £1 per week as his pension. The widow of another who died on the job in 1971 receives – even now – 37 pence per week.

But for every canalman or woman who dies, one is born. A canal christening was always a celebration, and not one which required a hostelry. Instead, it was a chance to get out the best clothes; which were rarely, for practical reasons, kept on board the boat, but instead were left with a relative who had a house on the canal bank, perhaps a sister would have left the boat and married a maintenance man, or a widow who, with the bit she had saved – and the women could save – had got herself a little cottage somewhere. The best clothes out and pressed, the boat polished and maybe repainted for the occasion, the horses tackle shining in the light, they would arrive at the wharf.

'During the time my grandfather, John Bate, was licensee and owner of the "Queen's Head" and wharf, Stoke Pound, Worcestershire, 1869 to 1901, he arranged several times with the vicar of Stoke Prior church to take an open air service for worship for boat people at Stoke Wharf. My grandfather was organist at the time at Stoke Prior church and he would let the vicar, the Reverend Oldham, know when boat people were likely to be congregated at the wharf for a service (Sunday afternoon in the summer) and to baptise the baby of a boatman and his wife. Sometimes there would be more than one baptism. I have heard my father say the vicar would borrow a small table and bowl or basin from a residence on the wharf and take some water out of the canal and bless the water and then baptize the baby. There were good voices to be heard at these services, those of the boatmen and their wives and, generally, locals joining in to the accompaniment of a harmonium organ brought out at the wharf . . .'[13]

A wedding, too, wasn't just a case, as the navvies did, of

jumping over a chair, but instead an excuse – and little was needed – for both folk and boats to be 'dressed up'.

'When two persons of the boating population wished to get married, the parents of the couple, or friends, would decorate the boat that was going to be used for their livelihood with bunting. After the couple had been married, generally in the local parish church nearest to the canal where their boat was moored, the bridegroom would carry his bride onto the boat, and they would be cast off to float or drift to some secluded place for a day or two . . .'[13]

One likes the discretion inherent in the 'drift to a secluded place'. This was probably the only time when the boat-couple would be completely on their own at night, for aside from the necessity to stop at stables for the horse, there were only a given number of lay-byes where a boat could be moored 'out of the road'. It is perhaps a vestigal atavistic instinct that leads the remaining boatmen to congregate at Braunston, Sutton Stop or Bedworth today. When the boatmen died then, and only

A wedding party

then, did they have absolute right of way. This probably wasn't because of any unpleasant reason, plenty of old women along the cut knew well enough how to preserve a body for a few days, but as a mark of respect. Usually, but not always, the boat was bowhauled, otherwise a 'steady' horse was used, the boat invariably was swathed in black crepe, and on one occasion at least black lines were used; while the boat was not clothed up (covered) except in inclement weather conditions. According to the district the coffin could be strapped on the fore-mast beam, on the floor, or 'with the coffin slung up to the beams of the boat'.[13] The whole essence of the treatment was one of respect; no matter if he had been a 'villainous, uncouth animal'. In earlier days at least, it was the custom for the boatman to be laid at rest with his boat's line and shaft beside him; what accompanied his wife is unrecorded.

Whether or not canal boats should be in use on a Sunday was, until recently, a matter between the clergy and the boatmen. Now it is a matter between anglers and pleasure-boaters. Early records tell us that boating on Sundays was forbidden – an Act of 1641 prohibited bargemen from working on Sundays 'unless their barge be in great peril', another of 1650 tightened this up

'. . . that no person shall use . . . any Boat, Wherry, Lighter, Barge either in the City of London or elsewhere (except it be to or from someplace for the service of God) . . . upon pain that every person that shall use such Boat, etc. shall for every such offence forfeit the sum of Ten Shillings and that every Boatman etc. shall forfeit Five Shillings.'

This clause was renewed at various times – although to little effect – until 1827 when it was expressly removed in the Watermen's Bill.

However, on the Somerset Coal Canal one August day in 1809, the Reverend John Skinner, tells us in his Journal that[36]

'Whilst walking in the village, as I generally do between Morning and Evening Services in order to see things are tolerably quiet, I saw a boat laden with coal going down the Canal. On enquiring whose it was I found that it was under the direction of William Goold, junr, who carried coal for his brother, Joseph Goold. I told the boys who were with it how improper it was to be boating on a Sunday, and begged they would tell their master I should notice the impropriety of this behaviour. The name of the barge was "Vulcan No. 7". On Monday I went to Goold's, found he was with the boat, and was not expected home for a day or two. I desired they would send him to my house when he came home. Friday he came up after breakfast, said he was very sorry for what he had done, but was fearful he should not get his coal up into the country if he had not done as he did, as there was likely to be a stoppage on the canal; that he knew I might have him fined, but if I would not proceed against him he never would be guilty of the like in future.'

One result of Sunday working was that a boatman had little time – even assuming he had the inclination – to go to church. There were exceptions: 'A respectable boater told me that there were boaters who read the Bible, and had family prayers daily.'[19]

To what extent the lack of religious upbringing affected the boat-children's approach to the subject I know not but: 'A boatman, a local preacher among the Wesleyans in Tipton writes me that they have two mission-houses in Tipton, and a few boatmen attend'[19] while in London:

'. . . in the Paddington basin . . . I myself counted on Saturday last over 60 boats, barges, &c. and 49 on Sunday, and I was assured that there were nearly 20 more at the Amberley and Carlton Wharves . . . the number of boats "tied up" in Paddington parish will average 60 per day all the year round . . . Mr. Norman, a gentleman in the employ of the Grand Junction Canal Company, and who looks after the canal at Paddington, states that the trade and number of boats there has, if anything, increased during the last twenty years, and to say it has declined is a mistake . . . I must leave it . . . to your readers to say if the "Boatmen's Mission" can be called a success amongst boaters, when only two or three of that number are to be found there . . . There may be houses built between the institution and the basin, to prevent the children seeing it, I admit. If its "flag floating on the breeze" will drawn the children, by all means get it; if not, I think it would be worth while trying to collect the children, to take them to some place in a boat. Suppose a boat, or, perhaps what would be better still, a floating school, was to call for the children every Sunday morning at nine o'clock, bring them home to dinner, call for them again at two o'clock, or at any time the most suitable – but to school they should go, at whatever cost.'[19]

The mischance that coupled religion and education together no doubt had an effect upon both; no (normal) child would willingly exchange the freedom of a canal boat for a Mission Hall. Education had, prior to 1870, been in the hands of voluntary schools, mostly run by the Church, sometimes aided by small State grants. One argument against education for all was that 'them below' would ape 'them above', but supporters of general primary education argued that if a man was to vote then at least he should be able to write! The latter caucus led to the Education Act of 1870[39] but under this however local authorities *could* make education compulsory for those children under its jurisdiction, not all did and furthermore by way of their nomadic life boatmen were rarely of fixed abode and thus slipped through the net. Not until 1880 was primary education compulsory for all; free schools not being general until 1891. Prior to this 'An Act to provide for the registration of Canal Boats used as dwellings' had passed through Parliament in 1877,[38] and *inter alia*, this provided for compulsory registration of boats, fixing of the number of inhabitants and more importantly perhaps stated categorically that:

'A child in a canal boat registered in pursuance of this Act, and his parent, shall for the purposes of the Elementary Education Acts, 1870, 1873, and 1876, be deemed . . . to be resident in the place to which the boat is registered as belonging . . .'

However, it also allowed that providing a certificate was obtained from one school (at, say, a regular tying up place), the

'. . . child shall be deemed for the purposes aforesaid to be resident in the school district in which the child is so attending school . . .'

All very well and good but, as ever, there was a fly in the ointment; that of human nature.

'In general a man has to carry his children with him, and, as he is nearly always on the move, he can only send them to school for a day or two occasionally. If he choose to set the law at defiance – and sometimes he does, partly because he is indifferent to the future, and partly because his offspring, when they grow big, complain tearfully of being put among the "babies" in a Board school and of being laughed at as dunces – it is very difficult to prevent him. To track one of his youngsters a "kidcatcher" has to display the tireless persistence of a bailiff laying siege to the domicile of a suburban debt dodger and the agility and fleet-footedness of a 120 yards' runner.'[22]

Boat people, possibly because of the solitary nature of the work, but mostly because of their sure knowledge of the work they carry out, are a proud, independent people; and small wonder no child would willingly go to school when they knew they would be laughed at. In 1968 a young boat-girl[23] told us:

'I can't read and write at all, there is a school on the cut, but I have never been to school at all because if you went to that school you had to stop there in London. We only had trouble with the authorities once and we had to send Muriel but they couldn't send me because I was looking after the boats when Dad was ill, she only went for a couple of weeks . . . When I was on the boats I didn't find it was any disadvantage but when I worked in a shop and the people I worked with knew I couldn't read and write they made fun of me – on the boats no-one took any notice because they were nearly all the same.'

Their pride plays them false once they leave the cut for:

'That's why I hate it at the canteen, when I was working for my Dad I went my own way and I did what I liked, I knew the job, but when you've got someone bossing you around all the time . . .'

And, of course, the inherent trouble with missionaries was that they had to pry. If someone came aboard your pleasure boat without so much as a by-your-leave and started asking questions, might you not be aggrieved? and when the questions included your name, number of children, who owns the boat, when was it bugged, do you tie up on Sundays, can you read or write, why do you swear, why is your horse so thin and the like, you would either run to the nearest telephone for a doctor or, if a boatman, clout the inquisitor hard on the nose. Unfortunately our boatman could not do either – for the latter a sentence of seven years hard labour would be the least he could expect, but he could avoid going to church. For this and other reasons canalside religious missions have waxed and waned through the nineteenth and twentieth centuries, reaching their heyday in the period immediately prior to the First World War. From 1869 – when the first canal mission was established at the Worcester Wharf, Birmingham – until 1914, the influence of the Incorporated Seamans and Boatmans Friendly Society steadily grew. In its later days at least, it could boast of a regular journal called *The Waterman*, and the missions extended from Plymouth to Newport, and from Seacombe to Bristol. Of special importance to canal people were those at Hednesford (1885); Top Lock, Birchells, Walsall (1901); Sheffield (1903) and Leeds (1900). Regrettably, their efforts were a little too strenuous and somewhat overdone. *The Waterman* was printed in an improbably small type, written more for the sound of 'pretty' words than readability. A few extracts will serve to show that gulf and lack of mutual comprehension that has always existed between canal people and those on the bank. The first page of the April 1910 issue is almost entirely devoted to a self-congratulatory article on the Leeds Branch of the Society having survived ten years, although: 'I found a number of young boatmen enjoying the various games provided – billiards, bagatelle, etc.'

A later issue, addressed to canal children, tells us the Union Jack, once a symbol of patriotism, stands for 'Unity, Faith and Love in Jesus Christ'. How many boat-children would even have seen a Union Jack? While further on: 'Perhaps the most startling event of the evening was the speech of a Keel Captain, called to the platform to "say a few words". This brother, Captain Albert Downing, gave one of the most terse and pithy speeches that ever I heard a sailor or bargeman make. Manly, distinct, logical, he bore testimony to the grace of God to save and keep and empower for service. Our friend spoke up well for his own class, referred gratefully to our Society's labours amongst them, and made a most pleasing impression on us all.'

Of some interest, and perhaps proving that the Society's work was not even popular with the natives, is the story concerned with the founding of the first mission. Initially the Society had rented a part of a building on Worcester Wharf, Birmingham. Worcester Wharf was, we are told, crowded with boats and the boat-people stood in some 'urgent need for help and moral stimulus'. Be that as it may, despite good congregations, when the Midland Railway Company decided to open a new goods station to deal with increased material traffic, the Society, which of course dealt solely with spiritual traffics, was ejected. However a good fairy by the name of Miss Ryland emerged and:

> 'Through her influence the Worcester Canal Company gave a piece of land to the Society, situate on Worcester Wharf, and there the first Boatmen's Hall was erected by the munificent generosity of Miss Ryland, and cost upwards of £2,000 . . . and the present building was opened in the year 1885. Under Mr. Cusworth's vigorous and intelligent leadership the local branch of the Society soon became a vital force among the canal boatmen. New ideals were brought into their lives, watchful care was exercised over the children, and for twenty years prior to the passing of the Canal Boat Act a day school was held, to which the children were admitted free of cost. In many other ways much was attempted to ameliorate the conditions of canal life.'

Yet in 1910 – twenty-five years later – they still spoke of the hope that 'a solid foundation has been laid for the moral, social, and religious improvement of the Boatmen on our local canals.'!

A rather sanguine view of the effects of the Society's work among the canal boat people was expressed by Joel Cadbury in 1911. Estimating that there were still upwards of 50,000 persons employed on boats, he considered that while legislation had played some part in improving the 'conditions of life' on board boats, nevertheless:

> '. . . we claim that, through the efforts put forth by this

Society, much has been done to elevate the social, moral and spiritual life of our boat-people and their children. Today nearly all have homes ashore, and have elevated ideas of home life. Immorality, once the rule, is now the exception, and it is regarded as a disgrace by nearly everyone. Spiritually, they groped in darkness, but today elevating influences are thrown about their life, and the change is evident to all who have any association with them.'

Whatever good the Society may or may not have done, it seems that even in 1912 they were still optimistically trying to convert boatmen from their natural ways; albeit by way of a homily. To cynical modern eyes this story is 'overdone' but the sincerity of the writer, Mr E. Clarke, is not to be denied, and, at least, we are no longer on a canal made up solely of mud and stenches.

'Job Trinder has been a fool to himself, and worse than a fool; and deserves richly all he has got! The wonder is, that he's alive on God's earth today; that he hasn't been swallowed up in the pit long ago – poor miserable Job Trinder! These bitter words fell from the lips of Job Trinder himself, as one bright Sunday morning he wandered in most abject mood down the towing-path of the canal where his boat was "tied-up" . . . a slave to strong drink . . . Hardly a day passed that did not find him worse for beer. What little money he earned when sober went mostly to the publican's till. No wonder, therefore, that he frequently staggered home late at night to a cabin, fireless, foodless, and cheerless in the extreme . . . The sun shone brightly. Trees, fields, and hedges were decked in loveliest spring green. Birds sang merrily in the branches overhead, and all nature seemed to rejoice in her wealth of beauty and innocence. It was the reverse with Job Trinder . . . Job Trinder had been drinking more heavily than usual the day before: and, to make matters worse, had quarrelled and fought with his companions, who had worsted him in the fight; and late at night had sent him reeling to his cabin all bruised and mangled . . . He awoke the next morning to find himself in a most pitiable condition. His head throbbed with pain, his pockets were empty, his cupboard bare, his cabin dirty in the extreme . . . His path ever after was a downward one; he went from bad to worse. Drinking, swearing, gambling and fighting were his common sins. He speedily lost home, health and friends. To crown all, death snatched from his cruel hands the young wife and child . . . But the time was now come when in the mercy of God, he should be a fool no longer . . . Stooping down, he picked up what appeared to be the soiled and torn pages of a tract . . . his eye caught the words: "God's Mercy" printed in large type at the top of one of the pages, "God's Mercy" repeated he with bitter emphasis . . . In an agony of mind he cried out: "Is it true? True that God will have mercy upon me? True that God loves me? True that I may get rid of my sin, and become a better man?" . . . Job Trinder fell on his knees, and with hands clasped, and tears streaming down his dirty and blood-stained face, and a heart ready to burst, he cried out: "God have mercy on me, save me, a miserable sinner: help me to break away from the drink: help me to be a better man for Jesus' sake." Job rose to his feet with a lighter heart . . . God had heard his simple, broken prayer . . . He was to become a better man. A resolution formed itself . . . he could sign the temperance pledge; and here (sic) once more the sound of the preacher's voice.'

By this time, of course, for Job Trinder, Mr Clarke and all those in the canal world, civilization as they knew it, had only two more years to run.

Immediately prior to the First World War a boatman's wages stood at £1.19 for a 48-hour week, where they were regularly employed. A bargemaster, day boatman, or other 'Number Ones' (owner/drivers) were paid 'trip' money: a piece-work system, whereby the more work you did the more you were paid. A tug-captain, no doubt on account of both the skill involved and the unsocial hours, which involved starting work at 5 a.m., received rather more, at 31/6d per week (£1.57½p). On the Monmouthshire & Brecon Canal each man in the crews of the Market Boats earned £1.10p per week, but for effectively a 4-day week. The Leeds & Liverpool boatmen on the other hand received £1.20p, with some payments when hindered by ice. The Trent Navigation Company's scale of

☛ **Popular Mission Services**

AT THE

BOATMENS' HALL,

—Bridge Street, Birmingham,——

Every Sunday

At 7 p.m.

SPECIAL SINGING.

You are most cordially invited.

Boatmens' Rest Mission,	Weather Forecast.
TOP LOCK, WALSALL.	**AN APPEAL.**
	WINTER—Cold Winds, Biting Frosts, Rain, Snow, and severe weather generally.
SUNDAY SERVICES :— Sunday School, at 10.30 a.m. Afternoon, at 2 p.m. P.S.A., at 3 p.m. Evening Service, at 6.30 p.m.	**THE POOR must need be clothed.** Those old and cast-off garments, &c., for which you have no further use, would shield our poor during the cold weather, and the giver would be happier in the knowledge that someone was warmer for their gift.
Monday, at 3 p.m., Women's Meeting. Monday, at 8 p.m., Bible Class. Tuesday, at 7.30 p.m., Band of Hope. Thursday, at 8 p.m., Prayer Meeting.	**PARCELS** will be gratefully accepted, acknowledged and distributed by the— **Rev. and Mrs. W. WARD, 26, Gough Road, Edgbaston, Birmingham.** - - - -

Welcome to the mission (Courtesy of the Waterways Research Centre)

wages, dated 1895, remained almost constant until the 1914 war and stated that : '. . . uniform weekly wage (per week of 7 days) will be paid . . . and no Voyage Money.' A captain received £1.50p and a mate £1.20p but 'When the Tug, Boat or Horse with which any Man is engaged is detained for a longer period than three days owing to ice, flood, fog or wind, such Man will be paid one-half his usual rate of wages . . . .'.

Canal boatmen, being only human, often got up to devilry and sometimes got caught. On other occasions tricks were played on them; a boat lay at the 10th lock of the Aston flight in Birmingham one winter's day. Snow, ice and more snow came blustering down but the two sons of the lock-keeper thought nothing of it until they got home and found the house cold.

'No fire, Mum? "No, not till yer Dad gets 'ome, got only one lump of coal." Where's Billy? (the boat captain). "Off up the pub." With no more ado the lads got out the wheel-barrow and started to rob the boat. This particular captain always stacked his coal so that the big (1–2 cwt) lumps were outside and the small stuff in. The biggest lad "copped 'old" of a massive lump and heaved and worried it away. Crash went the small coal and the boat lay over on her side. The coal in the outhouse, except the big lump which wouldn't go in! And a roaring fire when Dad came in. "Coalman bin?" "No, lads got it – and more in coalhouse." Dad goes to see falls over the lump "base over apex" and ends up in the snow, fortunately laughing. The snow continues until Billy and his mate come out of the pub. When they see the boat lying over "they starts a-cussin' and a-blindin' and bashes on the door." "No," says Dad, in response to their vehement enquiries. "No, they'm down the Mission, bin there all evening." '

Normally these boatmen, of whom it was said 'they wouldn't give you a splinter off of a knob of coal' reckoned to 'make' a ton to be sold to lock-keepers en route, wetting the load to put the weight back, this time it was the biter bit!

Boatmen were, and still are, curiously reactionary, a point born out when

'. . . about 1908–9 the complaint was made several times by the residents of Edgbaston about the exhausted state of the horses and donkeys towing the boats along the canal uphill from Kings Norton. So the authorities tried out the long towing of boats from Tardebigge to Birmingham [14 miles] and Birmingham to Tardebigge. It was not a success, the more boats on tow, the slower it became. The boatmen did not take to it and it didn't help them when they were going into the BCN after unloading at Bridge Street warehouse, as they then had to walk their animals alongside the tow anyway. As might be expected, some boatmen would deliberately steer their boat into shallow places to slow down the tug, or when meeting a down fleet the boats being towed would get tangled up with the other string and so get stemmed up. This did not last long before the towing went back to the original way, but not before the canal lost a good many number-ones [owner captains] never to return.'[13]

When war came, boatmen, stunted, drunken, etc. etc. alike, volunteered to serve in His Majesty's forces to such an extent that when nature joined in the battle on the Kaiser's side chaos reigned. In January 1917, the hardest frost for many a year began to freeze the canals, and:

'. . . this at a period when anything that interfered with or interrupted navigation on the canals was nothing short of a national disaster in view of the fact that the exigencies of the great war were straining our resources to the very utmost, and war stores of everykind were vital, if our armies in the field were to but hold their own . . .'[24]

The Birmingham Canal Navigations were particularly hard-hit and being unable to crew all their iceboats due to the shortage of skilled men, and of horses, many of which were dying in foreign mud, decided to abandon all ice-breaking on the Tame Valley Section, Rushall Locks and the Daw End Branch and instead to devote all their energies to keeping at least one route open to the collieries, that via the Hednesford Arm and the Wyrley & Essington. However, by 30th January, in a letter to the Board of Trade, appealing for assistance from the army it was stated that '. . . the canal is completely stopped as far as the Cannock Collieries and Hamstead are concerned and also the Tamworth Section of the B.C.N.', this in addition to the other colliery lines. On the following day a meeting was arranged between officials of the B.C.N., the Board of Trade and the local Officer Commanding His Majesty's Army and:

'. . . the proof that the grass was not allowed under our feet is that by the very first train the next morning 25 men, with an officer and sergeant [a number which grew into hundreds] complete, detrained at Great Barr Station, and well before lunch time they were all busily employed either in clearing the ice or helping with the ice-boat, and continued the good work for several weeks. In this way the Tame Valley Canal was not only re-opened, but kept open, and the value of it all cannot be measured in mere £.s.d., because of the intensely critical conditions prevailing at the time, for every available ton of fuel was worth more than money could possibly buy, as it meant the means, and only means, of combating the great peril with which the world was menaced.'[24]

A Board of Trade department, the Canal Control Committee, was set up in 1918 rather too late for practical purposes. The basic idea was to organize the traffic on the canals, so that it might be increased as much as possible in order to relieve the congested condition of other means of transport, especially the railway.

The biggest problem, as they admitted

'. . . had been the great shortage of labour at the present time, the canals having lost a large percentage of their staffs through the enlistment in the Forces before the canals were controlled, and through their leaving canal work for more remunerative employment, such as dock work and munition factories. The Canal Control Committee have, however, taken steps to retain the services of all men who are indispensable for work on the canals . . . By arrangement with the War Office, applications can be made for men over 25 years of age who have joined the Army for their transfer into the Transport Workers' Battalions, whence they are drafted back temporarily to their previous employers on the canals, although they still remain in the Army. In order to provide experienced boatmen, of which class there is a considerable shortage, men from the Transport Workers' Battalions without previous experience of the canals are now being trained on some of the Canals.'[25]

One unorthodox aspect of a boatman's life could occur only in wartime.

'During my early days of working at Tardebigge we used to have wounded soldiers come down from the local village hall, it had been turned into a hospital. They used to be interested in the making of the lock gates, also to have a ride on the steam tugs to Shortwood and back. On several occasions I would be steering the material boat through

Tardebigge Tunnel behind the tug when these soldiers would give vent to their feelings by singing some of the songs and ditties of the first world war. It would sound very pleasant, vibrating from one end to the other of the tunnel (the steam tugs never made any noise from their exhaust – you would only hear a gurgle of water now and then from the movement of the propeller). One song I became particularly fond of runs something like this: "Where are the boys of the village tonight, where are the pals we knew, in Piccadilly or Leicester Square, no not there, no not there, taking a trip on the continent, with their rifles and bayonets bright, going across the water to see the Kaiser's daughter, that's where they are tonight"; and another one, sung to a well-known children's hymn tune: "What a friend we have in Jesus," ending up "When I get my civvy clothes on, no more soldiering for me, no more church parades on Sunday, no more asking for a pass, you can tell the sergeant major to stick the pass up his ***" and so on!'[13]

One result of the rising cost of living and the labour shortage was an increase in wages in 1919 – allowing for the War Bonus – a boatman received between £2.84p and £3.22p while a tug captain had £3.29p and – oh horror – a writer in 1920 nearly had an apoplectic fit for not only had further 'demands' been made on the Canal Companies for a minimum wage (Captains £4.50p) for a 47-hour week, but 'In addition, the men are seeking for all public holidays on full pay and six days' holidays per annum with pay, the provision of clothing for boatmen, and other special allowances'.[24] But, given a moderate approach there were still some who hoped for better days on the canal.

'My grandfather and uncles all worked boats and barges on the canals, and when I left school they took me with them, as men were scarce. I should like to see a few alterations. I would have Sundays observed strictly – no alcoholic drinks, plenty of good refreshments instead, and I would sell corn, food, etc., to the watermen and show some interest in them. The canals should be well dredged and cleared of coal, ironstone and sand which someone is always throwing in, and men should be appointed to watch and report. If these things were properly attended to, with the water so near to all the wharves and warehouses, and all other things needed, I believe, with steady, consistent watermen, it would be a pleasure to all and very profitable to all concerned. I believe in all labour being well paid, but we must not go beyond and cripple our industries. I think that with good management, with engines in the boats, all in good repair, and a Benefit Club to help our watermen to take interest in the water work we should make everybody happy, and prosperous. This is my firm conviction, for the water trade is healthy and can be made more so.'[24]

However, in May 1920 a boatmen's strike took place, reflecting how important canals then were.

'The effect of this strike is, of course, disastrous, and must become more and more serious as the strike period continues. Not only Birmingham, but what is known as the Black Country is largely dependent upon canal transport for fuel and other commodities essential to the many industries represented. This is especially the case with the iron trade, whose works are practically all situated on the canal side, and whose sole means of securing adequate fuel supplies are by means of the canal.'[24]

Boating traffics never truly recovered from this, coupled with the general strike and the availability of cheap ex-WD lorries. The run-down of horse drawn boats was very fast – the new Gardner, Widdop, Petter and Bolinder semi-diesel hot bulb engines offered a faster turnaround at a lower cost. Fewer boats and hence fewer boatmen could be utilized to carry the same tonnage. Stables closed; leggers disappeared totally, the few horse-boats were pulled through tunnels by tugs or a passing motorboat instead; canal pubs went into a decline.

The Second World War became almost a pale carbon copy of the first; boatmen left to join the services, or were called up; many of them ending up on trawlers, or in minesweepers, others with the IWT in Britain and later in France. The young boat-man who might have kept traffic going after the war, having seen something of the world, and having had, probably for the first time, money of his own, was disinclined to return to the cut; and having married a girl 'off the bank' too often settled

30 Looking over the Barton Swing Aqueduct on the Bridgewater Canal to the Manchester Ship Canal below, 1970. *(Courtesy of L A Edwards)*

31 A compartment boat suspended over the breach of the Manchester, Bolton and Bury Canal at Prestolee in 1942. *(Courtesy of the Waterways Museum, Stoke Bruerne)*

32 Braby's Chemical Factory alongside the Coventry Canal, 1974

33 The pleasure craft *Day Star* being repaired at Tardebigge Dry Dock on the Worcester and Birmingham Canal

down to a council house and a factory job. Those who did return found the girls off the cut had gone on the bank and joined the Landgirls or the WRACs: the converse then applied. The older 'Number Ones' struggled on for a while, but some at least lost heart when faced with forms and coupons they could not read. The difficulties were great enough for someone with a fixed abode and regular shops; always on the move and regarded as 'pariahs' boat-people had no chance. Having lost boatmen, a training scheme was again set up; a few men came, less stayed, and a brief abortive experiment using girls was tried. In so far as, at best, there were only eleven pair of boats wholly crewed by these girls of which three were still in use at the termination of hostilities, the publicity has been out of proportion to the results. In her book[26] Eily Gayford mentions the disapproval with which the scheme was met, one reason having been the use of some unemployed merchant seamen as boatmen during the previous war. Although these men had been on the cut for over 20 years still they were 'sailors' to be ignored. Soldiers too had been used in that same war:

'In 1917 quite a large percentage of boatmen had been taken for the Army . . . As a consequence many boats were out of commission through want of repairs and lack of crews. To meet the labour deficiency arrangements were made for the employment of men from the Transport Workers' Battalion [and] the results proved very satisfactory, for, after a short period of training, the soldiers took the place of experienced canal workers, not only in the matter of loading and unloading boats etc., but also in the vastly more difficult work of navigating boats along the canals.'[27]

Initially, Miss Gayford, who was to receive the MBE for her work, together with another girl worked in 'double harness' with a regular boating couple, but finding this unsatisfactory to both parties they took their own pair and worked four handed with two 'trainees'; the crew per pair of boats being reduced to three as the trainees became independent, although strangely the last six girls working were those who first joined in 1941. Miss Gayford says, 'Time went on while trainees came and trainees went; sometimes, however willing and eager a girl might be she found she was just not strong enough to do the work, or perhaps because of her family she had to leave.' One difference between boatmen and 'trainees' was that the latter were paid a minimum weekly wage, whereas boatmen were paid only by the trip.

'Our greatest trouble, when working a continuous flight of locks, is to keep ahead of the boats behind. Some days we find ourselves quite alone and everything is pleasant and peaceful. Another day we may be overtaken by a fast working crew and we usually feel bound to "loose them by" as they say. This is rather a nuisance; it loses us about 10–15 minutes and gives us a lot of trouble in keeping our boats off the mud banks on the sides of the canal. However, boaters work on a piece rate, earning so much freight per trip, so the faster they work the more they earn and if you want to keep the goodwill of the boaters it is no good hindering them . . . We have some fierce arguments on this subject and on the whole the boaters are not displeased when we refuse to give in to them. A really good fight often precedes a firm friendship; we sometimes feel that it acts as an introduction.'[28]

The problems, aside from ice, were manifold for these girls:

'It is horrible when the rain pours down all day, our feet are sodden and water trickles down our sleeves when we move our arms. Bitterly cold winds beat on us unmercifully and our only comfort is the warmth which rises from the cabin stove' but, 'On the other hand it is very pleasant to be able to lie in bed in the morning, by which I mean 6 a.m. and put the kettle on the oil stove and light the fire without having to get up. It is easy to throw on one's clothes, let go the ropes and be off in the first light, starting one's day without any of the preliminary transport difficulties of the city workers.'[28]

Whether, in view of the time and money spent, the results were worthwhile is difficult to judge; most of the trainees were on the coal run to London; although they carried to Leicester and Northampton also. The use of female labour stopped in 1945, while the training scheme for men was reintroduced after 1947.

Traffics moved in the war, however, proved the value of canals:

'Although the capacity of the canals is severely limited, they still carry twelve million tons of cargo every year. What is the cargo? Half of it is coal, coke and other fuel. In Birmingham they will carry 100,000 tons of coal a month, on the Leeds and Liverpool canal, 80,000 tons a month. The railways who own canals carry nearly 30,000 tons of coal a month by water. Four hundred and fifty thousand tons of coal are carried every month by the boats and barges. The other cargoes are, of course, the simply bulk cargoes, like tar and oil – tar is important, granite, gravel, grain and many other food-stuffs for home consumption, steel and cement for our industries, and every month over 400,000 tons of these are carried from the ports and the depots to the storage places and the factories. The important relief which the canals give to the enormous war-time pressure on the railways is obvious.'[29]

During the war boatmen met with one extra hazard; the attention of Generalfeldmarschall Göring's Luftwaffe, which sank or damaged quite a number of craft. James Yates, a Director of Yates Brothers, gives his experiences:

'Regarding the sinking of canal boats in enemy raids, we had three boats destroyed. The "Oak" at Birmingham at the HP Sauce Works, on hire to W. J. Hayward of Tipton, in May 1940. The "Sunlight" and the "Wren" on hire to Samuel Barlow Coal Co. Ltd., were blown up at Coventry Power Station in the air raid there. We had out on hire during and before the war 350 to 400, mostly day boats. We worked day and night repairing the craft carrying fuel to munition factories, power stations, etc. Working upon the canal craft it was surprising where shrapnel had penetrated. I think a lot of it was from our own anti-aircraft guns. I have found it under cabin floors and stuck in the boat bottoms. It was a pity the trade went but we have many pleasant memories of the Birmingham Canal with no casualties.'[30]

In a sense it was just retribution that on a number of canals prisoner-of-war labour was used to supplement the remaining maintenance men. Generally speaking, Germans were the most popular, and, seemingly, were left to get on with whatever job

was involved virtually unsupervised; one at least ending up
boating, complete with English wife. On the Stratford Canal
Italians were given work, especially at Earlswood, where the
so-called 'Lakes' act as a reservoir for the canal, from which in
turn steam-railway-engines could draw water. Although the
work was not strenuous, nevertheless Signore Martinelli,
Giampiccolo, Serra, Rizzini, Tata, Casalnuovo, Del Pra,
Venturi, Biasco and Dellarocca were still held here, doing a
six-day, 52-hour, week, as late as 10 May 1946, and might
reasonably have been disgruntled at not being repatriated.
The prospects for boatmen after the war were grim. Although
a few 'Number Ones', such as John (later Sir John) Knill with
'Columba', started bye-trading, often using their war gratuities,
the first blow was struck when canals were nationalized, as
from 1 January 1948. The well-known story of the D & IWE
man who, when told that canals came within his aegis exclaimed, 'Oh Lord, do we have to have them as well' is all too
well-founded. Docks always had precedence and worse, most
of the officials were ex-railwaymen. The second blow was the
freeze of 1947, which gave the *coup-de-grâce* to many boatmen –
and the canals they used. However, after a while the D & IWE
decided to make the most of a bad job and in March 1952 were
proud to claim:

> 'On inland waterways controlled by the Executives the
> originating traffic rose to 12,155,000 tons – an increase of
> 4% over 1950, and nearly 2 million tons more than in 1947,
> the year before the inland waterways were taken over. Oil
> and other liquids in bulk contributed largely to the increase
> in 1951, and the tonnages of coal and general cargo were also
> appreciably higher.'[31]

Shortly after the war another form of 'missionary' work was
commenced; that of the Salvation Army. This operation was
run by Brigadier and Mrs F. G. Fielding, who made a sensible
approach by using a converted diesel-powered butty-boat,
Cornwall, subsequently renamed *Salvo*, which was fitted out
with both living quarters and a small 'chapel' or meeting room.
Living as they did entirely on the boats – the *Aster* was obtained
later – the officers were constantly in touch with the boating
families, and Mrs Fielding was often with the mothers when

their babies were born. Their claim was that 'Our prime concern was, not to get youngsters to join the Salvation Army, but
to bring them the Good News of the Gospel, together with a
social Ministry and practical service', and it is true that children
were the prime interest, to their advantage. For example, they
were taught elementary reading and writing, while entertain-
ment consisted of puppet shows, films, blackboard lessons and
various other visual aids, together with social evenings and
parties; the children often taking part in interviews for the
press, radio and, on one occasion at least, material was provided
for 'Sunday Break' a Granada Television programme. The
Salvation Army was granted the use of a wooden building at
Sutton Stop [Hawkesbury Junction] 'which served during the
winter months as a club-room, Sunday-school, and meeting
room, being open every day and evening, for the benefit of the
families old and young'. This hut was known, especially on the
long, dark, winter nights as 'The Lighthouse'. 'The children
were all known to us, and we gave them small presents and
cards on their birthdays, the highlight of the year being a great
Christmas Party held in the canteen of the Coventry Power
Station (permission being granted by the manager).' The adult
boat population were not forgotten, the provision of first aid
facilities, supplies of cheap (but new) clothing, practical
assistance and advice being very welcome.

It is pleasant to record that 'Now the children, and young
people of the boats are scattered and have settled in various
towns and villages, quite a number have in fact linked up with
the Salvation Army and have become active members of our
organization', while the old Toll Office at Norton Junction
(near Buckby, Grand Union Canal) has been converted into a
small but picturesque cottage as the home of Brigadier and Mrs
Fielding. On occasion, moored nearby will be the motor cruiser
Pilgrim in which they make journeys to various points along the
waterways 'visiting the boatmen's families and keeping in
touch with those splendid people whom they were privileged
to serve'.

Steps were also taken at official levels to improve conditions
for boat children, a new hostel (to supplement day schools at
Bulls Bridge and Brentford) was set up at Wood End Hall,
Erdington. By 1952:

'The venture has started promisingly. There are now 16 children, in some cases brothers and sisters, of ages ranging up to about 11 years, and they have settled down happily in a homely environment. After the unavoidably cramped life on the narrow boats, they are delighted with the sense of space, different recreations, their own beds, night clothes, regular baths and other amenities which are apt to be taken for granted. Recently one of the boys celebrated his eleventh birthday. A cake with candles was provided and the children had the excitement of their first real birthday party . . . There is room for more children at the hostel, and it is hoped that other boatmen, though naturally enough they like to live with their children, will welcome this opportunity of a proper education on modern lines for them. They can be confident that their boys and girls will be happy and well cared for.'[31]

This exercise was to be, as far as future boatmen were concerned, self destructive; the children simply would not return to the 'unavoidably cramped life'. Two years later the D & IWE started a training scheme to 'stimulate recruitment of boatmen for British Waterways canal craft operating in Yorkshire and Lancashire'. A barge, the *Weaver*, was especially converted to carry a crew of two men plus an instructor. 'Training occupies six to eight weeks, during which the men are encouraged to become fully self-reliant in learning out canal routes, navigation, boat and lock operation, cargo-stowing, etc. Practical experience is gained on the trips the *Weaver* makes carrying cargo between Liverpool and Blackburn. At the end of their course, the trainees should be sufficiently accomplished to become mates on other British Waterways barges operating particularly on the Leeds and Liverpool Canal.'[32]

Now there is virtually no commercial traffic on the Leeds & Liverpool Canal for as Charles Hadfield says: '. . . traffic continued to decline, and in 1963 British Waterways, who had acquired Canal Transport Ltd's fleet, ceased most carrying as part of a national policy.'[33] On the last day of December 1954, the D & IWE ceased to exist, the inland water transport division thereafter being renamed British Transport Waterways. Many boatmen must have taken heart when they were told that some canals, including the Grand Union (above Berkhamsted), the Leeds & Liverpool, the Shropshire Union, and the Trent & Mersey Canal would be retained as commercial waterways as long as they could be made to pay. Typifying the new attitude is the story of the narrow boat captain ambling up the Trent. Suddenly he found himself under the nose of a coaster whose mate told him, more or less politely, to 'b- off out of the way'. The boatman looking up, answered 'Ere, Mr Mate, speak to your equals, she's up the stern a-steering'. But the wages paid were still insufficient to retain the men and the handling conditions, relying as the boatmen did on a tonnage basis, were very far from the ideal, as evidenced by the following, drawn from the 1960 diary of a hard-working boatman:

Trips with loaded boats	109½ days
„ „ empty „	63 „
Waiting orders	37½ „
Engine repairs	17 „
Awaiting loading	16½ „
„ discharge	47½ „
Emptying and loading boats..................	27 „
Miscellaneous (floods, customs and maintenance stoppages)................................	19 „
Holidays and off sick	28 „

Summarizing, this gives 109½ days constructive boating, with 109 days more or less unavoidably lost. Totally lost (wasted) time occupied 118½ days – over one third, or four months of the year! The diary does also show what could be done: from Brentford to Birmingham (150 locks, 131 miles) a man and wife could shift 55 tons in 59½ hours running time, giving an income of £18.33p. Other running times – effectively disproving the claim that canals are too slow, were:

Bedworth to Colne Valley (53 tons @ 23.75p per ton) coal, 44½ hours;

Newdigate to Croxley (52 tons @ 23.33p per ton) coal, 40¾ hours;

Bulls Bridge to Tyseley (50 tons @ 63.75p) tomato purée, 55¾ hours;

Pooley to Croxley (53 tons @ 26.67p per ton) coal, 50½ hours;
Brentford to Wellingborough (45 tons @ 30p per ton) wheat,
    45¾ hours;
Coventry Collieries to Apsley (55 tons @ 23.75p per ton) coal,
    35½ hours;

and so on, and these were consistent times. Other loads included wood pulp, long steel, sheet steel and case oil. The
frightening loss of time was incurred mostly by 'waiting'.
Two typical examples are:

'Monday, 25th July	arrived Bulls Bridge 9.15 p.m.
Friday, 29th July	orders for Dock [Regents Canal Dock]
Saturday, 30th July	arrived Dock 10 a.m.
Tuesday, 2nd August	loaded 2 p.m.

***

Friday, 12th August	arrived Bulls Bridge 2 p.m.
Tuesday, 16th August	orders for Brentford
Wednesday, 17th August	left 5.30 a.m., Brentford 8 a.m. Loaded 4 p.m.
Thursday, 18th August	arrived Nash [Paper Mills] 5 p.m.
Sunday, 21st August	empty 12 midday.'

Then 'They' said narrow boat carrying could not pay! This
particular boat captain, seeing the writing on the wall, left in
1961 – to work in a factory. It is fortunate that even the worst
happenings never alter a boatman's humour. Often when they
took to the bank some readjustment in their way of life was
necessary, but patience with idiots was never a strong point.

'We had a bloke who if he stood by his shovel and stood still
he went to sleep, he was that type of man. If he sat down he
went to sleep, if he turned round and you didn't speak to
him he was asleep! . . . I woke him up once. We were working at Rushall, we had the top end gate open, we was going
to drive the binding pin out, top and bottom, and put a new
'ead on, and we got Joe on the top on a line on the gate to
keep it in position just until we got it spragged [propped] up,
you see. Well, this gate wouldn't stay still, every time we
touched it, it went one way or the other. So I had got a
sledge-hammer in me 'and, my favourite as you know, and

200

I walks 'alf-way up the ladder and when I looks there's Joe fast asleep on the balance beam and the ropes just lying slack! I was a bit impetuous then. I said "I'll bloody wake 'im up, you watch". You know the bead-iron that runs along the balance beam, I thought I'll give that a clout and make that ring that'll wake him up. I swings this bloody sledge-hammer full length and I 'it this bead-iron, next minute Joe's about five foot up in the air. The blokes says, "Bloody 'ell, that's woke 'im up" and the next minute we see Joe, he's a-holding 'is backside and 'es a-goin' round and round the lock-side. What 'ad 'appened I'd pinched 'is arse between the bead-iron and the balance-beam! He'd got about a three inch blood-blister across 'is bottom. He didn't go to sleep anymore that day! He couldn't sit down!'

Unfortunately this did not always make for popularity.

When the canal froze solid for 9–13 weeks, according to area, in 1962/3 the authorities heaved a sigh of relief and could, finally, stop carrying on narrow canals. The October 1967, the British Waterways Board magazine *Waterways* summed up the future:

'Yes – the curtain of uncertainty that has so long overhung the smaller waterways has lifted at last and the size of the network of the canals to be retained for pleasure cruising is established for the future. At 1,400 miles it is virtually the entire system as it exists at present and the Government is providing the finance to retain and develop it for recreational purposes.'

So the ring has gone the full circle, commercial carrying – and boatmen – still operate, no longer family boats, on the broad canals of the North, most try to go home for a night, to dig the garden, to watch television or to tinker with their cars. Not all can – one we know is so determined to that he takes his motorbike with him – but no longer does the old-time boatman putter along; instead, the job and responsibilities of men who navigate the Aire & Calder, the Gloucester & Sharpness, the Trent, especially with new developments appearing all the time, is more akin to that of the captain of a coaster.

New times, new ships, new men.

Modern tug meets cruiser

9 *Is there a Future?*

Amenity use of waterways is not new, it has already been shown
that around the turn of the century pleasure cruisers on the
River Thames took priority over commercial boats; similarly
on the Broads the hire of wherry, yacht, rowing boat or canoe
was commonplace.

> 'There are, we were told in 1904, numbers of suitable yachts
> for hire . . . The larger craft sleep four ladies and four
> gentlemen, and the hire is from £10 to £12 per week,
> according to the season. Attendants are included, but are
> boarded by the hirer. The four-ton boats, sleeping three, are
> £4 10s. a week with the attendant . . . Wherries are fre-
> quently hired by private parties, the hatches are raised a
> plank or two higher to give greater head-room, the clean-
> swept hold is divided into several rooms, and a capital float-
> ing house is extemporized.'[1]

The alternative – would we could still do this today – was

> 'to give a wherryman a small sum to take you with him when
> he makes a passage. There are always numbers of wherries
> leaving Norwich and Yarmouth, and if you hail the one you

fancy, you will be readily taken on board. Thus you might sail from Norwich to Yarmouth one day, up to Wroxham the next, back to Yarmouth and up to Beccles, at an expenditure of half-a-crown a day and refreshments.'[1]

There were, reasonably enough, rules to be observed by the man or woman pleasure bent, not the least:

'It is also a point of prudence not to cross a wherry's bows too closely, as they would smash up a yacht. If you are civil to a wherryman he will be most civil to you, and don't slang him if he doesn't at once give way for you to pass him.'[1]

Life on these Victorian and Edwardian cruisers was quite different from the frenetic rush of today, for example when shopping:

'it would be as well to take our man with us, and replenish our larder here [Stalham]. There is a butcher's, a baker's, an ironmonger's (who keeps a supply of fishing tackle), a capital grocer's, a chemist's, and several other handy shops. Having made sundry and very miscellaneous purchases, we send the man back to the Staithe, accompanied by a boy, both heavily laden, while we take a walk to Ingham, one mile to the east.'[2]

Akin to nattering to aged boatmen today, was a recommendation that 'if you have a short time to spare, you may while it away with the old seadog, Galbraith, who lives in the little tarred, wooden cottage, adjoining the churchyard. He will yarn you till you are both dry; but be not alarmed at that, for the inn is next door'. Now, alack, you couldn't even get in the pub! However, if perchance you were Fens cruising on your own on St Mark's Night (5 April) and saw a young maiden sitting in front of a mirror singing:

> Come, lover, – come lad,
> And make my heart glad;
> For my husband I'll have you,
> For good or for bad.

and you looked over her shoulder then you might gain an inexpensive crew member. Immediately prior to the 1914 war, motor boating on canals became a possibility for the adventurous. They had also to be wealthy, for not only was the boat expensive but a crew was necessary – none of yer 'Arrys and 'Arriets working their own locks! Not only had the would-be cruiser to be adventurous, but also meticulous in his approach.

'Preparatory to starting on such a journey as this, one would hardly realize the amount of work involved in corresponding with all the respective companies and parties concerned to procure the necessary information as to the arrangements of each canal. The writer thinks he must have indited some 50 letters before setting out. Then, again, there are the hotel plans to see to as one progresses so that really it becomes in a way an undertaking which one would little imagine.'

This particular voyageur[3] claims to be going on a 'voyage of exploration to waters hitherto unknown to the motor boat' and apart from himself and his two friends required a 'motoneer' (sic) and a handy man 'the latter being much sought after at times as the provider of all good things in the way of light refreshments, etc., necessary for the voyage'. Notwithstanding the five men on board, after leaving Sapperton Tunnel on the Thames & Severn canal 'We had the service of lock-keepers nearly all the way down, or got assistance, otherwise it would have entailed a heavy day's work'. This more or less typified the laziness of a canal cruise, while they considered themselves 'venturesome' when 'becoming adepts in motoring into the locks instead of working in with boathooks'. But in fairness to those men of yore they did manage to cover some ground; 381 miles and 291 locks in 15 days was reasonable, especially as they were governed by having to stop nights in hotels.

The alternative treatment was to hire a working boat, complete with a man – and a horse! – and, as it were, emulate the professionals. The best known of these hirers was E. Temple Thurston who in his book[4] tells us of his problems in convincing canal officials that he wished to risk going on the cut. But still he, and many like him, enjoyed their holiday.

During the interwar period the number of boats used solely for pleasure boating rose steadily, despite the fact that it was still an expensive pastime. On the LMS railway controlled canals, including the Shropshire Union, Lancaster and the

Early cruiser

Birmingham Canal Navigations, rates were calculated on a mileage basis with differing tolls for differing boat types. At a time when a clerk's wages would be £3 per week, the minimum one-way toll for a motor boat using locks was 40p; an amount which only covered 46 miles of cruising; thereafter an extra ½p per mile had to be paid. From Hurlesdon Junction on the Welsh Canal to the terminus at Llantisilio and back cost 60p; an annual licence for a 30-foot boat (1975) is only £24.50, go where you will.

To take even a canoe on GWR property was hardly more economic, on the Monmouthshire & Brecon from Newport to Brecon, without using locks, a single ticket cost 75p; a 3-month return £1.25. The 1975 annual charge, allowing its use on almost the whole network is £5. Almost contemporaneous with the nationalization of waterways, 1947 saw the formation of the Inland Waterways Association, which has over the years passed through many vicissitudes and changes of detail policy. The prime objective of the D & IWE appears to have been to make a profit, while Inland Waterways Association members have always more or less adhered to their policy 'to advocate the proper maintenance of all British navigable rivers and canals, and their full use by both commercial and pleasure traffic'.

The trend of the D & IWE's thoughts towards canal traffics

was well shown in January 1952:

> 'This close tie with the ports is emphasised by the traffic carried on inland waterways. Most of the 12 million tons dealt with each year consists of imports and exports, either foreign or coastwise. A considerable tonnage of the waterways' chief traffic, coal, is waterborne from Yorkshire collieries and shipped at Goole Docks by means of the remarkable "Tom Pudding" system. Outstanding among imports is the growing oil traffic carried inland in modern tankers, particularly on the Severn and Trent. Other traffics discharged overside at ports for conveyance by inland waterways include timber, metals, wool, minerals and foodstuffs. From the purely sentimental point of view there is something satisfying in the idea of, say, a consignment of Australian wool brought by sea to Hull completing its journey to destination by waterway. The inland industrial centres or storage and distribution depots served by waterway are, in effect, miniature ports, complete with cranes, trucks, warehouses, distribution facilities and, in some cases, dry docks. Though on a different scale, unloading waterway craft at such centres as Leeds, Sheffield, Nottingham, Worcester, Stourport or Winsford on the River Weaver in Cheshire, is not dissimilar from discharging cargo boats at seaport docks.'[5]

No mention of Birmingham, Coventry, Oxford, Northampton or Leicester; only wide-canal or river-fed ports are listed.

In the 1950s we had a triangular struggle between the 'fill em in' brigade, mostly 'political' councillors, hysterical mothers and yapping journalists; the D & IWE (and their successors from 1955 the British Transport Waterways) who sought to keep canals open only where they were financially viable, versus the Inland Waterways Association and kindred bodies who would not budge an inch from their belief that all waterways should be kept alive.

The first of the three was typified by a Councillor, J. H. Wardle of Wolverley, who said, *à propos* of the subsidy required by the BTC in 1956 for keeping all waterways open:

> '. . . many of the canals are nothing more than dirty, stinking ditches. If five and a half million pounds can be spent in

keeping these dirty, stinking ditches in being, where rats
thrive and cats are killed – and where even children are
drowned – it is absolutely disgusting,'[6]

while in Stourport more or less simultaneously, one R. F.
Abbotts described the Staffs & Worcs canal as 'nothing but a
disease carrier. You can see dogs and cats disintegrating in the
water.'[7] The year 1956 seems to have been a bad one, as even
the normally unbiased *Yorkshire Post*[8] tells us that:

'What was expected to become a derelict canal in the West
Riding is likely to be beautified by the British Transport
Commission. It is understood that the Commission plans to
make the Ripon Canal into an attractive feature of the
countryside. It is planned to break down the deep and
dangerous locks, and to build waterfalls in their place . . .'

In 1958, the *South Wales Argus*, writing on the Monmouthshire Canal, said 'It could possibly be made attractive by the
spending of a good deal of money, and so become an added
amenity to the new town. Better still, however, is Lord Brecon's
suggestion that it should be piped. In that way it would be out
of sight.'[9] A year later the *Beckenham and Penge Advertiser*[10]
reported that 'The Penge and Annerley Ratepayers' Association are to back Penge Council in their efforts to fill in the Betts
Park Canal [old Croydon Canal]. Mr C. G. Priest said at a
meeting of the Association on Monday that the Canal was
"disgusting", and that "many people would like to see it got
rid of, as it was nothing but a filthy stretch of water".'[10] Two
years later the same paper pursued the theme, reporting that
Councillor John Read said 'It stinks something terrible' and he
was sure that 'any improvements would result in danger to
children . . . to me it is just a horrible stretch of water'.[11] Meanwhile, in 1960, the *Oldbury Weekly News* reported Councillor
G. H. Price as saying 'I hope we shall be able to speed up the
filling in of this abominable canal which flows through the
middle of Oldbury. I see no reason why it should not be dealt
with very quickly.'[12]

Sir Reginald Kerr, General Manager of British Transport
Waterways, was a man who was probably more popular with
the rank and file of canal men than any other such officer, past

or present. Although an ex-BRS man, Sir Reginald brought
fire to waterways, mainly because he had a habit of popping
up here and there without fuss, but woe betide the slacker! He
would speak to anyone and everyone on the canal whether
boatmen, maintenance staff or the cleaners at Watford. Furthermore he possessed, and used, his own boat. In 1955, too, the
report of a special Board of Survey appointed to look into the
future of British waterways appeared and was accepted.
Broadly, it divided canals into three classes; more or less as they
are today. In the first group were those navigations 'which are
likely to be of real value to the country's transport system'.
Totalling 336 miles, these included the rivers Trent, Weaver
and Lee (below Enfield Lock), part of the Grand Union, the
Aire & Calder, etc., and were to be developed. The second
group, totalling 994 miles, were 'to be retained for the present –
their future depending on whether they could be made to pay
or not.' Among those listed were the Birmingham Canal
Navigations, Coventry, Grand Union Canal, Shropshire
Union Canal (main line only), Oxford (Northern only) and
the Trent & Mersey. The rest, some 771 miles, including the
Kennet & Avon, 'Welsh' canal, Oxford (Southern – Napton to
London) 'contains those which are either not used for navigation or carry so little traffic that there would be no point in
keeping them open.' Now that they at least knew what they
had to do, and had the money wherewith to do it, the BTW got
into gear. Under the heading 'Getting on with the Job', works
in hand were listed in their magazine each month. Typical,
was that for May/June 1957:[13]

Trent Navigation – Tender for the construction of two new
all-welded traffic craft costing £31,544, to be con-
structed by Richard Dunston Ltd at Thorne shipyard,
near Doncaster.
Grand Union Canal – Bank protection work at Paddington,
Southall, Uxbridge, Denham, Harefield, Apsley, Cow
Roast and Hatton.
Weaver Navigation – Repairs to river wall of Hunt's dry dock,
and the development of Hayhurst Yard, Northwich, for
Southern Carrying fleet repairs.
Gloucester & Sharpness Canal – Bank protection by steel piling

34 A pleasure wherry on the Fens at Barton Broad, 1890.
(Courtesy of the Waterways Research Centre)

35 Primeval man-haulage on the Worcester and Birmingham
Canal, below Astwood Locks, 1973

36 A canal loading wharf, owned by E J and J Pearson, at
Amblecote Works on the Stourbridge Canal about 1930, showing a
tramroad, a horse and carts, and eleven boats, some laden with
bricks. *(Courtesy of Price, Pearson Refractories Ltd)*

37 Both in retirement, about 1936. *(Courtesy of the Geographical
Magazine)*

at points along the canal.

Aire & Calder Navigation and Sheffield & South Yorkshire Navigation – Bank protection work by steel and concrete piling at various points.

Lee Navigation – Construction of towing path wall on the Limehouse Cut, in mass concrete for 1,500 ft. Work is being carried out by Leonard Fairclough Ltd. Also bank protection work at Tottenham with 2,400 feet of steel piling. Both these projects are part of the Lee Navigation development plan.

Shropshire Union Canal – Bank protection with concrete piling at Norbury and Great Stanney.

Forth & Clyde Canal – Purchase of new Priestman 'Wolf' excavator.

Trent & Mersey Canal – Construction of narrow raised footpath for a length of 600 yards in Harecastle Tunnel.

South Eastern Division – Purchase of six new steel-welded butty boats, to be constructed by the Thames Launch Works Ltd. Also the purchase of four Petter McLaren air-cooled diesel engines for carrying craft.

Leeds & Liverpool Canal and Shropshire Union Canal – Purchase of two new hydraulic dredgers to improve dredging output, particularly in bridge-holes.

Severn Navigation – Acceptance of Demolition & Construction Company Ltd's tender for bank protection work at Upper Lode Lock, Tewkesbury.

Trent Navigation – Repairs of Beeston weir.

Sheffield & South Yorkshire Navigation – Renewal of electric light and power installation at Canal Wharf, Sheffield.

In all, £5½ million was to be spent modernizing 325 miles of 'esturial' waterway, but as Sir Reginald said: 'We have the organization, we have the experience, we have the people with the know-how. We must now go all out to get the trade.' On 17 June of that year a new depot was opened at Knostrop on the Aire & Calder Navigation, 1¼ miles from Leeds, which it was claimed made the 'Port of Leeds now a reality'. Although in 1958 the new yachting basin at St Pancras was opened and the 'Heart of England' cruisers did well, trouble was in store on the amenity side. There were – and are – two schools of thought; the first, that whoever runs the waterways (whether it be D & IWE, BTW, BWB, Uncle Tom Cobley or Fred) should do just that and no more, while moorings, hire craft and amenity services should be provided by private individuals. The other is that all services whatsoever should be provided by the governing body. This latter caucus claimed that while it was true that the canal owners could, using government money, steamroll their way over any private company since they could undercut prices indefinitely, the canal network would nevertheless be developed as a unified whole, rather than piecemeal. The other party believed that a timely injection of private money would lead to improved facilities coming sooner and where they were most needed.

This latter view eventually won, and the results are now all too apparent. You may be charged 50p a night for tying up on the towpath – you may have to pay a 'service fee' of 20p for the privilege of emptying your chemical closet – you may find half-a-mile or more of private moorings occupying both banks of the canal where no tying up is permitted, however much this may obstruct the only access to shops. In 1974 during a working trip up the Ashby Canal (22 miles) a boatman found only one usable water-point as the rest were appurtenances to private boatyards, where boats were moored nose-to-tail.

In the meantime the Inland Waterways Authority was generally nudging the nationalized bodies into using all canals. Possibly the most cynical canal statement ever, appeared in their *Bulletin 51.*[15] Written at the time of the ill-fated Suez episode, it raises a query: 'Sir Brian Robertson [head of the BTC] has gone to see the last British soldier leave Egypt. Is it true that Colonel Nasser is being invited to see the last boatman leave British Waterways?'

One of the most prolonged battles fought under the umbrella of the IWA was that to save the Derby Canal. This was a privately owned waterway and in 1961 was still 14½ miles long. The 1960 estimates of the Derby County Borough Council included an item:

'of £36,000 to fill in half a mile of the previously abandoned Little Eaton Branch of the Derby Canal. This section was officially closed in 1935: the half mile recently filled in is the only part of the four miles of the section to have been dealt with in any way.'

Note the £36,000 required for just half-a-mile! By contrast, the opinion of the IWA was that:

'The Derby Canal, a wide waterway connecting the industrial centre of Derby with the South Nottinghamshire coalfield and the Humber Ports, should, under a rational system of transport, be a busy artery of trade. Such a waterway, emanating from the heart of a town and leading with surprising speed, to the quiet of the countryside, should be expected to attract fishermen and ramblers, naturalists and pleasure boaters. The value to waterside industry of a large quantity of cheap water, and to the fire service for emergency supplies, should not be underestimated.'[16]

In 1888, traffic totalled 85,484 tons; 11,200 in 1929, and as late as 1942, 3,350. Maintenance was almost non-existent and when in 1945 a pair of boats, loaded with coal destined for the I.C.I. works at Spondon, were brought to the Sandiacre entrance locks to the canal, notice having duly been given of the intention to navigate the canal, the gates were found to be padlocked by the company, and a policeman was on duty to ensure that no navigation took place. Despite the fact that the canal was not legally abandoned, in one year several lock cottages were bulldozed into their locks, gates were destroyed, and the famous 'Long Bridge' which carried the towing path across the River Derwent, was destroyed, and extensive filling was permitted in the Gas Board works at Litchurch. The cost of restoration was quoted in 1961 thus:[16]

Locks	Four new gates at each lock @ £720 per lock, including fitting	£6,480
	Repairs to chambers, weirs, paddles etc. @ £200	1,800
Dredging	19,000 cubic yards per mile @ 2/6d. per cubic yard	34,437
Puddled Clay	8½ miles rolled clay 12" thick @ 4/3d. per yard	12,342
Contingencies		5,000
		£60,059

Abandonment was estimated at £1,200,000. Based on calculations by a then canal carrier, J. K. Ebblewhite, potential annual income was estimated at:

Commercial and Wharfage	£14,630
Pleasure traffic	2,803
Angling	300
Water	1,000
Land drainage	3,000
Public donation	100
Annual subscription	500
	£22,333

That particular battle was one the IWA lost; the canal being formally abandoned in 1966. Anyone in the vicinity of Derby would do well to take a look at the 'superb re-development' of the waterway – rats, stinks, dereliction and all.

By contrast with this sad story, the (Southern) Stratford Canal has been restored. In the words of the IWA:

"It was a good idea to bring your mother this year, Ethel!"

Trouble was in store on the amenity side (Courtesy of the Sunday Mercury, Birmingham) 'after years of neglect by the former Great Western Railway Company, and by the Company's successor, the British Transport Commission, this beautiful waterway, was, after a long, hard and costly fight, saved by the Inland Waterways Association from abandonment [by] the Warwickshire County Council, that Council being perfectly prepared to close the whole navigation in order to lower a single road bridge across it. Subsequently, the canal has been leased to the National Trust, which set about restoring it, largely by public subscription and by voluntary effort, both being forthcoming mainly from the Association . . . and in July, 1964, the complete rehabilitated navigation was formally reopened by Her Majesty the Queen Mother, amid memorable scenes of rejoicing.

The case, obviously remarkable enough in itself, is of national importance also because of the attendant circumstances. The Stratford Canal at the time of the lease was about as far gone in dereliction as it would be possible for a canal to be while still remaining a canal at all; and it is in any case a narrow, winding, rural waterway, with a quite exceptionally large number of locks. The British Transport Commission's own published figure for closure was £119,000; providing not for filling in, which would have cost many millions, but merely for the first aid measure to prevent leaking, flooding, and crumbling (though not to obviate the dangers of an unused waterway) and to deal with compensation claims. The National Trust and The Inland Waterways Association undertook to restore and reopen throughout, and complete to the requirements of the original navigation statutes, for £50,000; which despite much inevitable official scepticism, has been done . . .'[17]

The Ashton, Upper Avon, Peak Forest and other waterways have been brought back to life using volunteer labour, initially to reduce cost and latterly because they were also found to be more efficient than contractors. This change of attitude was influenced by a complete *volte-face* on the part of the Government. In 1965 the British Waterways Board published a report[18] on the viability or otherwise of canals. This divided the future possibilities into a number of headings: present (1964) costs, reduction to a water channel with locks weired and navigation impossible, or total elimination. A few examples will suffice (all figures £1 UK).

Canal	Receipts 1964	Expenditure 1964	Profit/Loss 1964	Water Channel per annum	Elimination per annum
Ashby	1,388	9,522	−8,134	−7,500	−7,900
Coventry	16,737	28,854	−1,217	−4,700	−7,300
Cromford	1,470	7,190	−5,720	−7,200	−6,000
Erewash	7,241	9,491	−2,250	−600	−6,000
Lancaster	37,010	27,963	+9,047	+8,000	Not possible
Oxford (North)	8,335	31,780	−23,445	−9,500	−8,600

The British Waterways Board summaries were that:

(1) at least for a large number of years to come there is no prospect of pleasure craft activities paying for themselves in a true commercial sense;

(2) there is no true business future for the 'narrow boats', for which such nostalgic claims are still made;

(3) the most serious and over-riding fact emerging is that, even if the whole of the 'rest of the system' were to be ruthlessly treated (without any regard to social welfare) and every possible canal were to be either eliminated altogether or reduced to minimum water channelling flow – whichever was the cheaper – the exchequer would still be saddled with a bill equivalent to about £600,000 a year. And this, the survey reveals, is not an optional 'subsidy' but an inescapable minimum exchequer charge.

In 1967 a White Paper entitled *British Waterways. Recreation and Amenity* was published. Briefly, this said that the lengths of canals to be retained for pleasure purposes (1,400 miles) would have their deficit underwritten by the Government. 'A Subsidy for Sentiment', 'All Aboard for the Waterways'; 'Go-cruising Boost'; 'Holiday Charter for the Canals', were newspaper headlines of the time. Two years later a new division 'Amenity Services', with Allan Blenkharn as manager, was formed by the British Waterways Board. At the time Mr Blenkharn stated his objectives: 'One of my chief aims in this exciting new post will be to swell the numbers of pleasure craft owners and hirers. I want to ensure that the canals are always in a pleasant and acceptable state for the enjoyment of these people as well as anglers, naturalists, ramblers, industrial archeologists – and those who just want to stroll along the canal towing-paths.'[19]

A cautionary note appeared in an IWA Bulletin, December 1967. A writer in the *Sun* newspaper, 23 September, had complained: 'Ill mannered people on cruising trips go past anglers, with blaring radios, at fast speeds, carrying away keep nets, ruining bait and getting tackle awash,' the IWA warned that

'Not our Members, we hope; but the increase of use of waterways by all interests does bring in a lunatic fringe who may care only for their own pleasure – and both new anglers and new boaters can be equally inconsiderate. It is up to their own old hands to put them right; internecine strife between the two sports is not necessary, and if prolonged, neither side will win, but both will surely lose the public's goodwill (it's the taxpayers' £340,000) and ultimately the waterways.'

Unfortunately, the at times undisguised, imcompatability and dislike of the two groups, boaters and anglers, can show an ugly face. When in 1974, the Oxford Canal from Napton southward was closed, ostensibly at least, because of lack of water[20] a member of the Coventry & District Anglers Union told me in all seriousness that the C & DAU had had the canal closed as they had complained to the Board to the effect that fishing was impossible, whereupon the canal closure had been arranged. These kind of statements hardly improve relationships. It is undeniable that non-angling pleasure boaters often do all they can to torment anglers especially if there is a contest on; but having paid perhaps £150–200 to hire a boat for a week, or at least £35 for a boat's licence, no doubt they feel they are in the right; to fish for the season (roughly 15 June to 15 March) in those waters under the care of the Trent River Authority costs a mere 50p in 1973/4. A survey one morning in July 1973, over a three-mile length of the Stratford-on-

Avon (Northern) canal, showed there were 5 boats on the move, 49 anglers on the towpath, 22 walkers picking their way through the anglers' bits and pieces, 5 cyclists, a party of 6 youths using canoes and three yobs carrying or using shotguns; two were trying, successfully, to shoot a swan while both anglers and, regrettably, walkers looked on. Obviously the BWB did not have this kind of usage in mind when opening canals to the public, but notwithstanding all the platitudes coming from official sources no one in daily contact with waterways can help but notice that all kinds of vandalism is on the increase.

This is not, of course, a problem found solely on waterways, but is one of British Waterways Board's problems. Between 10 per cent and 25 per cent of their maintenance costs are incurred by vandalism; in effect money spent just to stand still.

A far more pleasing subject is that of canal societies. There were, in 1975, at least 360 such bodies, some dealing with one individual waterway or groups thereof; the B.C.N. Society, which hangs on to each and every length of the Birmingham Canal Navigations and is known for its unorthodox rallies, often held in God-and-BWB forsaken stretches of waterway; the Ashby Canal Association which, unusually, is strengthened by having anglers among its number who actually want to encourage commercial boats in order to deepen the channel and clear weeds; the Pocklington Canal Amenity Society whose aim, simply, is to restore their canal; these are only three, it is almost true to say that there is one for each (amenity) canal. Then there are the research bodies dealing more in abstract matters, not necessarily historical. The Canal & Barge Development Society looks entirely to the future, advancing well-thought-out plans for the future of canal carrying; the Waterways Research Centre deals with problems that range from a study of South Wales tramroads to the buoyancy problems involved in a boat-mounted dragline used for dredging purposes; while the Railway & Canal Historical Society has been described as a 'living museum of documentary evidence'. There are now a number of canal museums either in being or coming, from the Waterways Museum at Stoke Bruerne to the Black Country Museum. The regional societies are, in the main, co-ordinating bodies; the East Anglian Waterways Association, whose Hon. Secretary is L. A. Edwards (among other things the Editor of that indispensible book *Inland Waterways of Great Britain*) work closely with the Great Ouse Restoration Society but as they say:

> 'The price of Freedom is eternal vigilance and nowhere is this truer than in the sphere of our Waterways. The freedom of the individual to enjoy the beauty and amenities of the rivers which are such an integral part of the English scene is being constantly threatened. It is to every man and woman who is by birthright a heritor of the beauties of our countryside that we appeal most earnestly for support. Whether your interests are in yachting, canoeing, fishing, the preservation of wild life or just a simple desire to enjoy our Broadland and Fenland Waterways and to keep them unspoiled for future generations, we need your help . . .'

The doyen of all national societies is the Inland Waterways Association whose branches cover the country. They are best known to the public for their National Boat Rallies whose location has varied from Stratford-upon-Avon (1964), Blackburn (1965), Liverpool (1968), Birmingham (1969), on canals, to Guildford (1970) and Northampton (1971), on rivers.

Less well known but, if that is possible, possessing an even more devoted membership, is the Inland Waterways Protection Society. Their aims are, in their own words,

> 'to campaign for the Restoration, Preservation and Development of the Inland Waterways of Great Britain'. Formed in April 1958, their first move was to stop the lowering of Wilmcote Bridge on the Stratford-on-Avon canal: 'One of our engineer members viewed the bridge and planned an adequate structure at statutory height to replace the inadequate bridge the Council wished to demolish, and our plan, costing less than the Council's proposed culvert-level affair, was presented to the W.C.C., accepted and their Bill seeking the closure of navigation, withdrawn.'

From 1959 the BTW made attempts to close various canals:

> 'In the case of each threatened canal members of our Society made a detailed survey of the whole length, and an economic

survey was carried out . . . From this detailed work our Society drew up a scheme for the canal's restoration and multi-purpose usage, proving that the full use of the restored waterway could provide an income sufficient to pay, in a few years, for the waterways complete restoration. In due course each of our detailed Schemes was submitted to the Minister of Transport, as well as to most of the Local Authorities concerned. Happily, more than 45 threatened canals were, as a result of our determined efforts, removed from the Sessional Bills, which meant that each remained as a statutory navigation however derelict. Unfortunately, we failed to save four waterways – the Chesterfield Canal, the Darne & Dove Canal and two of the Birmingham Canals . . . It was in 1960 that we realised the threat to the Sheffield Basin, the head of the Sheffield and South Yorkshire Navigation. We started work at once, and a year or so later learned that a road, at a level of a few feet above the water, was to be built right across the Basin. We stopped that! The traffic into the Basin was then run down; but we spiked further plans by getting the two warehouses [built in 1819] at the head of the Basin 'listed'. Our work to save the head of the Navigation and have the whole Canal modernised to take 1,350 tonners, continues . . . In 1961 when working for the removal from the Sessional Bill of the three canals the Macclesfield, Ashton and Peak Forest, we realised the importance of the long derelict head of that group, the Buxworth Basin. After about $1\frac{1}{2}$ years of 'nattering', the British Waterways Board eventually agreed to permit the Society (with no help of any kind, except the provision of clay) to completely restore the derelict Basin. A difficult engineering task, working only at weekends with voluntary labour. The restored '1st 100 yards' won one of the European Conservation, 1970, Awards.'[21]

The most ambitious scheme put forward by the IWPS was for a 'Leeds to London Direct Route Canal'. This first appeared in 1961, and is still, with slight modifications, perfectly feasible. This would follow the route Leeds-Wakefield-Barnley-Swinton-Rotherham all on extant (however disused) canals. A new cut 9 miles long would bring boats to Killamarsh. From there to Chesterfield it would incorporate the Chesterfield Canal, with

a further new cut 14 miles long to bring the line to the Pinxton Branch of the Cromford Canal. Langley-Mill/Loughborough/ Leicester/London would, again, absorb existing routes. The staple traffic would be coal, but having connections to Sheffield, Gainsborough, Nottingham, etc., almost anything could be offered and carried at both a reduced rate, and using less oil.

In the 1970s, due to the attitudes of the media, the only word which is automatically associated with canals is amenity, but this obscures the true facts. There are a few philanthropic individuals concerned with waterways but in the main the whole concern of amenity is Big Business.

Basically there are three types of boat designed for cruising. First, the whole or cut down trading boat. With a few exceptions these are bought outright as a hull, the owner fits a cabin and goes on his way in an amiable manner. The second, often indistinguishable from hire-boats, are hulls built to 'commercial-style specifications'. In 1975, prices varied according to finish, from £1,000 to £10,000, and it has been estimated that 50–60 per cent are bought on 'credit' sales. The greatest number of pleasure boats are moulded from plastics. Being mass produced, the common nickname is 'jelly-moulds'; the early models were very akin to 'bubble cars', but later, rather squarer types, do show some styling. Nevertheless, they are indistinguishable one from the other save by name and, possibly, the colour permutation used. One large boatyard manager told us he would die of shock if such a boat were bought for cash, and anyway he relies on the percentage he receives from the hire-purchase company to boost his profits. Most steel hulled boats have diesel engines, and at least half these are British made, but this isn't so in the case of plastic boats for nearly all have outboard engines. There are good British engines but you do not see many – the chances are they will be American, French or Japanese, a situation which can only exacerbate our balance of payments troubles.

Inasmuch as it receives a good income from taxes, the Government has a vested interest in the continuing use of petrol-driven outboard motors, as have the fuel companies. It cannot be denied that the rise in pleasure boats has been phenomenal: in 1970, 12,607 licences were issued rising, by 88 per cent, to 23,729 in 1973. The British Waterways Board's

balance sheets, however, bring to light some other interesting
and very relevant statistics relating to their income:

	1970 £000	1971 £000	1972 £000	1973 £000	1974 £000
COMMERCIAL:					
Tolls & Dues	622.2	548.5	524	512.9	479.9
Water charges	898.9	953.2	976.3	1071.2	1234.2
	1521.1	1501.7	1500.3	1584.1	1714.1
AMENITY:					
Pleasure craft licences etc.	170.3	196.9	246.7	298.7	368.4
Rents	37.6	41.3	57.1	68.9	90.7
Angling	22.2	22.7	26.4	27.2	30.5
Miscellaneous	−2.2	−2.8	−3.2	−4.6	−0.8
	227.9	258.1	327.0	390.2	488.8
MISCELLANEOUS	264.6	260.2	404.0	410.5	482.5
TOTALS	2013.6	2020.0	2231.3	2384.8	2685.4

It will be seen that commercial traffics are still bringing in a
far greater cash income than amenity; the anglers seem to have
a greater say in the running of waterways than they deserve.
One other relevant statistic is that the 'Grant-in-aid' to keep
waterways open rose from £1,850,000 in 1970 to £5,300,000
in 1974.

The manpower position is a little odd for despite the re-
opening of stretches of waterway for amenity use, and the
increase in pleasure craft numbers, the maintenance staff
remains almost constant at about 1,500; half of the total
employees of the BWB. Wages, naturally, have risen; in 1974
salaried staffs received an average of £2,248 per head, manual
workers £2,018. The Chairman was paid £6,591, an increase
of £1,341 from 1971; the other seven members of the board
collected £6,961 between them.

Obviously with the losses the British Waterways Board incur
it would be unreasonable to expect them to view plans for

modern canals with much optimism. Nevertheless they cannot do other than realize the importance of the commercial traffics they have.

The arguments against extending the canal network by the introduction of a Grand Contour Canal, as propounded by J. F. Pownall[22] as long ago as 1942, verge on the childish. Water transport is slower than by road yelp the vested interests, aided and abetted by Government ministers of all parties. But what goods are concerned? Oil, fuel, chemicals, coal, iron-ore, limestone? We see the effects of a fuel tanker overturning on the road but how much are the indirect costs of the police and firemen who have to clear up the mess? While we hear of ocean tankers and ore carriers sinking, canal boats would be British owned, built and have British crews. Container traffic? If the Government have their way it will soon all come by road. Boats laden with goods for Birmingham once went to Stourport, then stopped at Worcester, then Gloucester, now Sharpness. Why not, say the road interests, Avonmouth? Or better still why use a boat at all? Ask people who live near Dover or Felixstowe what it is like to have 32-ton lorries (the present maximum, 60-ton limits are being sought) crashing through their streets every minute of the day and night. By the Contour Canal it would only take 24 hours to transport 1,350 tons from London to Birmingham – what goods need a faster time than that? Manchester–Birmingham 19 hours, Bristol–Nottingham 27, Southampton–Nottingham 33; these are typical times by a modern waterway. Another argument is cost. The rate, inclusive of all charges, London–Birmingham (1975) would be a maximum of 90p per ton; Manchester–Birmingham 70p, and so on. These rates would be reduced if a proposal for floating containers could be implemented; these would travel as a raft and only need a small tug for propulsion.

We are told by the media that children will drown. Swimming is taught in most schools – although we are told is not so popular once girls are in their teens, lest they spoil their hairdos – but while a child may swim out of a canal, very few can withstand this kind of collision: 'A 13-year-old boy died when a lorry skidded on ice at Batley, Yorkshire, mounted a pavement and crushed him against a wall.'[23] In any case with the traffic we should have on the canal, the child would not have to swim long before a barge came! The biggest bugbear of both canal and rail transport has been transhipment, but where no feeder canal exists adjacent to the premises concerned 'mechanical horses' would be kept ready to collect and deliver; it would be in the interest of everyone, barge-owner, wharf and warehouse owners, and the customers to keep goods moving. Incidentally, not all containers go straight through by the same lorry; visit any road hauliers depot for proof of this! In certain circumstances cargo lifting helicopters might be used for collection and delivery, but as there are arguments against these in terms of noise pollution, if the owner is so desperate to save a couple of hours a punitive surcharge would be payable. In due course the planners would, of necessity, site new buildings for industry right on the canal banks, each with its private wharf and loading facilities.

Amenity useage of the Contour Canal would be important; at suitable points en route 'Aquadromes' would be cut, offering all facilities for the public, as well as being handy reservoirs, and craft with competent crews would be allowed on the canal line, although commonsense says certain safety requirements would have to be met.

A vital service which this canal could provide is that of water supply. Pownall recommended a slight gradient (one foot in twelve miles; 1:63360) imparting a slight velocity upon the water sufficient for the waterways to act as a 'grid', drawing from such copious sources as the Wye and Dee and supplying water-short industrial areas.

We are told[24] that oil from the North Sea will not now be cheaper than from the Arab States, but a boat would carry 250 tons of goods a distance of one mile on a consumption of just one gallon of fuel; a lorry will only carry 58 tons over the same distance for this one gallon.[25] On the Contour Canal the speed travelled will be 6 mph (9.6 kph) and the minimum size of the barge 350 tons – the equivalent of at least ten lorries.* We must not overlook the cost and availability of the sump, gearbox and back-axle oils used by 10 lorries, compared with the one sump/reduction box of the barge. Furthermore, it takes 7 gallons of oil to make one tyre for road use, whereas the only use a boat

---

* Minimum 350 tons; normal 1350!

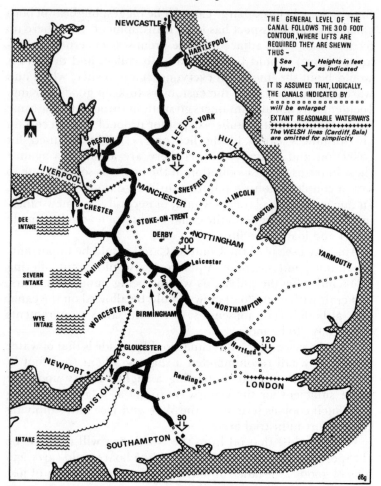

The Grand Contour Canal, as proposed by J F Pownall in 1942

has for tyres is as fenders. Most lorries are built by American firms; British boats can be built from our own steel and they can use our own British built engines.

Another argument is that to build new barge canals would only cost (at present) roughly £3 million per mile, as against a minimum of £5 million for each mile of motorway. Is it not logical, therefore, to stop building motorways and, for the sake of every man, woman and child in this island, build these

224

waterways instead? Think of the advantages. In the short-term, further unemployment, water-shortages and road hazards could be eliminated. In the long-term, transport costs would be vastly reduced, amenity facilities made available and, instead of black, bleak, tarmac, green fingers would span the country.

Shall it be? Or was George Orwell right to ignore waterways as he did in his novel *Nineteen Eighty Four*? Are they so insignificant? Are they just history?

Notes

These source notes relate to extracts or statistics used in the text. The majority of the books can be borrowed through Public Libraries; occasionally Public Record Offices have photocopying facilities available. Where an entry is shown as 'private mss' or similar, these are unpublished.

Two requests addressed primarily to 'students': With the ever increasing cost of postage it is courteous to enclose a stamped addressed envelope with queries to any research body; in some cases if this is not sent then there will be no reply. The second matter is not to waste the time of staff employed in Record Offices and Libraries; both suffer from an ever increasing workload. Typically, it has been estimated that 87 per cent of the letters received at the Waterways Research Centre in the course of a year (some 800 in all) contain queries which could be answered by opening almost any book on the subject of waterways; a situation repeated throughout the country, which must in time lead to the withdrawal of some facilities.

The following abbreviations have been used:

BPP: British Parliamentary Papers
(County or Town) RO: Record Office
(County or Town) RL: Reference Library; usually Local
    Studies Department
JHC: Journal of the House of Commons
IWA: Inland Waterways Association
BTHR: Public Record Office, London. British Transport
    Commission Historical Records
Lock & Quay and *Waterways* were staff magazines of the
    nationalized canal bodies and are not generally available
    for study.

Notes

CHAPTER 1

1 Shaw S. *A Journey to the West of England.* 1789.
2 Hutton W. *An history of Birmingham.* 1781.
3 *Gentleman's Magazine.* December 1789.
4 Priestley J. *Navigable Rivers and Canals.* 1831.
5 *8 Geo. I.* 1721.
6 *30 Geo. III* c. 82, 1790. *36 Geo. III* c. 69, 1796.
7 *46 Geo. III* c. 75, 1806, 7 & *8 Geo. IV* c. 87, 1827.
8 Langford A. *A Century of Birmingham Life.* 2 vols. 1868.
9 Pratt E. A. *A History of Inland Transport and Communication.* 1912.
10 *Leicester Journal.* 31 October 1794.
11 Shaw S. *A Journey to the West of England in 1788.* 1789.
12 Rees A. *The Cyclopaedia.* Vol. VI. 1819.
13 Baines (Ed). *A History and Gazetteer of the County of York.* 1822–23.
14 Throsby J. *Select Views in Leicester.* 1790.
15 Dodd W. *The Factory System Illustrated in a series of letters to the Rt. Hon. Lord Ashley.* 1842.
16 BPP 1842. *Children's Employment Commission* – Appx. Pt. II – Vol. XVII.
17 Clark G. F. C. *The Curiosities of Dudley and The Black Country.* 1881.
18 Howitt W. *The Rural Life of England.* 2 Vols. 1838.
19 Sidney S. *Rides on Railways.* 1851.
20 James J. *History of the Worsted Manufacture in England.* 1857.
21 BPP 1844. *State of Large Towns. Rules for the Management of Liverpool's Corporation Baths.* Appendix to 1st Report. Vol. XVII.
22 BPP 1866, *Children's Employment Commission* (1866). Vol. 24.

CHAPTER 2

1 Watts S. *A Walk through Leicester.* 1804.
2 Thacker F. S. *The Thames Highway.* 1914.
3 *21 Jac. I* c. 32.
4 Willan T. S. *River Navigation in England 1600–1750.* 1964.
5 Yarranton A. *Improvement of England by Sea and Land.* 1677.
6 *Proceedings of the Institution of Civil Engineers.* Vol. IV. 1845.
7 *32 Geo. II. c. 47.*

8 Rudder S. *A New History of Gloucestershire.* 1799
9 *16 Geo. III.* c. 21.
10 *The Glocester Journal.* 5 June 1790.
11 *28 Geo. III.* c. 8.
12 Obituary of Henry Berry in the *Liverpool Mercury,* 7 August 1812.
13 *Williamson's Liverpool Advertiser.* 9 December 1774.

CHAPTER 3

1 *7 Geo I.* c. 15.
2 Priestley J. *Navigable Rivers and Canals.* 1831.
3 *34 Geo. III.* c. 37.
4 Redding G. *England in the XIXth Century.* 1842.
5 Anon. *The History of Inland Navigations, Particularly those of the Duke of Bridgewater in Lancashire and Cheshire and the intended one by Earl Gower.* 1769.
6 Many Acts in fact specifically excluded the navigation from any direct benefit should minerals be found; even today a waterway lease can still reserve this right for the British Waterways Board.
7 Banks A. G. and Schofield R. B. *Brindley at Wet Earth Colliery.* David & Charles. 1968.
8 Aiken Dr J. *A Description of the Country from Thirty to Forty Miles Round Manchester.* 1795.
9 Creswell Rev. J. *An Account of Runcorn and its Environs* c. 1809.
10 Malet H. *The Canal Duke.* 1961.
11 Chaloner, W. H. *James Brindley (1716–72) and his remuneration as a canal engineer.* Published in the Transactions of the Lancashire & Cheshire Antiquarian Society. 1965–6. Vol. 75 & 76.
12 Annual Register, 1807.
13 Letter from Northwich to John Rickman. 9 June 1810.
14 *Glocester Journal.* 7 October 1793.
15 BTHR. Gloucester & Berkeley Minute Book. 8 May 1820, 14 July 1818 and 8 September 1811.
16 Fosbrooke. *History of Gloucestershire.* 1807.
17 Rolt L. T. C. *Thomas Telford.* 1958.
18 *7 Geo. IV.* c. 95. 26 May 1826.
19 Cobbett W. *Rural Rides,* Vol. 2, 1853. Reprint Everyman's Library 1967.

20 For details of the problems involved in building the Birmingham & Liverpool Junction Canal see *English Canals*, D. D. Gladwin & J. M. White, Pt. 2, Engineers & Engineering. The Oakwood Press, 1968.

CHAPTER 4

1 *Taunton Courier*. 27 April 1811.
2 BPP 1843 Midland Mining Commission. First Report Q.54.
3 BPP 1830 Report on the State of the Coal Trade Vol. VIII.
4 Shaw S. *A Journey to the West of England in 1788*. 1789.
5 Willmore F. *A History of Walsall*. 1877.
6 BTHR. Liskeard & Looe Union Canal Minute Book. 19 July 1825.
7 *Annual Register*. 1805.
8 *Aris's Birmingham Gazette*. 6 November 1769.
9 MacGill P. *Songs of a Navvy*. 1912.
10 *Annual Register*. 1816.
11 Lecount P. *The History of the Railways Connecting London and Birmingham*. 1839.
12 *Taunton Courier*. 25 April 1811.
13 Priestley J. *Navigable Rivers and Canals*. 1831.
14 Davies W. *General View of the Agriculture and Domestic Economy in South Wales*. Vol. II. 1815.
15 Berkshire RO. *Berkshire Sessions Order Book*. 1791–1795.
16 *Gentleman's Magazine*. September 1800.
17 Southampton RO. D/PM 6/3/11–13.
18 Southampton RO. D/PM 6/11/6 & 7, D/PM 6/2/1 87–92, D/PM 6/8/16.
19 BTHR. *Lancaster Canal Letter Book*.
20 *Proceedings of the Cotteswold Naturalists' Field Club*, 1868–1870. Vol. V. Article by J. H. Taunton.
21 Tomlinson V. I. The Manchester, Bolton & Bury Canal Navigation. *Trans. Lancashire & Cheshire Antiquarian Society*. Vol. 75 & 76. 1965–6.
22 BTHR. MBB 4/1. *Journal of R. Cunliffe, Agent of the Company*. 19 October 1835.
23 Southampton RO. D/PM 6/8/15, D/PM 6/11/10.
24 *Aris's Birmingham Gazette*. 8 June 1767.

25 *Aris's Birmingham Gazette.* 15 July 1767.
26 *Aris's Birmingham Gazette.* 6 November 1769.
27 BTHR. *Birmingham Canal Minute Book.* 20 October 1769.
28 *Aris's Birmingham Gazette.* 6 December 1769.
29 *Aris's Birmingham Gazette.* 14 May 1770.
30 *Aris's Birmingham Gazette.* 4 January 1770.
31 *Aris's Birmingham Gazette.* 5 November 1770.
32 *Aris's Birmingham Gazette.* 19 November 1770.
33 Hadfield C. *The Canals of the West Midlands.* 1966.
34 *Aris's Birmingham Gazette.* 7 January 1771.
35 *Aris's Birmingham Gazette.* 27 October 1769.
36 *The Glocester Journal.* 9 February 1795.
37 *The Glocester Journal.* 7 October 1793.

References 24–26, 28–32, 34–35, may carry differing dates to those shown in the text as Aris's newspaper was a weekly publication, and notices were put out by Meredith almost daily.

CHAPTER 5

 1 Warner Rev. R. *Excursions from Bath.* 1801.
 2 *Gentleman's Magazine.* December 1789.
 3 Townsend T. (Ed.). *News of a Country Town.*
 4 Fosbrooke A. *History of Gloucestershire.* 1807.
 5 Report by Whitworth quoted in Dalby L. J. *The Wilts & Berks Canal.* The Oakwood Press. 1971.
 6 Swindon RL. *Letter Book,* 5 August 1828.
 7 Phillips J. *Memoirs of William Smith.* 1844.
 8 *To the Gentlemen of the Committee of Subscribers to the Proposed Canal from Bristol to Cirencester.* 1793. Bristol RL.
 9 *Report of Royal Commission on Canals and Inland Navigations.* December 1909.
10 Dalby L. J. *The Wilts & Berks Canal.* 1971.
11 Taunton J. H. *Report to the Company.* 14 May 1883.
12 Gardom E. T. (Clerk of the County Council). *A Brief History of the Thames & Severn Canal.* 1901.
13 *The Committee of the Thames & Severn Canal Trust in a Report presented to the Trust,* 31 October 1899.
14 *Wilts & Gloucs. Standard.* 16 March 1904.
15 *57 Geo. III. c. 63.*

16 Priestley J. *Navigable Rivers and Canals.* 1831.
17 Cobbett W. *Rural Rides.* Vol. II. 1853 edition. Reprint Everyman's Library. 1966.
18 *Annual Register.* 1816.
19 *Circular issued by the Committee of Management of the Portsmouth & Arundel Canal.* Portsmouth RL.
20 *The Sussex Weekly Advertiser.* 26 May 1823.
21 Read W. R. *Birdham – Notes on its Village Life and Natural History.* 1935.
22 BTHR. *Letter from Portsmouth & Arundel Company to Wey & Arun,* dated 5 April 1832.
23 Latimer J. *Annals of Bristol in the Eighteenth Century.*
24 BTHR. *Kennet & Avon Canal Minute Book.*
25 Waylen J. *History of Devizes.* 1859.
26 Rees A. *The Cyclopaedia.* 1819.
27 White F. *History, Gazetteer & Directory of Cheshire.* 1860.
28 Priestley J. *Navigable Rivers and Canals.* 1831.
29 Hibbard J. *Statements on the Great Utility of a Circular and Other Inland &c. Canal Drainage.* 1804.
30 Billingsley J. *A General View of the Agriculture of Somerset.* 1794.
31 Freeth J. *The Birmingham Poet.* Privately held mss. c. 1770.
32 Southampton RO. *Letter to the Clerk of the Salisbury & Southampton Canal.* 4 September 1793.
33 Rickman (ed). *Life of Thomas Telford.* 1838.
34 *Felix Farley's Bristol Journal.* 6 April 1793.
35 *Sherborne Mercury.* 2 January 1797.
36 Dorset RO. Acc. 9455.
37 *Rennie's mss report on the Dorset & Somerset Canal 1799* (Institution of Civil Engineers).
38 Phelps. *History & Antiquities of Somersetshire.* 1836.

CHAPTER 6

1 Priestley J. *Navigable Rivers and Canals.* 1831.
2 Sandars J. *A Letter on the Subject of the Projected Rail Road between Liverpool and Manchester.* 1824.
3 Head G. *The Manufacturing Districts of England.* 1835.
4 McCulloch J. R. *Dictionary of Commerce.* 1841.
5 Killick. *Early History of the Leeds & Liverpool Canal.* 1897.
6 Transcript of the diary of V. V. Venner. (Privately owned.)

7 Potter L. *Lancashire Memories.* 1879.
8 *Canals & Waterways Journal.* February 1924.
9 Lewis S. *Worcester General & Commercial Directory.* 1820.
10 Boyle T. *Hope for the Canals.* 1848.
11 BTHR. *Oxford Canal In-letter book.* 13 March 1832.
12 Pickfords' *'Company History'.* (Privately owned.)
13 Hackwood F. W. *History of Tipton.* 1891.
14 *Glocester Journal.* 9 February 1795.
15 *The Courier.* 27 February 1824.
16 *Aris's Birmingham Gazette.* November 1769.
17 *59 Geo. III.* c. 27. 1819.
18 *3 & 4 Vic.* c. 50. 4 August 1840.
19 Hassell J. *Tour of the Grand Junction Navigation.*
20 Booker Rev. Luke. *Dudley Castle.* 1825.
21 BPP 1845. *Report on the Sanatory Condition of Bradford.* Vol. XV III Pt. 2.
22 Dodd W. *The Factory System Illustrated in a Series of Letters to the Rt. Hon. Lord Ashley.* 1842.
23 Davies V. L. & Hyde H. *Dudley and the Black Country 1760–1860.* Dudley PL Transcript No. 16.
24 Kay J. P. *The Moral & Physical Condition of the Working Class.* 1832.
25 Vince C. A. (MA). *The History of the Corporation of Birmingham.* 1902.

CHAPTER 7

1 Boyle T. *Hope for the Canals.* 1848.
2 Gardom E. T. *A Brief History of the Thames & Severn Canal.* 1901.
3 *Port of Manchester. Illustrated History of the Manchester Ship Canal,* 1708–1901.
4 This and other statistics in this section are drawn from or based on those quoted in *Port of Manchester* published by Hind, Hoyle & Light Ltd. c. 1901. (Privately owned.)
5 Newport PL Acc. 27115 SMOOO (386).
6 Newport PL Acc. 27111 MOOO(626).
7 BTHR. Shropshire Union Railways & Canal Committee Minute Book. 14 October 1903.
8 Dunwoody R. B. *Inland water transport.* A paper read at

Birmingham on Friday, 12 September 1913 before the
Economic Section of The British Association.
9 *Canal Control Committee (Board of Trade) Handbook on Canals.*
November 1918.
10 *Canals & Waterways Journal.* June 1919 & August 1920.
11 Hadfield C. *The Canals of the West Midlands.* David &
Charles. 1966.

CHAPTER 8

1 Thacker F. S. *The Thames Highway.* 1914.
2 Plot, Dr Q. *Oxfordshire.* 1677.
3 Proceedings of the Institute of Civil Engineers. January
1856. Vol. 15.
4 Nightingale J. *The Beauties of England & Wales and Delina-
tions.* Vol. 13. 1813.
5 Simmons J. (ed). *Journeys in England.* An Anthology edited
by Jack Simmons. 1951.
6 Laird M. *A Topographical & Historical Description of the
County of Worcester.* 1814 & 1818.
7 Thurberville T. C. *Worcester in the 19th Century.* 1852.
8 BTHR. *Grand Junction Canal Minute Book.* 10 November
1825.
9 Head G. *The Manufacturing Districts of England.* 1835.
10 Leifchild J. R. *A Traveller Underground.* 1859.
11 BPP 1833. *Report on the State of the Coal Trade.* Vol. XX.
12 Sims G. R. *Living London.* 1903.
13 Bate, George. Unpublished mss. 1972.
14 *The Waterman.* November 1911.
15 Hutton W. *An History of Birmingham.* 1781.
16 *Windsor and Eton Express.* 28 December 1822.
17 The late Jack James.
18 Mills J. of Tipton in *Some Historical Notes.* November 1911.
19 Smith G. *Our Canal Population.* 1875.
20 Robertson H. R. *Life on the Upper Thames.* 1875.
21 Meade T. L. *Water Gipsies.* 1850.
22 Young D. *On London's Canals.* 1903.
23 Janet Harris – ex boatwoman.
24 *Canals & Waterways Journal.* February, May, July and
August 1920.

25 *Canal Control Committee (Board of Trade) Handbook on Canals.*
November 1918.
26 Gayford E. *The Amateur Boatwomen.* David & Charles. 1973.
27 *Canals & Waterways Journal.* June 1919. August 1920.
28 Ramsay C. M. *On canal boats in war time.* Geographical
Magazine. June 1945.
29 *Transport Goes to War.* Issued for the Ministry of War
Transport by the Ministry of Information. 1942.
30 *Waterways.* Vol. 14. No. 139. March 1969.
31 *Lock & Quay.* Vol. 4. No. 3. March 1952.
32 *Lock & Quay.* Vol. 6. No. 3. March 1954.
33 Hadfield C. & Biddle G. *The Canals of the North West
England.* David & Charles. 1970.
34 *Birmingham Daily Mail.* 5 March 1875.
35 *Birmingham Daily Mail.* 12 March 1875.
36 Skinner Rev. J. *Journal of a Somerset Rector, 1803–1834.*
Reprinted Kingsmead Press, 1971.
37 *Sunday at Home.* Published by the Religious Tract Society.
August 1878.
38 *40 & 41 Vic.* c. 60. 14 August 1877.
39 *An Act to Provide for Public Elementary Education in England &
Wales. 33 & 34 Vic.* c. 75. 9 August 1870.

CHAPTER 9

1 *The Handbook to the Rivers & Broads of Norfolk & Suffolk.* ND.
2 Suffling E. R. *The Land of the Broads.* 1892.
3 Bonthron P. *My Holidays on Inland Waterways.* 1916.
4 E. Temple Thurston. *The Flower of Gloster.* 1911.
5 *Lock & Quay.* January 1952. Vol. 4. No. 1.
6 *Kidderminster Shuttle.* 6 July 1956.
7 *IWA Bulletin,* No. 52. October 1956.
8 *The Yorkshire Post.* 5 January 1956.
9 *South Wales Argus.* 11 November 1958.
10 *Beckenham & Penge Advertiser.* 17 September 1959.
11 *Beckenham & Penge Advertiser.* 5 October 1961.
12 *Oldbury Weekly News.* 2 June 1960.
13 *Waterways.* Vol. 2. No. 11. May/June 1957.
14 *Waterways.* Vol. 3. No. 18. April 1958.

15 *IWA Bulletin.* No. 51. July 1956.
16 *The Derby Canal Restoration Scheme.* Prepared by the Derby Canal Restoration Committee of the Midlands Branch of the Inland Waterways Association Ltd. 1961.
17 *The Future of the Waterways.* Published by the Inland Waterways Association. ND.
18 *The Facts About the Waterways.* Published by the British Waterways Board. 1965.
19 *Waterways.* Vol. 14. No. 140. April 1969.
20 *British Waterways Board Press Release.* PR1/189. 16 August 1974.
21 Personal communication from the late Mrs P. J. Bunker, the then Honorary Secretary of the Inland Waterways Protection Society.
22 Pownall J. F. Grand Contour Canal. 1944.
23 *Daily Mail.* 20 February 1975.
24 BBC Radio 4 News Programme. 12 December 1974.
25 *Onward* No. 67. January 1975.

Our thanks must be expressed to the following authors and publishers for permission to reproduce copyright material:

Willan T. S. *River Navigation in England 1600–1750.* Frank Cass & Co. Ltd.
Lancashire & Cheshire Antiquarian Society: Transactions.
Dalby L. J. *The Wilts & Berks Canal.* The Oakwood Press.
Pickfords Removals Ltd. *Company History.*
Davies V. L. & Hyde H. *Dudley & The Black Country 1760–1860.* Dudley Public Libraries, Transcript No. 16.
H.M.S.O. *Handbook on Canals.*
H.M.S.O. *Transport Goes to War.*
The Geographical Magazine. Article on Canal Boats in War Time.
British Waterways Board. *Lock & Quay: Waterways; The Facts About the Waterways,* and Press releases.
Skinner Rev. J. *Journal of a Somerset Rector 1803–1834.* Kingsmead Press, Bath.
Inland Waterways Association Ltd. Bulletins and other documents.

If, inadvertently, any copyright holders have been omitted – peccavi! Upon advice I would be pleased to rectify this in any future edition, and can only offer apologies.

General index

This index is deliberately divided into a number of main headings and sub-headings, generally speaking if the subject required relates, for example, to boats and more specifically to their use in wartime, the entry is shown as:
Boats:
    Wartime conditions and occurrences
To avoid excessive bulk individual carriers are only listed where they are of considerable importance, thus Pickfords have their own sub-heading while James Bromley does not, the latter being found under:
Carriers:
    Services offered
As not all canal societies are concerned solely with amenity use of waterways, they are shown under the name by which they are best known, i.e. East Anglian Waterways Association.

General Index

General Index

Railways:
  Competition from 130–3, 144
  Credit terms offered 131
  Great Western 144–9
  London & North Western 131, 138
  Manchester Ship Canal 140
  Purchase of canals 130–4
  Rate War 131, 138–9
Rate war, *see* Railways
Riots and commotions:
  Caledonian Canal 50
  Devizes 87–8
  Nine Locks, Brierley Hill, 121
  Sampford Peverell 49, 57
  Sapperton Tunnel 66
Roads, conversion of canals into 155
Royal Commission on Canals and Waterways
  (1906) 150–1, 153–4

Salvation Army 196–7
Shares 71, 73, 74, 84, 88, 92–4
Sheffield Basin 218
Skinner, Rev. John 179
Staunch (boat) 82–3

Telford, John 50
Telford, Thomas:
  Apprenticeship 43
  Birth 43
  Canal works 44–8
  Characteristics 43, 44, 45, 48
  Death 48
  Hours of work 43
  Non-canal works 43
Thefts from boats 112, 121, 122
Tipton Slasher, *see* Perry, William
Tokens, *see* Wages
Tolls:
  Animals 99
  Comparative 35–6, 86, 131
  Drawbacks 97, 115, 147
  Exemptions 96, 97, 99
  Rates fixed by Parliament 96
  Rates fixed by Railway Companies 83
Tom Puddings, *see* Boats
Towing Paths:
  Lack of 47, 160
  Severn 161
  Thames 159, 160
Traffics:
  Bricks 134
  Cider and Perry 134
  Coal 16, 17, 33, 35, 69, 83, 92, 125
  Corn 16, 83
  Cotton 121
  Gold 86

Gravel 82
Growth, microcosm of 13–15
Iron 14, 16, 97
Lime 16
Manure 16, 96, 97
Marble 86
Milk 89
Oil 139
Rags in bales 135, 137
Road stone 83, 136
Routeing of 125
Salt 33, 34, 92
Statistics 133–4, 139, 142–3, 150–1, 153,
  155, 156–7, 195, 196, 199–200, 211
Timber 83, 118, 134, 135
Wines & Spirits 112
Wool 138–9
Transport Workers Battalions 190, 193
Trinder, Job, *see* Boatmen
Tunnels:
  Blisworth 114, 124, 162
  Crimson Hill 164
  Cutting methods 52, 65
  Dunhamstead 164
  Maida Hill 164
  Mine 164
  Sapperton 52, 65–6, 76
  Shortwood 164
  Standedge 162
  Wast Hill 165
  West Marlands 61
Turnpike Sailors, *see* Boatmen

Vandalism 72–3, 121–3
Volunteer labour, *see* Amenity

Wages and salaries:
  Butty system 51, 52
  Rates of pay 20, 21, 41–2, 44, 46–7, 50, 53,
    58, 59, 69, 91, 129, 149, 163, 186–7, 191,
    205, 221
  Riots over 49–50
  Shortage of coins 50
  Tokens, payment by 51
Warehousing and wharfage 67, 98–100, 107,
  115, 116–7, 120, 121, 147–8
Water:
  Pollution 80, 101, 126–7, 172, 173, 206–7
  Shortage 79, 135–7
  Supply 79, 95, 96
Waterways Research Centre 216
Weights and measures 35, 51, 96, 98
Wheatcroft N & G 107–8, 113
Wigan 126
William Thomas 25
Wolverhampton 126

239

Index of canals and navigations